To Dr & Mrs Herbert Phillips
with Cordial regards

Very sincerely
Edward Greenstreet

THE WAR CALLED PEACE

Books by H. A. Overstreet

ABOUT OURSELVES
INFLUENCING HUMAN BEHAVIOR
THE GREAT ENTERPRISE
THE MATURE MIND

Books by The Overstreets

THE MIND ALIVE
THE MIND GOES FORTH
WHAT WE MUST KNOW ABOUT COMMUNISM
THE WAR CALLED PEACE

Books by Bonaro W. Overstreet

UNDERSTANDING FEAR (HARPER)
HANDS LAID UPON THE WIND

THE WAR CALLED PEACE

Khrushchev's Communism

HARRY AND BONARO OVERSTREET

W · W · NORTON & COMPANY · INC ·

NEW YORK

CONTENTS

PART ONE

DESIGN FOR CONFUSION

ONE THE GEOGRAPHY OF COMMUNISM 11

TWO THE MEANING OF "PEACEFUL COEXISTENCE" 30

THREE IN THE WAKE OF AN ILLUSION 44

FOUR DICTATOR OF THE IDEOLOGY 61

FIVE THE SUCCESS KHRUSHCHEV NEEDS 78

PART TWO

STRANGE WEAPONS

SIX THE BODY AND SPIRIT OF A PLAN 103

SEVEN HISTORY AS A WEAPON 120

EIGHT COMMUNISM'S PRINTING PRESS 136

NINE SPEAKING IN TONGUES 156

5

TEN   BERLIN: A CASE STUDY   174

ELEVEN   EXCHANGE PROGRAMS: WHOSE WEAPON?   197

PART THREE

STRANGE BATTLEFIELDS

TWELVE   COLONIALISM: SOVIET STYLE   220

THIRTEEN   THE PARTY'S WAR AGAINST THE PEOPLE   241

FOURTEEN   THE MAKING OF COMMUNIST MAN   258

FIFTEEN   METHODS OF MIND-MAKING   280

SIXTEEN   THE UNITED NATIONS AS TARGET   302

SEVENTEEN   TOO LATE FOR CREDULITY   319

NOTES TO THE TEXT   337

BIBLIOGRAPHY   350

RESEARCH CENTERS   364

INDEX   365

FOREWORD

WHAT Stalin concealed behind a cryptic smile; what Lenin, before him, spelled out mostly for Communist consumption, Khrushchev has broadcast to the world. We can no longer avoid knowing the score. He has told it in words and revealed it in actions. His words, to be sure, are still designed to confuse; but his actions speak louder—and more unmistakably—than words. We can no longer doubt Communist intentions.

So a new phase of the war called peace begins. We can at last move out of our semi-confusions and begin to see Communism clear. The conviction grows among us that the free world today faces an issue of moral and spiritual survival it has never faced before. *Communist man* confronts *the free man.*

We have Khrushchev to thank for this growing conviction. He, more than anyone else, has made us see the complete irreconcilability of these two patterns of man; and in doing so, he has helped us to know where our loyalties and

7

our efforts must lie. This book is an attempt to explore what Khrushchev reveals.

To the many who have helped us in the making of this book we give our warm thanks. Some of them are named in footnote references and in the bibliography. But others are unnamed. We have consulted with them in our own country and in many places around the world; and we are deeply in debt to them for much which they have helped us learn.

In a very particular way, we wish to express our gratitude to a host of escapees from Communism. In London and Paris and West Berlin, in Nürnberg and Munich and Vienna, in New Delhi and Saigon and Hong Kong they have told us their stories. To these, who must remain anonymous, we give our thanks—for their insights and their courage.

Harry Overstreet
Bonaro Overstreet

Falls Church, Virginia

PART ONE

DESIGN FOR CONFUSION

ONE

THE GEOGRAPHY
OF COMMUNISM

W HEN Nikita Khrushchev came to New York, in
September 1960, to head the Soviet delegation to
the General Assembly of the United Nations, it was reported that he had brought two prepared speeches between
which to choose: one tough, one "friendly."

Whether or not this report was literally true, it would be
consistent with his record. Khrushchev has recast international relations into the form of a giant guessing game: *what
comes next?* The stakes are so high that no nation can sit
placidly on the sidelines. But if all free-world nations and
peoples have again and again to ask the question, there is
growing evidence that Khrushchev himself has to ask it, too.
He has committed himself to policies of which inner contradiction is the essence.

If, at times, he seems to be a veritable master of mood-
changing, able to make the rest of us hope or fear as he

11

wills, at other times he seems merely to be scrambling to get out of a predicament into which he has maneuvered himself.

However, there is a perverse Communist strength even in his weakness if he can keep the non-Communist world jumpy with indecision. The more he can keep us busy adjusting to changes of his choice, and the more he can keep us focused on his latest move, the more able he is to keep initiative in his own hands even when he is asking himself, "What comes next?"

In view of this fact, the safest course for all free people is to get perspective on what cannot change in Communist policy because of what never changes in Communism's "world view." To do this, we must look far beyond the hypnotic image of a ranting or a smiling Khrushchev. He himself helped us to gain perspective, by his own performance at the General Assembly of the United Nations, in 1960, and the contrast this posed to his "friendly" performance there just a year before.

Adopting the tough line, and setting himself to make old stereotypes yield new Communist gains, he invited us to borrow a phrase from his own vocabulary and to see him as a "lackey" of Marxism-Leninism.

Marx was two men in one. As dialectician, he pinned down what was "fated" to happen. As revolutionary, he said, "Then make it happen." Thus, he converted the dialectic into a promise that revolutionary action carried on according to his formula would pay off in ultimate victory. What he started more than a hundred years ago is far from being finished yet; and no part of the world is exempt from the struggle that he imposed upon mankind.

Action, even if justified by the dialectic, does not take place in the dialectic heavens. It takes place on earth. Moreover, revolutionary action is political action. Its aim is to gain control of the instrumentalities of power and coercion. It becomes, therefore, *strategic* action that takes place on an earth mapped out in political units. This is where Lenin fits into the picture—as strategist of the revolution.

This, again, is where Stalin fits in—prefacing his armed take-over of the Baltic States by mutual "non-aggression" treaties with these states; and seizing by armed force in East Europe what his subversive Parties had there made ready for him.

But this, also, is where Khrushchev fits in—practicing his Communist diplomacy in an effort to gain the fruits of war without the risks of war; and, at the United Nations, trying so to re-map the world into political groupings that Africa would be laid wide open to his "friendly" incursions.

Under the aegis of its "world view," in short, Marxist-Leninist Communism operates according to *a strategic view of the world.* In this view, ideology and political geography meet to make our planet a maneuvering-place: *this* can be made to happen here; *that* can be made to happen there.

If we hold in mind this Marxist-Leninist image of our planet, we emancipate ourselves from Khrushchev's zigzag efforts to choose our moods for us. While he, ranting or smiling, bids us fear or hope, we can be fitting his zigzags into a larger frame of policy. We can set ourselves to follow the ins and outs of his shifting course and to judge what—if anything—his brand of "peaceful coexistence" has to do with peace on earth and good will toward men.

The first thing we must know about Communism's ideological geography is that it cuts our world into two parts that are never to be reunited except on Communist terms. The Bolshevik *coup d'état* of 1917 transferred Marx's "class struggle," as revised by Lenin, from the page of the book to the face of the earth. This transfer has been made explicit times without number. We can take three examples from key periods of Communist history.

In 1919, Stalin, as spokesman for Lenin, said, "The world has split into two irreconcilable camps: the camp of imperialism and the camp of socialism." (1)

In 1947, in the wake of World War II, Zhdanov, Stalin's cultural commissar, brought the "two-camp" theory up to date: on the one hand, he said, there was the "imperialist camp," led by the United States; on the other, the "anti-imperialist camp," led by the Soviet Union and the "countries of the new democracy." (2)

In 1959, the Communist Party of the Soviet Union, in a Resolution adopted at its Twenty-First Congress, set forth Khrushchev's version: "Now there are two world social systems: capitalism, which is breathing its last, and socialism, which is brimming over with a growing vital force and enjoys the support of the working people of all countries." (3) The "two camps" have become "two world social systems"; but they are still *two* and they are still irreconcilable.

Khrushchev has made plain, time and again, just how irreconcilable they are. In September 1956 he made it plain in his talks with Tito. In that critical month he needed Tito's good will, for he wanted him to exert neighborly influence to smooth out the mounting unrest in Hungary. Yet he felt impelled to denounce Tito's effort to stay on good terms with both the Soviet Union and the West. Yugoslavia, he insisted, must join one or the other "camp." Her "natural place" was in the Soviet camp.

A year later, explaining "peaceful coexistence" to a Soviet audience, he said, "but of course we must realize that we cannot coexist eternally. One of us must go to his grave. We do not want to go to the grave. They (the Western Powers) don't want to go to their graves either. So what must be done? We must push them to their graves." (4)

Khrushchev's Summer of 1960, from the collapse of the Summit conference in May to the U.N. meeting in September, might be described as one long verbal debauch—in which he alternated calls for "peace" with threats of missile warfare and reassertions of the irreconcilability of Communism and "imperialism."

Many persons in the West have hoped that as the Soviet Union built up that "strong material base" to which it has aspired, it would become more interested in the practicalities of a going order than in Communist expansionism. The burden of this hope has been that "two-camp" recalcitrance would die a natural death as the Communists began to feel less anxious about the future of their own system: more secure and self-confident. The record does not support this hope. The Soviet people, we can assume, would be ready to drop the world revolution at any time. It was never of their devising. But the Soviet people do not make Soviet policy. The Communist Party does that.

If we return to their setting in history the "two-camp" statements which we have quoted above, one fact stands clear. Not one of them was stimulated by a sense of weakness, failure, or letdown. Each was stimulated by a heady sense of success—and of more success in the offing. Moreover, each was meshed in with a rallying of the world Communist movement for a swift push ahead to new victories.

Stalin's "two-camp" statement dates from 1919. What state of mind did it reflect? What type of action did it encourage? In that year, Lenin launched the *Comintern*—the Communist International—in an atmosphere of buoyant hope. In the history of Communism, 1919 was *a year of confidence*.

We tend to forget this; for Lenin was soon to learn that the recasting of human society in the mold of his choice was a harder task than he had thought. But on May Day 1919, the Executive Committee of the Comintern saw the climactic world revolution as just ahead: "The great Communist International was born in 1919. The great international Soviet Republic will be born in 1920." (5) Lenin himself saw July of that year as "our last difficult July" and predicted that "by next July, we shall greet the victory of the International Soviet Republic . . ." (6)

Under what circumstances did Zhdanov re-stress the "two-camp" theory in 1947? He did so as key speaker at the founding convention of the *Cominform*, that successor to the Comintern through which Stalin, having closed out his wartime alliance with the West, reintegrated the world Communist movement for a new drive.

Just as 1919 had been *a year of confidence*, so was 1947. Stalin had problems on his hands. But he felt able to take the offensive against them with the Cominform as an extension of his own will. He was not on the defensive. He was flushed with the success of empire-building. During the period of his mutual non-aggression pact with Hitler, he had seized the Baltic states and part of Poland. In the two years since the war, he had "liberated" Rumania, Bulgaria, Albania, and Hungary into the status of satellites; and he saw the "liberation" of Czechoslovakia and Poland as just a matter of time. They became his in 1948 and 1949—at which point NATO put a stop to that particular drive toward empire.

What was Khrushchev's mood in 1959? The Party Congress which inserted into its key Resolution the reminder that there are "two world social systems" might well be called Khrushchev's Congress. To it, with assured confidence, he brought the accumulated fruits of success; and at it, he had everything his own way.

He had, by then, effected that twofold consolidation of

power—Party and State—which alone, in the Soviet system, can be called *dictatorial*. He was both First Secretary of the Party and Premier of the Soviet State; and thus had under him two chains of command. He had rid himself of the so-called "anti-party" group—Malenkov, Molotov, Kaganovich, and the rest—who had opposed him on various policies. His Sputniks had startled the world. The Soviet economy had pulled out of its long inertia. Even his much challenged virgin-lands program seemed to be paying off. In 1958—the year which had ended just a month before the Congress —these lands had yielded a bumper harvest.

At the Congress itself, the delegates hailed him in terms that did not come too far short of those that had once made Stalin "infallible." They adopted his Seven Year Plan with "enthusiasm"; and every speaker who took the platform praised and echoed his words.

On another front, contacts with the outside world which he had been cultivating ever since his first visit to India, with Bulganin, in 1955, also showed signs of paying off—in the coin of respectability for the Soviet system and extended Soviet influence. He had launched his economic offensive in the area of trade and aid. And, not least, he thought he had found a diplomatic formula for securing, without war, what he wanted from the West: concessions with respect to Berlin; disarmament without controls; and the splitting up of NATO.

The world Communist movement—which had been thrown into divisive confusion by his own "de Stalinization" speech in 1956, and by the Hungarian and Polish uprisings in that same year—was again united and at his command. Representatives of seventy Parties outside the Soviet Union were present at the Congress; and they were ready to have their energies focused for the new expansionist drive that Khrushchev was ready to launch.

It was not, in short, a discouraged Khrushchev, nor a Khrushchev starved for success, who reminded all Communists that the world is irrevocably divided into two "social systems." It was a Khrushchev who was riding the crest of the wave; and who planned to use the concept of the dichotomized world, just as Lenin and Stalin had, to try for a swift conversion of prospective victories into accomplished victories, by spurring the world Communist movement to the requisite effort.

Khrushchev did not, in 1959, set a date for Communism's climactic victory—as Lenin had in 1919. But by the Summer of 1960, during his visit to Austria, he was ready to be at least half serious in saying, "Life is short, and I want to see the Red flag fly over the whole world in my lifetime."

Success, in short—Communist style—does not inspire in the Party or its dictators any will to join together, except on Communist terms, the "two camps" which the dogma has put asunder. On the record, success *achieved and anticipated* has the opposite effect: it stimulates the desire to forge ahead toward the fulfillment of Marxism-Leninism's "historic mission."

We of the free world, then, should recognize that in this Khrushchev era of expanding Soviet strength and self-confidence we must reckon, as heretofore, with this first aspect of Communism's political geography: the "two-camp" theory. Khrushchev can be expected to go right on talking about "peace"—to encourage the non-Communist world to disarm in mind and in fact. But he cannot be expected to stop pressing toward a Communist goal that he sees as accessible, now, *because of Soviet strength.*

There is a kind of moral in all this. The "two-camp" concept is calculated to defeat in advance any normal effort we can make, under present conditions, to achieve a trustworthy, really friendly peace. It defeats, also, any normal effort on our part to persuade the Communists that their derogatory opinion of us is unjustified. In their eyes, our national character is not defined by what we do. It was ideologically defined a long time ago—and for keeps. Whatever we do, short of submitting to Communism, will be "warmongering" and "imperialist"—because we belong to the "camp" designated by these terms.

And this is where the "moral" comes in: namely, that we do better to match our policies to our own beliefs about the life of man on this earth than to shape and trim them in the hope that we can persuade the Communists to credit our good intentions.

Here, again, history lends perspective. Our Marshall Plan did more than any other one thing to save the economies of postwar Western Europe from collapse and start them toward vigorous growth. But Zhdanov, in his 1947 speech, denounced this as an American plan "for the enslavement of Europe"—because it got in the way of Stalin's plan for exploiting economic chaos. Remembering this, we can feel less impelled to try to clear up the "misunderstanding" when Khrushchev says of our current foreign aid programs, "The imperialists use their economic relations with the underdeveloped countries as instruments of blackmail and distortion . . ." (7) Just as our national character has been defined for keeps, so have our motives been: they are those which "inevitably" mark "capitalist imperialist exploiters."

Our motives for giving aid, as for our other undertakings, need to be understood by ourselves; and also by other free-world nations and peoples that have a direct or indirect stake in them. Here, we must try to clear up misunderstandings; and must try, also, to counteract Soviet misrepresentations. But it is something else altogether for us to set out to convince Khrushchev that we are not the "imperialist warmongers" he takes us to be—as though his description stemmed from simple ignorance or misunderstanding. It does not. It stems from the ideology which undergirds his power—and promises a further extension of it.

Some of Khrushchev's statements, taken in isolation, would seem to make the above unduly pessimistic. Thus in *Pravda,* on September 27, 1959, he struck a note wholly unfamiliar in the Communist press: namely, that the American *government,* as well as the *people,* wanted peace. Did this mean that, at last, he felt reassured enough to relegate to limbo the old "two-camp" theory?

It did not—to judge by his subsequent actions. Rather, it would appear, he was announcing to the Communist "camp" that his controversial policy of "peaceful coexistence" had been proved "correct": just as he had predicted, he would be able to get what he wanted from the West without war. In any event, what he proceeded to do, as soon as he felt assured that we wanted peace, was to step up the pressure on Berlin and to make another bid for disarmament *on his terms,* with no adequate inspection or control.

When he became convinced, by late Spring 1960, that peace did not signify to the West a policy of making concessions to him on point after point while he made none in return, he plunged the world back into cold war.

The second aspect of Communism's view of the world *as maneuvering-place* adds to the theory of two irreconcilable "camps" the dictum that all contact between these "irreconcilables" must be controlled from the Communist side. This dictum is made manifest in the intricate machinery of the Iron Curtain.

The dividing line that stretches across the world from the juncture of the Soviet Union and Norway to that of North and South Korea is not merely *boundary,* but *barrier.*

The degree to which it is "open" or "closed" varies from point to point, and from one Communist "policy period" to another. But to the Communists, any point at which they *cannot* close it—as between East and West Berlin—is anathema. So is any free-world force—like Radio Free Europe or RIAS (Radio in the American Sector of Berlin)—that defies the machinery of cloture.

In reverse, however, this boundary that is "closed" against all unsolicited crossings from the non-Communist side is regarded as rightly "open" *from the Communist side* to all crossings that the Party may initiate. Any force within the free world which halts or exposes such crossings is anathema.

Yet the line is definitely not open from the Communist side to any crossings that the Party does not approve. If the Iron Curtain forms a barrier against the outside world, it also forms a "corral." The escapee who defies it is anathema. The extent to which he is anathema was made clear, in February 1960, by an event proudly reported in *Obrana Lidu*, organ of the Czech Ministry of Defense. A railway signalman and his wife, the article said, had just been decorated by the Czechoslovakian government for "exemplary cooperation with frontier guards": they had, over a period of years, foiled the escape across the Austrian border of three hundred refugees.

Just as our Western minds have preferred to rate the "two-camp" dogma as a "curable" product of Communist insecurity, so we have preferred to think of the Iron Curtain as just a manifestation of fear. According to this view, *Curtainism* is already becoming, in this Khrushchev era of growing Soviet strength, a leftover from the era of Stalin's paranoia and of the Soviet Union's "encirclement" by a hostile world. It is hopefully regarded, in short, as a vestigial remains.

It is far from that. It is part of Communism's design for success: for keeping matters under control. *Iron Curtainism—*

with all that it implies in the way of censorship, barbed wire, radio-jamming, and the rest—is one of the means by which Marxism-Leninism is projected upon that "maneuvering-place" which is our planet.

When Lenin created the Bolshevik Party, he ordained that it was to be "closed" and impenetrable: a hard-core party. What it did and how it did it was to be its own affair—with no uninvited witnesses. No "bourgeois," "reformist," or "revisionist" influences were to be tolerated within its ranks.

On the other hand, this Party was to regard all elements outside itself as open to penetration, and subject to take-over. To effect such penetration, the Bolsheviks could move in illegal secrecy; or they could work in the open, and even make temporary alliances with the "enemy." But penetration must be achieved: ". . . we must have 'our own men' . . . everywhere, among all social strata . . ." (8)

Iron Curtainism simply carries forward these Leninist edicts into the period when the Party has not merely a structure to call its own, but a portion of the earth. The orbit where the Party holds power is endowed with the same sacrosanct impenetrability that Lenin bestowed upon the Party. But the rest of the world is regarded as rightly open to penetration—because *it is future Communist territory.*

How do the Communists rationalize this one-sided design of *penetrating without being penetrated?* Within their frame of logic, this poses no problem. The immunities and privileges of the Bolshevik Party derived from its being the "progressive" element of the proletariat: the "revolutionary vanguard." It knew what was good for the "workers" better than they knew themselves—because they had only "trade union consciousness," not revolutionary insight. Moreover, the Party, armed with Lenin's strategies, knew precisely how to do what needed to be done to further the best interests of the "workers." For it to have shared authority, then, or any part of the planning function, with other less enlightened social elements would have been treason to the human future: a willful delaying of progress.

The Communist orbit is the working base of this "vanguard" Party. Why, then, should it be intruded upon by "retrogressive" influences from the outside? These have nothing to offer to the future, being themselves slated to recede into the past. They could only slow up progress: a poor service to mankind. This is one half of the logic of Iron Curtainism: the half which contends that the orbit must be guarded against penetration by "reactionary bourgeois elements."

The other half of the logic simply works in reverse: the "obvious" duty of those who have a Communist home base from which to operate is to work their way into the non-Communist orbit, there to make common cause with "progressive elements" and effect their eventual "liberation." To this end, they *naturally* have to move outward across the dividing line between the orbits: that line which is *naturally* closed to reverse crossings from the "bourgeois" side.

If we hold this logic of Iron Curtainism in mind, we will be rendered less dizzy when, for example, Khrushchev hotly denounces as "interference in the internal affairs of the Soviet Union" some practice in which the Communists themselves habitually engage with respect to other countries. *They* are not interfering. They are extending "fraternal" support to the dispossessed but rightful owners of the non-Communist orbit.

This same logic accounts for the double standard which the Communists apply to espionage. In the wake of the U-2 affair, for example, Ulbricht, Party chief in the Soviet zone of Germany, found that people were inclined to ask embarrassing questions about Soviet espionage, when the "correct" response would have been for them simply to denounce America. He explained sharply that "the collection of military information by 'peace lovers' was not spying, but a humane duty." (9)

This view was not his own hasty makeshift. The Soviet government itself has issued a propaganda booklet entitled *No Return for U-2*, which contains the pronouncements on the subject of the U-2 by Khrushchev and Gromyko. Among other things, it reports Gromyko's having been asked, by a correspondent of the Baltimore *Sun*, about the Soviet Union's own maintenance of an intelligence agency. One should not, said Gromyko, judge the Soviet Union by American standards. (10)

When we ask ourselves, "Why not?" we have to circle right back to the ideology for an answer: that ideology which makes it a "humane duty" for the Communists to penetrate the non-Communist orbit without letting their own orbit be penetrated.

Over a period of several years, Khrushchev has been making far more strategic use of the Curtain's "open" features than Stalin ever did; and has been playing down, but not eliminating, its "closed" features. As a result, there are more people in the free world today than ever before who disagree with one another as to whether or not the Iron Curtain is only a vestigial remains—if, indeed, it is in operation at all. For personal experiences with respect to it are far more varied than when Stalin was alive; and many of these variations in experience bear the trade-mark of Khrushchevism.

In the Summer of 1959, for example, Khrushchev was going all out to sell to world public opinion his brand of "peace." In late July and early August, the Communist Youth Festival was held in Vienna—for the first time outside the Communist orbit. Party members who manned the information booths gave one stock answer to all questions about the Iron Curtain: "There is no Iron Curtain." To give this answer a semblance of truth, the border most accessible to Vienna—that between Austria and Hungary—was "prettied up": the barrier of barbed wire and guard towers was partially, not wholly, dismantled.

In that same Summer, an unprecedented number of Western tourists visited the Soviet Union. The reports which many of them brought back were like surprised echoes of the routine answer given at the Vienna information booths: "There is no Iron Curtain."

But there was. A "mobile" form of it became abruptly visible at the Youth Festival itself. Delegates had been instructed to be "friendly." But when some of them began, as *individuals*, not as *Communists*, to show friendliness toward people of the host country and Western tourists in Vienna, and an interest in non-Communist printed materials, a "mobile barricade" was established.

Soon, delegates were being herded from bus to meeting place to living place; and unauthorized outsiders who approached their "corral" came under hostile scrutiny. Only the Poles stubbornly maintained, and patently enjoyed, relative freedom. The Chinese Communists, whose compound was guarded by dogs, were most rigorously controlled, with the Hungarians and Czechs as runners-up.

Shortly after this Festival, we ourselves, with two staff members of Radio Free Europe, drove out from Nürnberg to the Czecho-German border at Tillyschantz. This road used to run through to Prague. Now it ends as abruptly as if cut with a knife. The village of Tillyschantz, which once spanned the border, has been similarly amputated. Except for a few houses, well back from the line, now used as barracks, the Czech portion of it has been leveled.

We stopped—confronted by an Iron Curtain that was no vestigial remains. The barriers of electrified barbed wire were no sagging relic of Stalinism. They were taut; and the middle barricade had been added only a few months earlier. Behind the barbed wire, concrete "dragon's teeth" jutted up to forbid vehicular traffic; and they did not stand neglected among weeds. As we got out of our car and followed a path parallel to the border, we were scrutinized and photographed from Communist guard towers. Three such towers were in sight— so placed that the guards could watch not only every foot of the border but one another as well.

Turning back on the amputated road, we angled across country to another border point, at Waldhaus-Rosshaupt. Here, on the only highway still open between West Germany and Prague, there was two-way traffic, though slight in volume. Persons with passports and visas in order were halted only long enough for the routine formalities of entrance and egress: "There is no Iron Curtain."

What has happened is that the Iron Curtain—with no basic change in function, and with most of its Stalinist features still in use or in reserve—now presents to the non-Communist eye more contradictions than ever before. Only some knowledge of the ideological basis of Iron Curtainism can enable this eye to see as one whole the barrier at Tillyschantz and the "open" highway at Waldhaus-Rosshaupt; Khrushchev's well-publicized unjamming of Western broadcasts in the Fall of 1959 and the fact that he had two thousand jamming stations in operation just a year later; or the Communists' long invasion of the free world by Parties, "fronts," and press and the indignant complaint of Georgi Zhukov, Director of Soviet Cultural Relations with Foreign Countries, in October 1959, that the United States was trying to use exchange programs to "foist an alien ideology" on the Soviet Union and East European countries.

Here, then, are two aspects of Communism's ideological geography. First, it divides the world into "two camps": one occupying Communist territory; the other, *future* Communist territory. In the second place, it puts the boundary between the two wholly under Communist control—on the theory that while there can be no proper reason for the "progressive" camp to be penetrated by "reactionary" elements, the "fated" course of history demands that the "reactionary" camp be penetrated by "progressive elements." The elaborate apparatus for regulating the back-and-forth traffic of men, ideas, and materials is the Iron Curtain.

It remains to take stock of a third aspect of this curious geography—and one with which we shall deal more fully in later chapters. Again, it has to do with the "two camps"; but with the relation of areas and forces *within them* rather than with the division between them.

In Marxist-Leninist theory, the non-Communist orbit is incurably divided against itself: by the "class struggle" within each separate country; the cutthroat competition among capitalist countries; and the struggle of colonies to escape from imperialist control and establish their independence.

The prime characteristic of the non-Communist orbit, in brief, is its vulnerability to Communist attack. There are always points at which divisive wedges can be driven in. There are always points at which antagonisms can be heightened and exploited: between classes, races, allied nations, blocs of nations. The everlasting task of the Communists is to make a "correct" appraisal of opportunities, and then to work out a "useful" strategy. Attack can be by such standard methods as propaganda, infiltration, and subversion. But Khrushchev has added some insidious new methods of his own within the frame of "peaceful coexistence." By "lowering tensions," for example, he has tried to make room for a free play of mutual suspicions, irritations, and rivalries within NATO. Again, in September 1960, he tried to split the United Nations into colonial and anticolonial blocs.

Attack can be openly hostile—as in Khrushchev's vituperative denouncing of Eisenhower, in his Paris press conference in May 1960, and of Hammarskjold in the General Assembly of the United Nations. Or it can take place under the guise of "peaceful coexistence" and "peaceful competition"—if the capitalists can be persuaded to believe that being pushed into their graves without being shot first is more "friendly." But it is a Communist axiom that the campaign *to divide and conquer* must always be in process, by myriad expedient means, in myriad places.

Now, what of the Communist orbit? In theory, it cannot contain any deep tensions or antagonisms; for it has overthrown the system which breeds these: the "class struggle," capitalist competition, and imperialism are no more. Within each Communist country, "monolithic unity" prevails; and within the orbit, "socialist solidarity"—with the Soviet Union giving "fraternal guidance" to less experienced countries.

In practice, as we shall note in later chapters, the Communist orbit contains tensions galore: enough of them to keep the hierarchy forever nervous in a world of normal human diversities and to put a shrill edge on the Party's demands for a stepped-up war against "bourgeois remnants" and "revisionism."

Such tensions, however, have no *ideological* right to exist. Hence, they create a double crisis. The free world has to worry only about the practical consequences of mutual pullings and haulings, and about these only when they begin to get out of bounds. For the free world is a world of acknowledged diversity. But when tensions crop up in the Communist orbit, the hierarchy has to worry about *both* their practical consequences and their illegitimate presence. This makes life difficult; and it points to the war in which Communism is most deeply and persistently engaged: the war against the stubborn *variousness* of human nature and society.

Here, then, in broad outline, is Communism's peculiar system of ideological-political geography. It results from a translation of the Marxist-Leninist "world view" into a strategic view of the world: a view of the whole earth as a *maneuvering-place*. Into this scheme of things, we can now put Khrushchev's policy of "peaceful coexistence."

THE MEANING OF
"PEACEFUL COEXISTENCE"

A SOVIET Resolution on propaganda, dated January 10, 1960, states, "The party has in a novel way expressed the problems of peace and war under present-day conditions." (1) It has indeed. It has expressed them in so "novel" a way that it enables every well-schooled Communist to read the word *war* where the rest of us are invited to read the word *peace*.

Khrushchev is the author of this "novelty." The essence of it has been compressed into his trade-mark phrase, "peaceful coexistence."

When the Communist Party of the Soviet Union held its Twentieth Congress in 1956, "collective leadership" was still the order of the day. But Khrushchev claimed the spotlight by setting forth a new "creative development of Marxism." The world balance of power, he said, had so decisively shifted in favor of the "socialist camp" that a new possibility had been introduced into the "historic process": namely, that Communism's final take-over of the world might be achieved by peaceful means. That climactic war between the "two camps" which Lenin had pronounced to be inevitable had become avoidable.

He gave himself an orthodox "out": as long as there were "capitalist imperialist nations," there would always, of course, be the risk of their starting a war—in an effort to grab more power or to fend off an economic crisis. But the "socialist camp" had become a formidable counterbalance to "imperialism." If it could rally around itself all "peace-loving elements" everywhere, even the "warmongers" would have to think twice before launching a war which, for them, could only be suicidal.

While the "warmongers" were thinking twice, the "camp of peace" would be growing ever stronger. Since this "camp of peace" would not start a war, the great point of change in the "historic process" would come when the "imperialist camp" finally recognized the futility of starting one. At this point, the foundation would be laid for "peaceful coexistence between states with different social systems."

We cannot know how much impact this doctrinal innovation would have had if it had stood alone; for it did not stand alone. At that same Twentieth Congress, Khrushchev made his "de-Stalinization" speech; and, further, he declared that countries within the Soviet bloc should have more latitude than Stalin had ever given them to find their own proper "roads to socialism."

Thus, on three counts he seemed to downgrade the hitherto infallible. Throughout the Communist world, it was as though an earthquake had taken place along a hitherto unsuspected ideological "fault line." The resultant confusion was a mixture

of hope and dismay: hope among those, particularly in East
Europe, who felt that he had promised them a new measure
of personal and national freedom; dismay among those Communists everywhere who felt that he had cut the ground out
from under the "monolithic" system and the "historic mission."

Significantly, both the elated and the dismayed read into
Khrushchev's words more of "peace" than he had intended.
So did non-Communists in hopeful multitude. Khrushchev
had said that the Soviet Union needed peace in order to build
up its economy. This made sense. He had said that no sane
person could want nuclear war. This, too, made sense. Let
him go on talking, then, if he must, about "warmongers" and
Communism's "inevitable" victory. Time and the live-and-
let-live experiences of "peaceful coexistence" would take care
of the dogma.

Khrushchev was willing enough to have non-Communists
misread his meaning. But it was a different matter for Communists to do so; just as it was a different matter for them to
start claiming more freedom than the Soviet Union could tolerate their having. Before long, and emphatically after the
Polish and Hungarian uprisings, a step-by-step process of "re-
Stalinization" got under way; and Khrushchev devoted himself to a full-scale effort to make clear to Party members
everywhere that "peaceful coexistence between states with
different social systems" does not imply "ideological peace."
It implies war with new weapons.

Three years elapsed between the Twentieth and Twenty-
First Congresses of the CPSU (Communist Party of the
Soviet Union). For Khrushchev, they were crowded years. He
had to complete his own drive for power, ridding himself of
rivals and opponents. He had to make clear to Communists
both inside and outside the orbit what he meant, and *what*

he did not mean, by "peaceful coexistence"; and to reunite the world Communist movement around the meaning which he put into this phrase. He had to reassert the dominance of the Soviet Union over the satellites. On the home front, he had to make ready for the vast economic-ideological effort which was to be launched by means of the Seven Year Plan. And, not least, he had to shape up a Soviet foreign policy that would implement his doctrinal innovation, and to start selling his brand of "peace" throughout the non-Communist world—to both highly developed and underdeveloped countries.

By the time the Twenty-First Congress convened in Moscow, early in 1959, he had accomplished enough of what he had set out to do that he could speak from strength. When he gave his Report on the Seven Year Plan target figures, he did not need to fear that the delegates and visiting representatives from seventy Communist Parties would seriously misunderstand him when he spoke of "peaceful coexistence." That danger had been liquidated—at least, so far as the hard core of the Party was concerned.

Some among the assembled Communists—notably, the Chinese—might understand and yet disagree, both with his "creative development of Marxism" and with the foreign policy based upon it. But there was no danger that the Chinese would make the mistake which had proved so disruptive in East Europe in 1956. They would be *less* ready than he wanted them to be to establish expedient relations with the "enemy camp"—not *more* ready.

Thus, he did not have to be wary about saying, "All we want is an early end to the cold war. . . . Everything that obstructs peaceful coexistence between states with different social systems must be swept away. . . . We must eliminate the things which aggravate the international situation and obstruct peaceful coexistence." (2)

If the world press, reporting on the Congress, quoted these words, and if a multitude of non-Communists, reading them, uttered a fervent, "Yes"—*precisely because they did not understand what he meant*—Khrushchev was under no obligation to set them straight. He had said often enough, and openly enough, that Communism's final victory was as "inevitable" as ever.

If these non-Communists put their own meanings into his statements, and thereby proved to themselves that he was a "blessedly new kind of Soviet dictator"; and if they put pressure upon their governments to meet him half way, and not to go on talking war when he was talking peace, and not to go on building up armaments when he was ready to disarm, this merely went to show that the Party's "novel way" of expressing the problems of peace and war under present day conditions was "correct." It was proved "correct" by the confusion it wrought in non-Communist minds and by the divisiveness it introduced into the non-Communist orbit.

Khrushchev, however, left nothing to chance so far as the Congress delegates and the representatives from Parties around the world were concerned. For them, he spelled out just what he meant by "things which aggravate the international situation." Without exception these aggravating factors *as he detailed them* were "capitalist imperialist policies": for example, all Western policies with respect to Berlin. At no point did he suggest any slightest change that might be called for in Soviet policy.

Khruschev said, "We must eliminate the things which . . . obstruct peaceful coexistence"; but no single thing which was to be eliminated *by Communist action* lay within the legitimate province *of Soviet policy*. In each case, it lay within the "policy province" of the West.

Also, Khrushchev identified the instigators of war. Pronouncing the unity of the working class to be "the most reliable barrier" against war and fascism, he asked, "Who obstructs the unity of the working class? Imperialist reaction and its henchmen in the working-class movement, such as Guy Mollet and Spaak . . ." (3)

These were not the only villains: "In another part of the world—the Far East—the aggressive policy of the United States in regard to the Chinese People's Republic and other peace-loving states is the main source of tensions." (4) Also, there were the economic "imperialists" who were "bribing" newly liberated peoples into servitude by means of "aid" programs.

Again, the Yugoslav "revisionists" must not be forgotten. They "resent our telling them that they are sitting on two stools. They insist that they are sitting on their own Yugoslav stool. But for some reason this Yugoslav stool is held up by the American monopolies!" (5) Such "revisionism," Khrushchev made clear, became more dangerous than ever in a period of "peaceful coexistence," because it threatened "socialist solidarity" at the very time when this should be intensified.

In its totality, Khrushchev's Report to the Congress delegates was designed to fortify their understanding of the fact that "peaceful coexistence between states with different social systems" does not imply "ideological peace." The very practice of such expedient "coexistence" calls, in fact, for an urgent stepping-up of the effort to "instill Communist consciousness" and to "combat bourgeois ideology." The doctrine of "peaceful coexistence" must be understood not as one that would lead to a gradual easing of the class struggle, but as a bold doctrine for opening up opportunities to carry on that struggle along new lines, particularly the line of economic competition.

The policy built upon this doctrine was designed to gain

time for "socialist construction"; to create a world mood favorable to advantageous negotiations and trade agreements; to aggravate tensions within the "imperialist camp"; to convince "peace-loving" people within this "imperialist camp" that the best road to peace was that mapped by Soviet policy; and, not least, to extend the ideological province of Marxism-Leninism to embrace all economically backward countries that were seeking to move forward.

Here, Khrushchev issued a warning. It was not enough to avoid "revisionism." This merely safeguarded "socialist solidarity." To make "peaceful coexistence" pay off in positive gains for the "socialist camp," it would also be necessary to avoid "sectarianism": a rigid refusal to establish even expedient relationships with non-Communists.

"Great changes have now taken place in the world. There are countries that make up the world socialist system and countries forming the world imperialist system. But there are also countries that are not socialist, but which cannot be regarded as belonging to the imperialist system. Having won their national independence . . . these countries want to follow a path of their own, by-passing the capitalist stage of development . . ." (6).

To let "sectarianism" limit the Party's contacts with these countries would be a serious error. Every effort must be made to establish "friendly" relations with them and to keep them reminded that the Soviet Union itself managed to by-pass "the capitalist stage of development." They must be brought, step by step, to see in the Soviet Union an example for themselves; and also to see this "invincible camp of Socialism" as having "everything necessary to bridle the forces of aggression," and as "a mighty bulwark of peace and international security." (7)

If all comrades could be brought to understand the magnitude of their opportunity, and to do their part with "selfless enthusiasm," the results could only be good. These newly independent countries would then gradually come, *of their own accord,* to accept what the truly "progressive" elements within them already knew: namely, that for the "international working-class movement and for the triumph of Communism the ideas of Marxism-Leninism are what sunshine and warmth are for plants, for life on earth . . ." (8)

Thus, Khrushchev sent the CPSU delegates home to all parts of the Soviet Union with their work cut out for them. They were to build up "Communist consciousness"; to combat "bourgeois ideology"; and to stimulate the people to work "selflessly" for the fulfillment of the Seven Year Plan— which was to provide the economic base for the expansionist drive on the world front.

The visiting Communists who went home to their seventy Parties around the world also had their work cut out for them. In underdeveloped countries, they were to accomplish two ends, under the aegis of "peaceful coexistence." They were, in so far as possible, to "eliminate" non-Communist influence within these countries and to stimulate fear and hatred of the "capitalist imperialist" nations. And they were, by all expedient means, to convince the new nationalist governments that the Soviet Union had the secret of swift economic advance and that they could not go wrong in accepting "friendly" guidance from that great nation.

Parties operating within "capitalist imperialist" nations also had special tasks which stemmed from the policy of "peaceful coexistence"; and in behalf of these, they were to launch a new "united front" effort. They would, of course, continue to "politicalize" all the domestic issues of these "capitalist imperialist" nations: imposing upon them a Marxist-Leninist interpretation; aggravating them by means of agitation and propaganda; and discrediting "reformist" efforts to solve them. But also they must, by every possible means, work to set the NATO countries against one another; and they must work to effect in the public mind the closest possible identification of Soviet policy with peace.

Three additional comments may help, here, to round out this picture of the world Communist movement readied for its next drive. The first of these takes us back several months before the Twenty-First Congress and anticipates certain directives which Khrushchev later made explicit.

The October 1958 issue of the Moscow *Kommunist* carried an article by B. Ponomarev, "The International Communist Movement at the New Stage." On a number of counts, it put the minds of Party cadres through a dress rehearsal for their later orientation.

In the "so-called classical capitalist countries," the article indicated, it would be a waste of time for the Party to try to form a united front with the workers. For the time being, "the bourgeoisie and their right-wing socialist accomplices" had succeeded in their effort to "deceive" the working people. Thus, the working-class movement, in its interpretation of problems and its view of the world situation, was not currently accessible, in significant measure, to Communist propaganda or to efforts at collaboration—even in behalf of "peace."

This unreachability of organized labor was not too important, however. It did not stand in the way of reaching through either to "peace-loving" elements in the capitalist countries or to those whose good will could lead to profitable trade relations. Neither did it stand in the way of profitable diplomatic relations.

Taking the world as a whole, the article saw it as a most promising field of action: "New sites of revolutionary movement are being created all the time." In "the countries of the East, Latin America, and some European countries, the labor movement distinguishes itself by its militant character and solidarity; it displays examples of Marxist-Leninist vigor and is rising."

But, said Ponomarev, the labor movement in underdeveloped countries must not be thought of as always rising against the government. In some countries, the government itself must be rated as "progressive"; and in these, the labor movement is part of the national struggle for "liberation not only from the foreign yoke but also from social slavery . . ." The Communist Party, in each such case, must make certain that labor leaders draw their inspiration "from the treasure-house of socialist ideology," and that they rely upon this ideology for "operative perspectives."

One sentence in this article is so Leninist that if it were fitted into the text of *What Is to Be Done?*—which Lenin published in 1902—it could pass as part of the whole. In these countries striving for "freedom, peace, and social progress," the Party "gives the proper orientation to the working class, helps it to understand complicated events and to recognize the political intentions of one or another political grouping . . ."

Our second comment takes us back to the Twenty-First Congress, at which, after Khrushchev had given his Report, Mikoyan told of the impressions which he had gained from his scouting visit to the United States. From "both the ordinary Americans and the business men" with whom he had talked, he had received a "very friendly welcome." They had shown themselves interested in the Soviet people and in Soviet policy; and they had wanted "to get us right." In handling their questions, Mikoyan assured the Congress delegates, he had helped them do this. Also, they clearly wanted peace and would be responsive to any effort to insure peace.

Various persons in government circles, he was sorry to

report, had been less flexible. They had seemed unresponsive to the "favorable climate" created by the Soviet Union's bid for "peaceful coexistence"; and reluctant to work out "measures to end the 'cold war.'" Some had even "joined," apparently, "the campaign for fostering the 'cold war.'" In contrast, the people in general, and particularly "leading business men and industrialists," had shown "a gratifying wish for peace and mutual understanding." (9)

Our third comment takes us from the Twenty-First Congress, in Moscow, to New York City some ten and a half months later, to the Seventeenth National Convention of the CPUSA (Communist Party of the United States). We make this mental trip because it lets us take stock of Khrushchev's directives at one of the multitudinous points at which, throughout that year, they were being *translated into action;* as they have been translated into action ever since.

The keynote speaker at this convention—from which even the American press was rigidly excluded—was Gus Hall, newly elected General Secretary of the CPUSA. He built his speech around a question: "What is the role of the party in this entirely new situation?" Since the CPUSA had been represented at the Congress in Moscow, we need not regard as obscure the meaning of the phrase, "in this entirely new situation." Nor need we regard Hall's answer to the question as his own brain-child: to do its job, the Party must overcome its "isolation" and move out "into the broad stream of the people's movement."

Only thus could it convert directive into action: "We want to participate in, organize, and lead the broadest of united front movements . . ." (10)

If Khrushchev were simply a traditional power-seeker—the kind whose name is legion in history—he might have watched the well-instructed comrades depart from the

Twenty-First Congress and have said to himself in the words
of Shakespeare's Mark Antony:

> Now let it work: mischief, thou art afoot,
> Take thou what course thou wilt!

But Khrushchev is a *Communist:* an agent of that "historic
process" which, Marx stated, had been brought into being
by the first division of labor rooted in private property, and
which would continue until the communization of all property everywhere had been achieved. Moreover, he is a
Leninist: an agent of the "vanguard" Party. Still further, it
was as a *Stalinist* that he learned to "get results."

Nothing, therefore, could have been further from his mind
than to let "mischief"—or anything else—take its own course.
He had completed, for the time being, his pedagogic task.
He had made explicit the meaning of "peaceful coexistence
between states with different social systems"; and he had
made sure that all Party members, each in his own domain,
knew the nature of the task ahead. He himself, therefore,
could turn to his own next undertaking.

This undertaking called, we might say, for his laying off
his Congress role as head of the CPSU and the world Communist movement, and stepping into his alternative role: that
of Premier of the Soviet State and Chairman of its Council of
Ministers. For he, too, had to take the world as his province
—for personal diplomacy. While keeping an eye on the whole
Communist enterprise, he had to settle down to the business
of persuading the West that its relation with the Soviet Union
"should be built upon the foundation of friendship and . . .
should fully correspond to the principles of peaceful coexistence." (11) For it would not be enough for the Parties
around the world to perform their assigned tasks unless he
could deliver, by means of diplomacy, various advantageous
agreements with the West: on Berlin, trade, and disarmament.

During the fifteen months that lay between the Twenty-First Congress of the CPSU and the blasting of the Summit conference, in May 1960, the hope for peace got a stronger hold on Western minds than at any time since Stalin had begun to fill the postwar "authority vacuum" of East Europe with Soviet authority.

It was as though Khrushchev had insinuated into the atmosphere a "theme song" called *Peaceful Coexistence;* and as though people of all sorts had begun by contagion to hum snatches of the tune under their breath, or even to sing them out in full voice. When once Khrushchev's "theme song" had thus become, in effect, a folksong, its store of words grew by spontaneous additions. But the burden of it remained that Soviet Communism could now be lived with "because Khrushchev doesn't want war."

It could be lived with "because Khrushchev is a practical man; not an ideologist." It could be lived with "because Khrushchev, though he can't openly say so, is afraid of Red China and wants to build the sort of friendship with the West that he may need later." It can be lived with "because Khrushchev, while he learned how to *survive* under Stalin, is no Stalinist: he has no power-complex, and would rather run a tractor than a world empire."

It can be lived with "because education and technology are making the Soviet Union more liberal and democratic"; and, "because, as standards of living go up in the Soviet Union, the people are becoming more like us all the time"; and "because the Soviet Union under Khrushchev certainly isn't any worse than a lot of other dictatorships with which we've managed to get along." It can be lived with "because we have no alternative; we can't risk nuclear war."

Khrushchev himself, to be sure, kept introducing discordant notes: threats with respect to Berlin; charges of "aggression" and "interference"; obstructions to the very disarmament agreements which he said he wanted. But there might be, in each case, some point to the reasons he gave. Besides, the modern world is a discordant place. Even in the sphere of "peaceful coexistence," perhaps, it must be expected to produce a music after its own kind.

Then abruptly, in May 1960, with the U-2 incident as the ostensible cause, there came the crashing, climactic discord, with Khrushchev's voice adding invective to invective. Not only the Summit conference but a multitude of illusions were splintered by the impact of sound at this new pitch. The first era of "peaceful coexistence" was ended.

THREE

IN THE WAKE OF
AN ILLUSION

IN THE staccato weeks which followed the Summit debacle, there were days on end when the news had the
quality of machine-gun fire; and when the element of peace
in "peaceful coexistence" seemed due to reach the vanishing
point.

Before leaving Paris, Khrushchev reaffirmed the doctrine
of "peace." A month later, at the Congress of the Communist
Party of Rumania, in Bucharest, he did so even more strongly.
In the course of that summer of 1960, however—against a
background of riots in Japan, uprisings in the Congo and
Rhodesia, and myriad other signs that the world was heavily
heaving itself into a new position—he "scrapped" the Monroe
Doctrine and threatened a missile defense of Cuba if the
United States practiced "aggression" against that country;
threatened to bomb American bases in Europe; rushed Soviet
troops to the Congo; and accused both the NATO powers

and the United Nations of "conniving" to "re-enslave" that young nation.

He put a melodramatic end to the disarmament talks in Geneva by engineering a walk-out of the delegates from the USSR, Poland, Czechoslovakia, Bulgaria, and Rumania; used the occasion of a visit to Austria to make veiled threats against that country's neutrality; and carried to the United Nations the case of the Soviet shooting-down of the RB-47 plane, charging that its flight had constituted an "aggressive" act. When his charge was voted down, and when Great Britain proved ready to support, on the basis of independent evidence, the claim of the United States that the plane had been attacked in international air space, he refused to permit any international body to investigate the circumstances of its being shot down.

In mid-August, he—who has used Soviet embassies all around the world as espionage centers—(1) turned the trial of Powers, the pilot of the U-2 plane, into a mammoth, carefully staged "spectacular." In September, he induced a new crisis in Berlin; and he descended upon the United Nations with the largest entourage of fellow Communists ever to convert the General Assembly into a propaganda forum.

Yet these events did not comprise the full story of that summer and fall. Less obtrusive than the sense of crisis, but no less present in the atmosphere of the free world, was a curious calm. It might almost have been described as

> . . . the large and unclamoring peace
> Of a dream that was ended. (2)

For it was, in effect, the calm of making ready for the next long pull: for the second era of "peaceful coexistence"— which would be distinguished from the first by a sharp diminishment of the illusion that "peace" means peace.

On the very day the Summit meeting was canceled, this calm was signaled by a closing of ranks. There was no fanfare about this. It simply took place. Khrushchev, up to the minute of leaving Paris, continued to try to drive a wedge between Macmillan and de Gaulle, on the one hand, and Eisenhower, on the other. Not only did his effort fail—his making of it seemed part of his sudden divorce from reality.

It suggested an overweening pride in his own manipulative skill. Even more, it made him seem a drearily average product of that Communist thought-machine which has, for decades, been turning out the stereotype that "capitalist imperialist" nations can always be pried apart. Khrushchev stood revealed as a man who had not the slightest concept of the extent to which the three men with whom he was dealing respected the values which they had in common. While he went on trying to make the old stereotype prove out in action, they began looking ahead toward sustained efforts they could make to strengthen the organizations through which the unities of free men can find practical expression.

The Western heads of state closed ranks; and behind them the people closed ranks. They did not thereby relinquish any part of their right to criticize the policies of their own governments. They simply acted out once more one of the perennial dramas of democracy. By so doing, they too called attention to the Communist thought-machine and to Khrushchev as a product of it.

With a fine disregard for contrary evidence, this "scientific" machine has gone on, decade after decade, turning out the stereotype that the people and the government of a "capitalist imperialist" nation can always be pried apart, because their "true" interests are lodged at the two poles of the "class struggle." Khrushchev himself has made an enormous investment of hope in this stereotype which, stemming from the dogma of economic determinism, has never made room for the consequences of political democracy.

The Communists have talked endlessly about economic vested interests. Yet the world's top Communist has shown himself as unable as the least comrade to credit one of the most potent vested interests on record: that of a politically free people in a system that lets them keep up a running fire of criticism against it, because it is theirs, and they can always see things in it that they wish were different.

The closing of ranks of which we are speaking here is not to be taken as equivalent to the building of adequate free-world unities. The months that have elapsed since the collapse of the Summit conference have contained many evidences of how hard it is for nations to work out the practicalities by which their separate goals and their common goals can be reconciled by voluntary agreement. Nonetheless, and in spite of all the pullings and haulings, it seems fair to date from May 1960 a new urgency of conviction that common policies must be achieved.

One further aspect of this closing of ranks must be noted; for it received, we think, too little attention when East-West gains and losses were being added up. This was the abrupt closing of ranks on the part of the world's free press against what Khrushchev showed himself to be.

Prior to the events in Paris, newsmen had, on many occasions, enjoyed Khrushchev as a man to interview, as a good source of copy. They had found him blunt; quick on the uptake; ready to be made the target of their questions; and alert to make them and their countries the target of his answers. For all his dogmatism, and his abrupt angers, he had not shown himself to them as a man with whom it would be too hard to reach some commonsense agreements.

Then, suddenly, at the press conference in Paris, they were confronted by a sulfurous Khrushchev: a man of unleashed fury and mental brutality; a fanatic hater whom it was not too hard to visualize as a fanatic killer; and, not least, a dictator who might be much further along the road to megalomania than any of them had suspected. From being a man whose virtue was that of being nobody's fool, he had changed into a man whose vice was that of being evil.

The newsmen turned to a new enterprise. From weighing the pros and cons of the U-2 flight, and of our cross-purposed handling of the situation—to all of which they could revert later—they turned to the making of a different kind of estimate. They weighed what the Western heads of state represented as against what Khrushchev represented; and weighed their conduct *under stress* against his.

Their verdict could be called unanimous: Khrushchev was no safe man to have in control of other men's lives; and not much could be said for a system that would not only let him maneuver his way to the top but that would make him appear "liberal" by comparison with other elements in the hierarchy. As one witness to his performance said later, in conversation, "I got the sudden feeling that there just wasn't room enough on earth for both mankind and Communism."

In addition to this strange calm of closing ranks, there was the calm, also—at least, among experienced observers— of recognizing that while Khrushchev was on the warpath, he was not risking war. The strongest proof of this came almost immediately in the wake of the press conference, when he stopped off in East Berlin on his way back to Moscow.

Khrushchev had long since wrapped up the "German question" in a threat that was a promise to the puppet regime in the East zone: he would sign a separate peace treaty with this so-called German Democratic Republic and then leave it up to the Communist regime in this "independent" nation to eliminate the "cancer" of West Berlin.

When he left Paris, therefore, it seemed shockingly clear

that if he intended to convert into action the fury and hatred which he had there shown forth, East Berlin would be his most likely starting point. It was also clear that any action which he might start in this spirit could reduce to a shambles not a Summit meeting, but the world itself.

The German Communist leaders visibly hoped that he would make good, at last, on his threats and promises. Instead, he turned the powder keg into a pulpit from which to preach the virtues of patience. What, he asked, should be done at this moment of deadlock between East and West? And he answered: "We shall work for peace by negotiation, and we believe that negotiation should take place at the Summit in six to eight months' time." (3)

By thus urging patience upon the German Communist regime, Khrushchev gave the free world a yardstick by which to measure his subsequent threats. Thus measured, they all appeared to have one characteristic in common: they were not tied up with any specific commitment that seemed likely to unleash a war. When he threatened, for example, to defend Cuba even to the point of missile warfare, he stopped well short of defining the precise form of American "aggression" that would move him to this extremity.

None of this meant that his mounting threats could be laughed off. They had to be taken seriously—as the opening guns of a new major propaganda offensive. Their ostensible targets were the Western powers, particularly the United States. But their *propaganda* targets were the leaders of "national liberation" movements in underdeveloped, politically seething countries.

Thus, when he said that he would, even at the risk of war, prevent "aggression" against Cuba, he was not actually saying to the United States, "Stop. Be warned. Stay out of Cuba,

or else." There was no call for such a warning. The United
States was quite obviously preoccupied with the question
of how to defend itself *by means short of force* against
Castro's virulent anti-Americanism. Khrushchev knew this.
Therefore, to target minds in Asia, Africa, and Latin America,
he said, in effect, "The United States is at it again. Once an
imperialist always an imperialist. But now, fortunately, the
Soviet Union is strong enough to prevent the capitalist imperialists from enslaving weaker nations."

In its verbiage, Khrushchev's new propaganda line was
tediously old. The intensity of it was what drove home the
fact that it signaled a major shift in Soviet policy. This shift
would take place within the frame of "peaceful coexistence."
To this extent, it would be continuous with the policy it was
replacing. But it would represent a new deploying of Communism's forces, and a new constellation of strategies. Also,
apparently, it would cast Khrushchev in an altered role: that
of the outright Communist agitator. To this extent, it would
be discontinuous with what had gone before.

One era of Soviet foreign policy had spanned the entire
period from the time when Khrushchev, even prior to his
full consolidation of power, had begun to make that policy
his own unique creation to the torpedoing of the Summit
conference, in May 1960. The second policy era could be
dated from that point. What would be its character? What
had determined its timing?

Answers to such questions have to be looked for among
the eventful realities of the period that has produced Khrushchevism. One such determinative reality can be made to
stand clear by the substitution of one word for another: by
our talking, not about "peaceful coexistence," but about
"stalemate coexistence." For while Khrushchev's policy has
had little enough to do with peace, it has been inseparable

from the fact that an East-West military stalemate exists. Moreover, this stalemate exists at a level where the potential destructiveness of the weapons that are held back from use is in itself a further deterrent to their use.

It is no accident that one of Khrushchev's favorite words is *patience*—though his personal make-up is scarcely one that would seem to bring it naturally to his tongue. In a period of stalemate, the Communists have no choice other than to be patient with the fact that "capitalist imperialist" nations still encumber the earth and have to be dealt with by means short of war. Further, all expedient means that are available for breaking the stalemate, and for moving beyond it to a balance of power that will favor the Communists, are means that call for patience.

Khrushchevism is a design for so operating within the framework of stalemate as to gain some advantage which can, by many small or large accretions of added advantage, be made, in the end, *decisive*. Such a policy calls for a "correctly" paced exploitation of every opportunity to make a gain for Communism that will also be a loss for "imperialism": in self-assurance, internal unity, influence, prestige, markets, raw materials, alliances, territory, or military striking power.

Patience is the key word to Khrushchevism, not because Khrushchev is a patient man, but because he is a Communist; and there are two things which the Communists cannot do until some decisive shift has been made in the balance of power.

First, they cannot try to force any gain for themselves that would entail so great a loss for the "imperialists" that the latter would simply refuse to accept it as more tolerable than war. Here, we have the apparent reason why Khrushchev did not force the issue in Germany, in May 1960. Again and again, prior to that date, he had put out threats as "feelers." There seems to have been a time, in the wake of his visit to the United States, when he was almost convinced that he could safely move from threat to action. Then he was told otherwise.

On April 4, 1960, Secretary of State Herter, speaking in Chicago, warned Khrushchev not to repeat his threat about signing a separate peace treaty with the puppet regime in the Soviet zone of Germany if he hoped to reach any agreement with the West on the control of armaments. And on April 20, Undersecretary of State Dillon, speaking at an AFL-CIO meeting in New York, said that Khrushchev was "skating on thin ice" when he made this threat. Khrushchev complained that these speeches violated "the spirit of Camp David" and "reeked" of cold war. But in East Berlin, a month later—and in spite of his raging performance in Paris—he urged patience.

In the second place, until the stalemate is decisively broken in Communism's favor, the Soviet Union has to keep in moth balls its traditional method for consolidating power—the method which enabled Stalin to build his satellite empire. In at least some of the underdeveloped countries today, Parties, "fronts," and Soviet teams are preparing the soil for take-over quite as well as the East European Parties did at the behest of Stalin. But Khrushchev cannot do what Stalin did: *he cannot convert preparation into accomplishment by moving in with armed forces.*

Stalin's ability to act *as if he had a favorable balance of power,* and thereby to subjugate a hundred million people, was, we must recall, a gift from our Western selves. We trusted his motives enough, and were anxious enough to have the war ended, that we pulled out of East Europe the forces that could have insured stalemate. Thus, we lost the chance to include at least several of the East European countries in the Marshall Plan. There is every reason to believe that if we had not lost this chance, these countries today would be enjoying economic stability and political freedom as part of the community of Western Europe.

Khrushchev has never expressed other than admiration for Stalin's method of empire-building. Also, he has shown himself to be aware that the method would be a "natural" in many underdeveloped countries in the world if only the West were not so "rigid." The West, however, has not, this time, offered a favorable balance of power as a free gift. If, therefore, he is not to lose the unparalleled opportunity for Communist expansion which these countries represent, he has to find substitutes for armed force.

While his Parties, "fronts," agents, and teams have kept themselves busy with preparatory work in Asia, Africa, and Latin America, Khrushchev has, during recent years, devoted himself intensively to the effort to provide two decisive substitutes for armed force: *economic power* and *diplomatic success.*

There has been one area—that of Soviet economic development—in which Khrushchev has not made *patience* his watchword. Rather, this watchword has been *urgency.* For if the preparatory work to which his "outpost" forces everywhere have been devoting themselves is not to prove vain, the Soviet Union must be able to move in with full economic strength when the time is right. Meanwhile, through its programs of trade and aid, it has to make the best possible strategic use of its economic and technical resources to supplement the accomplishments of propaganda and agitation:

"First the easy credit terms from Moscow. Then barter deals that lock trade in Communist channels. After that, machine tools made in Russia that require spare parts made in Russia. And Russian technicians, Russian engineers, Russian economic consultants. Finally, it is time for Russian arms,

Russian military advisors, and pro-Russian governments that expropriate private investments and order the evacuation of American military power from 'neutral' soil." (4)

By this process, we must note, Khrushchev is taking leave of one of the historic axioms of Russian imperialism, Tsarist or Communist. Unlike Western imperialism, Russian imperialism, as developed under the Tsars and carried forward by Lenin and Stalin, devoted itself to the conquest of territory that was contiguous to territory already controlled. We shall take stock in a later chapter of the manner in which the Soviet Union has practiced this historic type of Russian imperialism.

Here, we wish to note that Khrushchev has invented a "novel" kind of imperialism. He is working to establish, at strategic points around the world, *economic satellites* that will, in effect, be also political satellites, but that will remain "neutral" and "independent." By this means he can accomplish two ends. He can acquire colonies without having to give up his propaganda line about Western imperialism. And he can swell the number of pro-Soviet votes in the United Nations—which he could not do by absorbing new territory into the Soviet Union or by openly reducing these economic satellites to colonies.

Thus, *economic diplomacy* is one of Khrushchev's two substitutes for armed force as a means of shifting the balance of power. The other substitute—to the cultivation of which he has devoted himself in his role as Premier of the Soviet State and Chairman of the Council of Ministers—is diplomacy with a Communist twist.

Ever since he got control of the machinery of State, in 1957, Khrushchev has exhibited a supreme confidence that he could negotiate advantageous agreements with the West. We must stress the word *advantageous;* for his aim has been to effect a favorable shift in the balance of power and thus to release from stalemate the Soviet Union's scientific-military apparatus of conquest. No agreement that was fair and equitable, but not *advantageous,* could serve this purpose.

He has tried to maneuver the West into making concessions with respect to Berlin that he would not have to match. He has tried to negotiate "fair and equitable" trade and exchange agreements with enough loopholes in them that he could, in practice, make them *advantageous.* And he has tried to negotiate the same type of "loopholed" agreement with respect to disarmament.

Here, his standard tactic has been to propose a disarmament agreement couched only in general terms, with the specifics of control and enforcement to be worked out *after it is signed:* an agreement, in brief, that would be just one big loophole. Offering such a proposal, he has declared the world's need of peace to be too urgent to have to wait upon technicalities. Thus, he has sought from "the people" a yes-response that would make the no-response of Western governments seem like a mark of "rigidity."

Here, then, in broad terms, is that strategy of "stalemate coexistence" which Khrushchev put into operation with increasing thoroughness during the several years that preceded the Summit debacle. With this "foolproof" plan in full swing, why did Soviet policy suddenly change—and change in a direction successively mapped out by Khrushchev's vituperative crudeness at the Paris press conference; by the multiple threats that punctuated the Summer of 1960; and by his September attack on Secretary General Hammarskjold and the very structure of the United Nations?

Because the change first became conspicuous in connection with the U-2 flight, it has been easy to overlook deeper reasons for its taking place—particularly, as Khrushchev has tried to divert attention from these. But the reasons were there.

One incisive reason was that Khrushchev's "infallible" plan for getting results from the West had turned out to be exceedingly fallible. Both his supreme confidence in his own diplomatic shrewdness and the stereotype that "capitalist imperialist" nations can always be pried apart had let him down. He had not obtained even one clearly *advantageous* concession or agreement; and he had not split NATO.

In brief, while Parties and Soviet agents in Asia, Africa, and Latin America had scored propaganda gains by means of their "anti-imperialist" drives, Khrushchev had no diplomatic gains to chalk up in relation to the West. That phase of his foreign policy *which was uniquely his own to execute* had worked out much as the Chinese Communists and his opponents in the Soviet Union had said that it would.

A second incisive reason was that, by the Spring of 1960, the Soviet people had begun to show a disturbing readiness to believe that "peace" meant peace. Khrushchev had assured Party skeptics that he could prevent this development. Instead, he had helped to bring it about. The prize souvenir which he had brought home from all his diplomatic adventuring in the West had been "the spirit of Camp David." Making the most of this—both as a substitute for what he had not been able to secure and as a promise of what he would secure—he talked about it, in speeches and in the press, with insistent satisfaction. The Soviet people liked it, too. The only catch was that they took it to be the spirit of genuine peace; and they showed themselves more than ready to scrap the Iron Curtain and enjoy being part of the world.

As early as January 1960, Khrushchev launched an all-out propaganda drive to counteract this "lowering of tensions" at a point where he did not want them to be lowered. But there is no evidence that the drive had much effect. By late Spring, it was obviously time to re-jam Western radio broadcasts and to launch a new dramatic anti-American campaign.

In the third place, it was time to threaten the West with missile warfare—as a reminder of Soviet military striking power. For Western governments, and even the Western peoples, had made a less than "correct" response to the policy of "peaceful coexistence." To be sure, the people had shown a "correct" hunger for peace; but they had stopped far short of putting mass pressure on their governments to come to terms with the Soviet Union. As for the governments, they had showed increasing signs of being convinced that Khrushchev would not risk a war—even though they were also convinced that his "peace" did not mean peace. In short, they were not making the concessions he needed *either* out of faith or out of fear. Some "rocket-rattling" seemed in order.

Actually, this "rocket-rattling" paid small dividends. For Khrushchev's program of scientific weaponry had not effected that basic shift in the balance of power which the Sputniks had initially seemed to promise. Developments had indeed continued; but they had not sufficed to open any decisive gap between Soviet and Western striking power. Therefore, in one sense, they had netted Khrushchev nothing.

Moreover, he was not able to make his new threats sound new: they were all too tediously familiar from past cycles of "toughness." Max Frankel, correspondent of the *New York Times*, who returned to the United States late in the Summer of 1960, after spending three years in the Soviet Union, has reported that even in Moscow neither officials nor the people at large saw the threats of war as increasing the likelihood of war: they saw them as signs of a shift in the propaganda line. (5)

Finally, the People's Republic of China was posing problems that could not be resolved by diplomacy in the West. While the Chinese did not openly challenge the Soviet

Union's leadership of the world Communist movement, they had begun, in highly practical fashion, to intrude upon the domain of this leadership. They were definitely out to sell to Parties around the world their own ideological views and their opposition to Khrushchev's "revisionism." Moreover, they were claiming a special aptitude for working with the peoples of Asia, Africa, and Latin America, and were sending their technicians and propagandists into the field.

All these developments together dictated a change in the Soviet line: a change in the direction of "toughness" short of war. By one of those curious signs that forecast coming events in the Communist orbit, we know that a policy shift of this sort was in the making by the end of April 1960, before the U-2 flight. Without that flight, the shift might have been made later, after the Summit meeting had been held. It might have announced itself less explosively. But it would have taken place.

While Soviet newspapers and magazines designed for mass consumption continued their build-up of the Summit conference and the scheduled visit of Eisenhower, the Party's theoretical organ, *Kommunist*, was preparing for a change in the line even before the U-2 flew over the horizon. In April 1960, Issue No. 7 of this journal was being put together for publication. The make-up was approved on April 29, so that the contents cannot have been influenced by the U-2 flight. The lead article was called, "The Solidarity of the Workers of All Countries Will Grow Stronger"; and its central theme was at an exceedingly far remove from "the spirit of Camp David":

"International solidarity is strengthened in the course of an active uncompromising struggle against the intrigues of the reactionary bourgeoisie. The imperialists are divided by insoluble contradictions, but at the same time they are united by a hatred of the workers of their countries . . ."

In this article—designed for the briefing of Party members—we find both the description of the West by means of which Khrushchev was explaining away his failure to deliver concessions and the new "tough" line in the making. However much specific pressure may have been focused upon Khrushchev by reason of the U-2 affair, it seems apparent that a shift from the first to the second period of "peaceful coexistence" had already been dictated by larger circumstances.

By mid-Spring, 1960, in fact, there were evidences of Khrushchev's being on the defensive about his failure to deliver tangible results through personal diplomacy. He had, apparently, deceived himself during the Fall and Winter of 1959 about the gains which his visit to the United States had netted him. Having practically invited Eisenhower to invite him, he seems to have interpreted the resultant amenities as Western readiness to sign on the dotted line the agreements he wanted with respect to Berlin and disarmament. By mid-Spring, he was beginning to complain that "the spirit of Camp David" had been deliberately calculated to deceive him.

One of the most penetrating appraisals to come out of the Summer of 1960—the Summer of mounting threats—was made in August, by Theodore Draper, who has so often pinpointed the meaning of the zigs and zags of Communist policy. Pulling together the various items of evidence on which to base a characterization of Khrushchevism, second phase, Draper wrote:

"The manner rather than the matter of the Soviet's new course best reveals the nature of the change. Even in his most diplomatic missions, Khrushchev has always behaved far more like the agitator than the statesman. Both at Paris and in his latest junket to Austria, the agitator really let himself go. He shed every pretense of correct diplomatic form. . . . He shifted the balance overwhelmingly in favor of the Communist party leader at the expense of the head of Government. In this case, the style is not only the man but also the policy." (6)

A month and a half later, during the meetings of the General Assembly of the United Nations, an article in the New York *Herald Tribune* made a similar point about Khrushchev's performance in that international body: *"The Soviet Premier has not been delivering a program for action in the General Assembly. He has been providing the Communist and pro-Communist agencies of propaganda around the world with slogans."* (7)

We do well to recognize that this is what we are going to be dealing with throughout the second phase of "peaceful coexistence": unbridled hostility; obstructionism; ruthless propaganda; and a dramatic pseudo-championing of the cause of "target" peoples. There is nothing here that we have not met before. This is Communism as it has been practiced, through the decades, by Parties round the world. What is new is that it is now being openly practiced by the Premier of the Soviet State: by a man who will put into it all that he has because he is a Communist; because he is, by his very make-up, far more of an agitator than a diplomat; and because he is moved to fury by the frustration of having failed to win one-sided concessions by diplomatic means.

FOUR

DICTATOR OF
THE IDEOLOGY

AT THE Twenty-First Congress of the CPSU, Khrushchev
was unanimously hailed as the Party's leading *ideologist*
and *theoretician*. Does this mean anything? Our Western
minds may say, "Not much." By comparison with his having gathered unto himself the key powers of Party and State,
his being given the right to propound the abstractions of
Marxism-Leninism may seem a prize anticlimax. It would be
easy to think that the Congress, in bestowing the title, had
merely shown itself to be hard pressed to find some new appropriate gift for "the man who has everything."

Such a reading of the event, however, would be a misread-
ing of what the ideology means to the Communist hierarchy.
It means so much that until a dictator can exercise the same
control over the "science of Marxism-Leninism" that he
exercises over the Party-State apparatus, he may be "the
man who has everything" and yet have nothing.

61

The image of Khrushchev as a practical man who cares less about the ideology than about a new machine or a good stand of wheat has been fortified by the fact that he talks like a man who wants to get things done. Leonard Schapiro has noted this with respect to the way he first presented, at the Twentieth Congress of the CPSU, his idea of "peaceful coexistence": "There was indeed a certain robust common sense about the speech: the old formulae were all there, but it was clear that no question of doctrine was to be allowed to interfere with the practical issues that mattered—the increase of production at home, the preservation and advancement of communist power abroad." (1)

Khrushchev, however, does not simply want to get things done. He wants to get Communist things done, by Communist means, in the service of Communist aims. He must, therefore, be able to plan for the defense and use of the ideology as well as for new machines and good stands of wheat. It was as a practical man, in short, that he arranged to have himself "spontaneously" hailed as leading ideologist and theoretician.

This brings us to a fact that is always slippery in our Western minds. Armed with its ideology, Communism can aspire to be *everything*. Deprived of its ideology, it becomes *nothing:* nothing, that is, except one more system of irresponsible power in history's tedious succession of these.

The "dictatorship of the proletariat" becomes simply dictatorship, and "democratic centralism" coercive rule from the top down. The "historic mission" fades into thin air; and the interminable killings which this has "sanctified" become murders. The demand that writers and artists dedicate themselves to "socialist realism" becomes trespass by a police state upon the free province of the human mind. "Class morality" becomes the immorality of violence, double-deal-

ing, and double-speaking. The hierarchy's control over all
the means of production becomes sheer expropriation of the
people's property. The "fraternal" relationship of the Soviet
Union to the satellites becomes imperialism. And Khrushchev, we must note, ceases to be "the head of the working
class." He becomes nothing more than a dictator who has got
to the top of the Communist heap by outmaneuvering his
rivals.

The Communist ideology, in brief, has to prop up a
gigantic, bureaucratic, expansionist structure of power. Yet,
paradoxically, it has itself to be forever propped up: by propaganda, indoctrination, and all the machinery for warding
off both criticism and experiential data. It is a sort of intellectual shack with an impressive false front designed to make it
look like a veritable mansion of philosophy, a veritable
academy of science.

In his *Communism and the British Intellectuals*, Neal
Wood observes that in the 1930's the "hesitating empiricist"
who stood "bewildered by the flux of events" often found a
sudden release from confusion not only in "scientific" Marxism but in Soviet Communism. He had, in loneliness, sought
answers without finding them. Communism had answers;
and because these all dovetailed to "make sense" within their
ideological "universe," he assumed that they would also
make sense within the frame of actuality.

Such a person might be well-educated on many counts.
But if he was a "political illiterate" at the time when he felt
the first tremendous emotional impact of the world's being
out of joint, his education could itself make him ready to be
impressed by a "universe" constructed of words. Instead of
making him critical of Communism, it could quite as well
make him see in it "a system of great human ingenuity,
indeed of architectonic grandeur, apparently logical, co-
herent, and reasonable." (2)

But now let us look at this "architectonic grandeur" from behind the scenes, where all the props and the nervous arrangers of these are in sight. In late 1956, Khrushchev faced the problem of making some expedient concession to intellectual unrest without unleashing forces of dissent and criticism that might come to focus on the ideology itself. On November 10, an official article in *Kommunist* "clarified" the Party line:

". . . the clash of opinions on a foundation of Marxist-Leninist principles must be thoroughly encouraged. . . . Of course, there can be no compromise with views and pronouncements hostile to Marxism. . . . But this, we repeat, does not exclude the clash of opinions—of course within the frame of allegiance to the Party and Marxism— a clash in the course of which incorrect tenets and conclusions are rejected."

Communism, in short, rests its "guaranteed" right to take over the world on a theory of "great human ingenuity" which has forever to be ingeniously defended against examination. Yet those who ward off all critical examination of it have themselves to change it, and change it again, in order to come to terms with changes in the real world that are not on the books of Marxism-Leninism. This double process of protecting and revising the "infallible" has not exactly authenticated the "architectonic grandeur" of the ideology or the system; but it has kept them going.

The fact is, as Edwin Arlington Robinson has pointed out in *Roman Bartholow*, that

> ". . . even a phantom house, if made unwisely,
> May fall down on us and hurt horribly." (3)

For more than four decades, the Communists have maintained their turbulent residence within the phantom house of Marxism-Leninism. All this time, they have exhibited both a fanatical belief that the phantom house is real—real enough to endure to the end of time—and a constant anxiety lest it fall down on them and "hurt horribly." Out of this ambivalence, they have developed to a high point the art of tearing the house down, board by board, and rebuilding it along different lines, while keeping inviolate the fiction that it was perfect and indestructible from the start and will remain so to the end.

Now, a vast apparatus of power would have to choose to *liquidate itself* before it could choose to liquidate the process by which it has contrived both to repudiate the ideology and to keep this inviolate. There is nothing in the present scene, nor on the horizon, to suggest that any such choice will be made.

We simply prepare to victimize ourselves and others if we rate Khrushchev as any less dependent than were Lenin and Stalin upon the reality of the phantom house; or any less committed to keeping it shored up; or any more likely, as a practical man, to become bored with it and preside over its demolition. He is now chief architect in charge of the house. He can remodel it. He can virtually rebuild it, if need be. But *preserve it he must.*

This is where our Western minds balk. *Why* preserve it? On the material plane, the Soviet Union is a going concern. Also, it is a world power. Why, then, does it still need the "architectonic grandeur" of a phantom house? Why must it still replace the warmth and variety of normal human discussion by stereotyped "parrot-talk?" Why must so much energy still be diverted into the spinning-out of polysyllabic proofs of the unprovable? Why does even the most common-sense shift in policy have to be proclaimed ideologically "correct" before it becomes legitimate?

Why, in brief, should any modern state, intent to advance, want to lug along the dead weight of an "infallible" dogma that is either irrelevant to or at odds with most of the facts that have to be dealt with in actual experience?

But this is where our minds show themselves to be very wide of the mark. *The Soviet Union is not a modern state; and the prime function of the ideology is to prevent its becoming so.* It exists in the contemporary world. But it is a totalitarian, monolithic state in which a self-appointed elite has spent more than four decades trying to acquire in full measure the resources of modern science and technology *without building a modern state in the process.*

No state is strictly modern. But those that best deserve the name are those which have best wrought into their customs and institutions certain concepts: the inviolable worth of the individual; the right of dissent; freedom of the mind to search for truth and to express its findings; freedom of religion; freedom of the press; freedom of association; respect for the social contribution of diversity; respect for the role of a "loyal opposition"; liberty under law; and the sovereignty of the people.

But the states which, by these standards, come closest to being modern are precisely those which the Communists are most intent to wipe off the face of the earth. Their "crime," from the Communist point of view, is not that they are "imperialistic" or "exploitative." They are far less so than the Soviet Union or the People's Republic of China. Their "crime" is a double one. They allow that very exercise of the human mind that would lead to the ideology's being tested by objective evidence—and made to look silly. And they refute Marxism-Leninism by proving that an evolutionary industrial system can provide a high standard of living within a framework of civil liberties and responsible government. Thus, they rob the monolithic state of its sole claim to legitimacy—that of being the elect agent of a fated process which is the only possible line of advance for mankind.

What all this comes to is that if the ideology were ever forced to prove its right to exist by its correspondence to reality, it would fall apart. But if it were to fall apart, the system would fall apart, too. Therefore, while it is unthinkable for *everyone* to examine the ideology, *someone* must. Otherwise, the disjunction between dogma and reality would itself become a threat. Someone has to be on the job of making expedient adjustment.

Khrushchev, with the machinery of Party and State at his command, knew what he yet lacked. He lacked the authority to effect a truce between the ideology and recalcitrant objective facts—and to call this truce a "creative development of Marxism." Also, he lacked the authority to get his practical policies "blessed" as ideologically "correct"—so that he could, in their behalf, set in motion all the forces of propaganda, indoctrination, and open and veiled coercion.

Khrushchev, we might say, is simply the latest of Communism's dictatorial *revisionists*. From the beginning, to misquote Marx, Marxism-Leninism has carried within itself the seeds of its own destruction. Therefore, to keep it sacrosanct, nondictatorial revisionists have had to be purged. But dictatorial revisionists have had to stay on the job, to keep the theory in working order.

Marx himself urgently sought evidence with which to support his theory, but wanted nothing to do with evidence that threatened either its logic or its revolutionary dynamism. Thus, even before his death, a gap was opening between what he had set down as absolute and what was taking place in the world. He himself, late in life, made a limited acknowledgment of this. But he kept it so limited that it merely gave his followers more contradictions among which to pick and choose in shaping up their own absolutes and calling them "Marxist."

Lenin took over from where Marx left off—and let expediency be his guide. By Marxist standards, Russia was far from being ready for revolution. But Lenin was ready for it even if Russia was not; and he felt capable of directing Russia on a short cut to Communism.

Lacking a proletariat schooled by industrial experience for the role which Marx had assigned *to that class alone,* he substituted his Bolshevik Party and called it the "revolutionary vanguard," the "progressive" element of the working class. To it, he assigned the task not only of seizing power but of enacting the "dictatorship of the proletariat."

To give this Party a "monolithic" strength comparable to the strength which Marx gave to an industrial proletariat unified by long struggle, Lenin invented "democratic centralism." He structured the Party, layer upon layer, in the shape of a pyramid; and the smaller the layer, the greater the power until, at the top, power became absolute. On matters where no decisions had been reached, *opinions* could, in theory, move from the bottom up—though anyone who expressed an unorthodox opinion soon became "unreliable." This theoretical upward flow of opinion was stated to be the "democratic" feature. But "centralism" was the dominant feature: *decisions* must always move downward; and they must, at each level, be given unanimous, unstinting support. To insure this, *coercion* also moved from the top down.

The Party, today—having "evolved" from a band of revolutionary zealots to the most powerful bureaucracy ever to exist on earth—is still structured on the principle of "democratic centralism." Khrushchev stands at the top; and he says of it, "The Communist Party, the highest form of social organization, the leading detachment and trusted vanguard of the people, gives leadership to all other organizations of the working people." (4)

Because Lenin thus substituted hard-core Party for class, while still holding to Marx's concepts of "class struggle," the "dictatorship of the proletariat," and the "guaranteed" outcome of the historical process, it was "not the unity but the disunity of theory and practice that began to be embodied in Soviet institutions." (5)

This same "disunity of theory and practice" became embodied in Communist verbiage. When Khrushchev calls himself "the head of the working class," he speaks in the letter and spirit of Lenin's revision of Marxism. When he says that the Soviet workers own all the means of production, he is saying that these means of production are controlled by those who have appointed themselves to enact the "dictatorship of the proletariat." When he talks about "democracy," he is talking about "democratic centralism."

After what Marx did to the full-range complexity of the human situation, and what Lenin did to Marxism, the sky was the limit so far as "licensed revisionism" was concerned —so long as the "revision" defended the system. It had become orthodox for the dictator to liquidate any aspect of the ideology that got in the way of expediency. The only requirement was that he must hide the corpse in a sufficiently dense thicket of verbiage.

This was no impossible requirement, as Stalin showed when he declared for the strengthening of the State beyond any point authorized by Marx or Lenin: "We stand for the withering away of the state. At the same time we stand for the dictatorship of the proletariat, which is the mightiest and strongest state power which has ever existed. The highest development of state power with the object of preparing the condition *for* the withering away of state power—such is the Marxist formula." (6)

Stalin further compounded the "disunity of theory and practice" by introducing the concept of "socialism in one country" and reanimating the very Russian nationalism and Pan-Slavism which Marx had deplored. Also, he declared it to be "correct" for social classes to continue in existence throughout the whole period of the "building of socialism."

When we add up these victories of expediency over "infallible" theory, there would seem to be too little left to Marxism to give the old phrases, any longer, even a propaganda value. Can a mountain which never was nearly as high as it was proclaimed to be, and which has now been quarried and eroded away until it is more of a hollow than a hump, still be made to inspire mountain climbers?

The Communist answer is, *yes:* a way must be found to keep people convinced, and to convince ever more people, not only that the mountain exists but that there can be, in life and history, no greater incentive, no higher goal, than to reach its top.

Khrushchev also says *yes.* Ever since he began his climb to power, he has been trying to make the ideology serve four purposes: to keep inviolate the "vanguard" role of the Party; to inspire the people to a "selfless" performance of practical tasks; to counteract, on the home front, the invading influence of "bourgeois ideology"; and to guide the world's "revolution of rising expectations" into Marxist-Leninist channels.

Khrushchev's "practical" attitude toward the ideology can best be seen, perhaps, in the way he has both revised and exploited it in behalf of the Seven Year Plan for economic development. On the one hand, he had scrapped, with remarkably little fanfare, any phase of the ideology that has proved to be a roadblock to production. Thus, some of Marx's most sacrosanct axioms with respect to wages, labor, and markets have simply gone by the board; and "capitalist" practices have been introduced—with no bow to capitalism—wherever they have promised to pay off. At the same time, however, he has launched one of the greatest ideological drives in the history of the Soviet Union—to try to make the people feel that they are performing their "international duty" to Marxism-Leninism when they put forth "selfless" effort to insure the Plan's fulfillment.

Khrushchev, in short, has exhibited a quite remarkable skill in tearing down the "phantom house" and rebuilding it along different lines while asking the Soviet people to be deeply moved by its unassailable "architectonic grandeur."

If, however, Khrushchev has demonstrated even more clearly than Lenin and Stalin how far "licensed revisionism" can go in the service of expediency, he has also shown *where it has to stop*. No revision must ever call into question: 1. that form of Party control which rests on the structure of "democratic centralism"; 2. the concept of the struggle between the "two camps" or "two social systems" as ultimately irreconcilable; 3. the "guarantee" that Communism will win in this struggle; 4. the kind of "class morality" that makes the end justify the means; 5. that concept of "socialist solidarity" which lets the Soviet Union direct, from the top down, the world Communist movement. These five aspects of the dogma must be preserved.

To see how rigorously they must be preserved—and at what cost to moral and intellectual integrity—we can turn back to an incident that took place shortly after the Twentieth Congress of the CPSU, in 1956.

At this Congress, we recall, Khrushchev "disposed" of Stalinism in what seemed an all-out fashion. Stalin had said that the class struggle would increase in violence *after* the "dictatorship of the proletariat" had been set up, because of the last-ditch stand which the bourgeoisie would make.

Khrushchev denounced this view as nothing more than an ideological excuse for terrorism. Stalin had said that the proletariat could seize power only by an armed uprising. Khrushchev said that it might do so by peaceful means. Stalin had denied that the "building of socialism" could take, in any country, a form other than that which it had taken in the Soviet Union. Khrushchev said, or seemed to say, that socialism could be built in ways that took account of the uniqueness of each country.

In brief, Khrushchev "refuted, one after another, all the principles Stalin had proclaimed and to which, only two days before, people, parties, and governments had sworn allegiance. . . . Things that, had they even been insinuated a few days before, would have cost the bold offender his life, were now enthusiastically approved by every delegate to the Twentieth Congress . . ." (7)

But there was one thing which Khrushchev did not do. Again and again, during the years, he had subjected hapless individuals to humiliating "self-criticism" for the merest word or act that had deviated from a line which he now pronounced to have been viciously miscast. Yet, spelling out in detail the brutal Stalinist crimes *in which he himself had been deeply implicated,* he uttered no word of regret or "self-criticism" for his own part in these. Neither did any word of "self-criticism" come from any other member of the hierarchy that had done Stalin's bidding.

Shortly after the Congress, however, Togliatti, head of the Italian Communist Party, made the "mistake" of drawing from Khrushchev's speech an "unwarranted" conclusion. He wrote that the "cult of personality" which Khrushchev had condemned was only the product of something else: "The roots are deeper. . . . If one were looking for the true Marxist explanation, one could not escape the logical conclusion that these crimes grow from the soil of the system itself." (8)

A "logical conclusion" of this type was outside the pale. *Pravda* accused Togliatti of "exaggeration"; and he was forced to exercise the "self-criticism" which Khrushchev had shown no will to exercise with respect to that servile adherence to Stalinism which had insured his own staying not only alive, but *ambitiously* alive, and on the make, where so many had died.

In summary, the original Marxist theory, designed to impose a revolutionary imperative upon the working class, was an oversimplified distortion of the human scene and the historic process; as Marxism-Leninism, it has been remade, time and again, to fit the purposes of the Communist power system and its current dictator; but it has, all the while, been kept "infallible"—because both the power system and the drive for world conquest would collapse without it. Khrushchev today, claiming the human future for Communism, speaks his piece as "caretaker" of an intellectually and morally bankrupt dogma.

The degree of bankruptcy in the dogma and the system is well indicated by the conduct of Togliatti himself. His own published words tell us that, in 1956, he recognized that the crimes which Khrushchev attributed exclusively to Stalin had, in fact, grown "from the soil of the system itself." Yet when it turned out that Khrushchev had intended, at the Twentieth Congress, to stage only a tactical retreat from Stalinism, Togliatti went through the cynical routine of "self-criticism"—and is still head of the Italian Communist Party.

This points to a still further characteristic of the Communist force with which we are now having to deal at this critical juncture of history. The years that have witnessed the compounding of expedient contradictions within the dogma and the ever greater consolidation of the power system have witnessed, also, the progressive weeding-out from the Party of all persons who respect the voice of individual conscience.

All around the world, after the Twentieth Congress, Party members were purged—and in Hungary, shot down—for not being able to do what Togliatti did: namely, reject what his own mind told him in favor of what the hierarchy told him. Members in comparable numbers had been purged, in 1939, for not being able to accept Stalin's pact with Hitler. But such "mass" purges have merely punctuated the ongoing policy, ordained by Lenin, of keeping the Party free from dissenters.

This "natural selection" has, by now, produced a Party in which the "still small voice" of conscience is not likely to be raised against the far from still small voice of Khrushchev. If anything was proved by the eventful Summer and Fall of 1960, it was that Khrushchev, as leading ideologist and agitator, can put on any kind of act that expediency, bad temper, or congenital boorishness may dictate: his puppets, his Parties round the world, and his controlled press will play "Follow the leader"—at least, until he is squeezed out by Kuzlov, Suslov, or, quite as likely, by some other rival who has not yet attracted the free world's attention.

When we thus review the whole cynical process by which the ideology has been defended, revised, and exploited, we feel the urge to ask, "How long, O Lord, how long?" How long can the Communists find target minds susceptible to the idea that Marxist-Leninist totalitarianism is "progressive" and holds the key to the future?

There is, of course, no answer to such a question. But we are tempted to suggest that two answers are, today, competing for validation. One might be phrased, "Long enough for Khrushchev to make the determinative shift in the world balance of power." The other might be phrased, "Not much longer. The time which the Communists have at their disposal may be running out."

The first answer is supported by the fact that angry unrest

coupled with political inexperience has always provided Communism's best opportunity; and that there are more such areas in the world today than have ever *simultaneously* existed before. It would be unrealistic for us to doubt that Marxism-Leninism will still have its ideological appeal to many minds in these areas. Where change in a hurry is called for, "packaged" solutions to all problems can exert a strong pull; and where civil liberties and popular sovereignty have never prevailed, a totalitarianism that poses as benign, and as anti-imperialist, and as economically efficient may seem to offer the best available type of "guidance."

The second answer, however, is also well-supported. It is supported by a fact which British Prime Minister Macmillan pointed out at the General Assembly of the United Nations, on September 29, 1960: namely, that the "sponge" of world opinion has become saturated, so far as Khrushchev's repetitive propaganda is concerned. There is increasing evidence that both his boastings and his denouncings have been carried to the point where they evoke less and less response. His incivility, moreover, appeals only to the uncivil; and it does not recommend him as a "guide" to those who are wanting to build their countries into stable, responsible members of the family of nations.

There is another reason, also, for believing that Communism's time may be running out: its dependence upon the ideology to justify the structure of power and the drive toward world conquest is making it look *dated* in a way from which no expedient "creative development of Marxism" can save it.

The Communist system, of course, has always been *reactionary*, because it is based on edict and coercion from the top down. But when we speak of it as *dated*, we are thinking along a different line. From the mid-nineteenth century to World War II, roughly speaking, the West was living through what has been called "the age of the ideologies": the age of all-in-one-package answers to the human predicament as modified by industrialism. Marxism was a product of this age. So was Leninism. But *susceptibility* to Marxism-Leninism was also a product of it. The "age of the ideologies" appears, now, to be slipping into the past.

What, then, of Communism's future? The Soviet Union is a vast power state. The Communist orbit is a system of power states covering one-fourth of the earth's surface—and insistently reaching for more. The world Communist movement circles the globe. But what will come to pass if, in the world's marketplaces of the mind, there are fewer and fewer customers for the "architectonic grandeur" of Marxism-Leninism?

In the Summer of 1959, in Hamburg, in the homeland of *dialectical* and *historical materialism,* the Socialist (not Communist) International held its Congress. Delegates from Socialist parties in thirty-eight free nations slogged their way through problems that they all acknowledged to be too complex for dogmatic solutions. In the course of all this, Marx's name was mentioned exactly once. The basic tenets associated with his name were dismissed as holding no key to the solution of today's problems and as offering no proper guidance to human idealism.

What happened at the Congress is simply one sign that the "age of the ideologies" is receding into the past. One reason, perhaps, is that the first tremendous impact of the modern world's "out-of-jointness" is also receding into the past. Complexity is becoming the "natural habitat" of the human mind; and all-in-one-package solutions are, therefore, losing their hold on this mind.

The future is yet to be made. But the drama of "experimental pluralism" appears to be regaining its hold. This drama, we must recall, has a far older and deeper root-hold, both in philosophy and in human experience, than has Communism. Also, it has far more in common with the authentic aspirations of the underdeveloped countries. For it can go at their needs in manifold ways; can size up these needs in their own right instead of making them support ideological stereotypes; can invite into the open the ingenuities of people; and can respect the diversity of independent nations.

Khrushchev can throw his weight on the side of this or that faction or power-seeker. He can appeal to the anti-imperialism of new nations. He can pose as peacemaker while blocking all practical plans for disarmament. He can work to get the economies of the new nations inextricably tied up with the Soviet economy. But in a world that is ready to go on the hunt, once more, for many solutions to the problems posed by the multifariousness of life, the Communist system alone remains fettered to its ideology—so that, in increasing measure, it looks *both* reactionary and dated.

FIVE

THE SUCCESS
KHRUSHCHEV NEEDS

IN CHAPTER ONE we reported Khrushchev's remark that
life is short, and that he hopes to see the Red flag fly over
the whole world in his lifetime. Now, we are venturing far
out on a limb—to say that if he does not realize his hope, or
make considerable strides toward doing so, the chances are
against any later Communist dictator's having that satisfaction.

If the free world can firmly hold the line for, let us say, another decade or so, while putting its creative mind to work on
problems attendant upon freedom's advance, it may become
too late for Communism to add further victories. To recall a
phrase that had great meaning for generations of Americans,
we may be able to give our children, and their children, and
the world's children a better chance than we have had:
namely, a better chance to live on a planet where they can
experience peace that does not need to be written "peace."

This prospect carries no guarantees. Khrushchev has the means of blowing up the world—as we have. If he cannot currently afford an all-out war, he has devised dangerous substitutes for it. Moreover, no one knows what form Communist desperation may take at the point where its "fated" victory turns out not to be fated. We will do well to see to it that any resort to all-out war is kept inexpedient.

Nonetheless, it would be a grave mistake for us to regard Khrushchev as always mysteriously able to lead from strength. He spends a very considerable amount of effort trying to keep the world's attention fixed where he wants it fixed—so that it will not stray to the problems he faces. But these problems define the types of success that he needs, and needs soon. To see what they are, and to see them in perspective, we can well take a backward look.

Marxism has existed as an ideological force for more than a hundred years: Leninism, as a "science of conspiracy," for sixty years. For more than four decades, Communism has had a base in the Soviet Union, and from this has operated a world movement. For a decade and a half it has had a satellite empire; and for more than a decade, an Asian base in Red China. Today, there are sixty-six Parties and a multitude of "fronts" outside the orbit. Propaganda coverage is worldwide and permeative.

All Communists are schooled in "politicalizing" issues— giving them a Marxist-Leninist interpretation, and placing blame on a designated "class enemy," whether this be the government of the United States or simply the least poverty-stricken among the farmers of a Chinese village. (1)

The Communists have had at their disposal the discontents, explosive demands, and unmoored idealism of an age of ferment. Throughout the decades, they have had at their disposal anti-Tsarism, inside and outside Russia; the disillusionment that followed World War I; the despairs of the depression years; the resentments and hopes of underprivileged minorities; the trust extended to the Soviet Union by its Western allies of World War II; the fierce anti-Nazism of countries overrun by Hitler; the anticolonialism of Asia and Africa; the restlessness of young people in an age when swift change has left an unbridged gap between the generations; and the verbalizing power of alienated intellectuals within both advanced and backward countries.

They have had at their disposal factionalism within all nations, exploitable liberties within all democratic nations. They have had the emotional letdown and general confusion which have marked various new nations at the point where a united struggle for independence has yielded place either to a divisive struggle for power or simply to the workaday task of making a society function. They have had at their disposal people's hunger for peace, and the guilty consciences of a multitude of "haves" in a world where most people are still "have nots."

Also—however much they may deny this—they have had an incredible tolerance extended to them by the "target" governments which they have worked to overthrow. Even today —when there cannot be much residual doubt about their aims, conspiratorial methods, and trouble-making propensities— half of the Communist Parties outside the orbit still enjoy legal standing.

Yet with all this long opportunity to tap not only the discontents and mutual antagonisms of men and nations, but also their hopes, idealisms, and unsuspicious decencies, the Communists have never won a country by free election. Theirs is the triumph of bringing under their control, by subversion and naked force, one-third of the earth's people and one-fourth of the earth's surface; *and theirs is the most colossal failure in all history.*

This is the fact which Communist propaganda, at home and abroad, has continually to mask. It has also to mask the fact that in no country where the Party has seized power has it been able to bring about a state of affairs in which it can let down its guard and rely on the support of the people.

Czechoslovakia is the satellite in which the Communists, at the time of take-over, came closest to marshalling a majority. They had on their side both anti-Nazism in its most intensive form and Czech resentment against the West because of the Munich pact. Thus, they could enact their role as "liberators" more convincingly than elsewhere.

Yet the Communist regime in Czechoslovakia, after being in power for more than a decade, still has to maintain on the border between that country and the free world that compound of barbed wire, "dragon's teeth," and guard towers which we saw at Tillyschantz. Also, it is the regime, we recall, which decorated the railway signalman and his wife for preventing the escape of three hundred refugees. And it registers a constant anxiety about any exchange with the West that might foster "bourgeois ideology."

The Soviet Union itself—where the Party has made all policies for more than forty years, and has always, according to Khrushchev, made them "correctly"—offers an even more striking case in point. Khrushchev talks about the "boundless love" of the people for the Party; but he still has to "prove" this love by rigged elections; still has to jam Western radio broadcasts; and still has to fill his controlled press with faked stories about a multitude of events in the outside world.

None of this means that either the Soviet Union or any of the satellites is currently confronted by revolutionary rumblings among the people. We are talking about something quite different: about the pettiness of the victories which Communism has been able to chalk up. It has never chalked up any except by conspiracy and force; and it has never been able to make even one victory conclusive enough that the Party can, in effect, sign a peace treaty with the people and, confident of their voluntary support, encourage them to grow toward individual maturity. Communism's grandiose plan for success would seem to lack something.

This lack in Communism is precisely why we must not let our fears or credulity cooperate with Khrushchev and give him what he does not have the means of winning by a free exchange of ideas or by free election. There is nothing "fated" about Communism's take-over. Yet there are at least five ways in which we could hand over to Khrushchev *in his lifetime* the makings of victory. All five of these we are going to call ways of *self-indulgence;* for we believe that each represents a selective evasion of issues.

First, there is that self-indulgent pessimism which says, "Communism is here to stay"—and which manages to make this pronouncement sound like the higher realism. Pessimism of this type can almost cheerfully encourage the free world to make one concession after another, without giving close regard to what shift in the balance of power results from each or who suffers in consequence.

The "higher pessimist" seems, often, to have been unwittingly infected by two aspects of the Communist outlook. He identifies the colossal and "monolithic" with the strong; and he takes history to be an unfolding process rather than one that is being made by man. Thus—even if he happens to be an "intellectual"—he reduces the human intellect to a point where it has to play second fiddle to both material forces and "fate."

Yet, pinned down, he will not actually say that the West was "fated" to hand Stalin a satellite empire by first crediting his word and then pulling out of East Europe. Neither, as a rule, will he say that any other single policy that has given the Communists a free hand *in the past* could not possibly have been otherwise. What seems to be "fated" in his mind is the *future*.

This is why we call this kind of pessimism *self-indulgent*. It seems to have at its core a proudly suicidal readiness to give up: to make the gesture of abandoning the long human struggle toward civility, mercy, and justice, and to call this gesture realistic.

In the second place, there is that self-indulgent optimism which sees industrialization in the Soviet Union, with a resultant rise in living standards, as bound to have a "liberalizing" effect. *Why* is it bound to have such an effect? What precise part of its monolithic power is the Party likely to yield first, and then second, and then third, until "liberalization" is effected?

Oddly enough, many persons who are thus optimistic with respect to the Soviet Union are gloomy about the effects of industrialization and high living standards in the United States. Here, these are said to have fostered "materialism" and "conformity"—both of which the Communist hierarchy in the Soviet Union is intent to encourage to the utmost. By what logic, then, or what "fated" process, are the same forces to have a "liberalizing" effect in the USSR—where the Party is in control and where there is no tradition of political democracy?

This kind of optimism, like the pessimism which we have considered, is a form of abdication. It, too, diminishes man to the stature of a being *to whom things happen*—and thus justifies itself in not assuming any responsibility for what happens. It differs from pessimism only in visualizing fate as prone to deliver happy endings.

Third, there is that self-indulgent sentimentality which asks the West to make the gesture of unilateral disarmament, or of disarmament on Soviet terms, with no provisions for enforcement—thereby leaving *the whole free world* at the mercy of a Communism which has always, to date, made success a stimulus to a further drive toward ultimate success.

We recall, in this connection, a talk we had with a man in South Vietnam in the Fall of 1959. Where he lives, the killing of peaceful villagers by Communist guerrillas is so common an event that when darkness comes down at night, fear comes with it.

Himself deeply involved in his country's effort to build a viable economy and to learn the skills of political independence, he said, "Anyone in Vietnam who dares to be an anti-Communist has daily reminders that he is signing his own death warrant if the Communist breakthrough comes. The one assurance that makes the risk seem worth while, giving us hope that we may yet have time to build our country in freedom, is the fact that the American Seventh Fleet is in the Pacific."

Almost invariably the person who recommends unilateral disarmament or disarmament without controls is also a person who has wanted the countries of Asia and Africa to gain their independence. Yet, now, he seems to find virtue in the act of putting their independence in jeopardy: of making ourselves helpless to defend them against a Communist take-over, with all the senseless slaughter which such a take-over always entails. For he chooses to disregard three facts: that the Soviet Union has never given independence to any inch of its colonial empire; that it has never been known to respect a treaty which it has signed; and that its expansionist drive has, in the past, been stopped only where it has encountered the strength, not the weakness, of the free world.

There has grown up among us a curious habit of posing the question of disarmament in apocalyptic terms: "Would you rather live under Communism or have the whole world destroyed in nuclear war?" But how about using our heads, consciences, and resources to avoid either alternative?

As Hugh Seton-Watson points out, in his analysis of problems of Western policy, in *Neither War Nor Peace,* "The choice is not between the certainty of destruction of the human race and the certainty of communist dominion but between the possibility of destruction, if the West retains atomic weapons, and the certainty of Soviet dominion . . . if the West unilaterally disarms." (2)

We shall have more to say about disarmament in a later chapter. But here we would merely emphasize that any design for disarmament which has enough loopholes in it to make it constitute *a free gift to Khrushchev of an altered balance of power* has to be rated as profoundly immoral.

The fourth way in which we can hand over the world to Khrushchev is by self-indulgent indifference to human needs and aspirations. Only if both compassion and a knowledge of what makes a society viable are kept on the job, on the world front, can we either hold our own against Communism or experience within ourselves the stimulus of an adventure appropriate to our time.

The fifth way of self-indulgence—and one to which we are singularly prone—is that of turning away from a still extant problem because we are tired of hearing about it. Those who are most ready thus to turn away from the problem posed by Communism's will to take over the world appear to be persons *who have heard too much about this without learning enough.*

Millions of persons who live under Communism are tired of doing so. We would do ill to let our boredom add to their number. We would do ill, also, to forget that the attention and effort now required for the prevention of Communism's total victory are infinitely less than mankind would have to put forth, after that victory, to regain even the slightest measure of freedom. It is hard to see any merit in the act of selling the hard-won customs and institutions of freedom down the river as a substitute for taking the trouble to preserve them.

It is on the record, as we have noted, that Communism cannot prove its case to the minds and consciences of men in open competition with other systems. Khrushchev's conduct at the General Assembly of the United Nations was, incidentally, a strong reminder of this fact: at every point where Soviet policy was concretely challenged in terms of the record, he chose to sidestep the issue by putting on a temper tantrum.

It cannot be said too often that Communism's past victories have been won by means of conspiracy, subversion, armed force, and free-world credulity. But for this precise reason, it cannot be said too strongly that *future* Communist victories could be added by these same measures. Our task is to prevent them by refusing to provide the credulity—and also by a steady forging ahead with freedom's enterprise. If we do this, Khrushchev's problems will have time to work against him. And this brings us back to the types of success he needs, and needs soon.

First, he needs economic success on a colossal scale. To an extent not dreamed of in the eras of Lenin and Stalin, the Khrushchev era has shaped up as one in which *products are proofs.* Khrushchev's policy, foreign and domestic, is inextricably tied up with *two* "revolutions of rising expectations." One of these, in the underdeveloped countries, he needs to exploit. The other, in the Soviet Union itself, he needs to keep within bounds. To do so he must deliver more consumer goods. But he must also preserve the Party's power to denounce as "bourgeois" a wide range of consumer desires; to determine priorities all along the line; and to subordinate consumer demands to those of "socialist internationalism."

To handle "correctly" these two "revolutions" Khrushchev needs an enormous output of goods. In our next chapter, we shall examine his Seven Year Plan for securing this output. But no amount of goods, however abundant, will give him the success he needs unless those who are on the receiving end of the goods, both at home and abroad, can be persuaded to see the abundance as made possible *only* by the wise leadership of the Party and the application of Marxism-Leninism.

This is the weakness of Khrushchev's position. The Soviet economy cannot be permitted to stand on its own merits, as a productive system now maturing in a world where other industrialized economies already exist and will continue to exist. It has to be made to "prove" that all other systems are obsolete. Khrushchev must be able to say, "Look what *Communism* has wrought."

The toughness of his task on this score is pointed up by a conclusion which Hugh Seton-Watson has reached as the result of a long study of the stages of Soviet development: the totalitarian dogma "may provide idealism and energy for the early stages of a revolutionary regime, but after a time it can only be an obstacle to progress. The Soviet Union has achieved magnificent successes by virtue of the great talents of the Russian people and the great resources of the Russian soil and sub-soil, in spite of the dogma of Lenin and Stalin." (3)

Khrushchev belongs to the era *when the ideology has become "an obstacle to progress."* His manifold economic innovations—to provide incentives, make capital more fluid, and cut through red tape—report this fact. Almost without exception, they have represented a piecemeal scrapping of the ideology. In brief, it is the ideology which has become obsolete—not those non-Communist economic systems which Khrushchev denounces as obsolete even while he is urging upon the Soviet people the need of "overtaking" them.

It is not going to get any easier, as time passes, for Khrushchev to prove that what has been accomplished *in spite of* Marxism-Leninism would be *impossible without* Marxism-Leninism. Yet this is what he must prove. The ideology must be proved indispensable, for it alone preserves the "legitimacy" of the power system and the dynamism of the world Communist movement.

The Communists talk as though the Soviet economy represented a forty-year miracle. But does it? In a land of rich human and natural resources which had made major contributions to world science even under the Tsars, and which began after 1905 to take swift strides toward industrialization, why has it taken *forty years* of manifold killings, unlimited coercion, forced deprivation, and mind-control, together with the stealing of scientific secrets from the West and the plundering of every captured country, to bring the productive system of the USSR to a point where the people can begin to hope, within the foreseeable future, for a minimum satisfaction of their basic consumer needs?

Once this question is asked, the answer emerges: at whatever cost to production, or to the people's welfare, Soviet economic policies have always had to "prove" and preserve the dogma; and in spite of Khrushchev's innovations, they still have to do so.

If Khrushchev cannot get control of the economies of the underdeveloped countries before the leaders of these countries start asking why it has taken the Soviet Union *so long* to get around to the production of consumer goods, he will lose his prize substitute for armed force as a means of takeover. After all, these underdeveloped countries are right up against the problem of having people in multitude to feed, clothe, and house. They need to produce consumer goods. But wherever Marxism-Leninism sets the pattern, consumer goods come in a bad second. The consolidation and extension of the power system come first.

Khrushchev's second problem stems from the changed character of the "unchanging" Party. It might be called a problem of bureaucratic dry rot. Lenin organized the Bolshevik Party as a tightly knit band of revolutionary zealots, and lived to translate it into the exclusive ruling body of the Soviet State. While Stalin subordinated the Party to his own dictatorial will, he preserved its structure; and under him, as Leonard Schapiro reminds us, it became elite in a new sense.

It set itself "to gather into its fold the great majority of men and women in the highest positions"; and its unity changed from that of a self-disciplined band of revolutionaries to that of a self-serving privileged class. Moreover, it carried "democratic centralism" to a point where all elections and decisions within the Party, throughout the whole Soviet Union, were dominated by "an apparatus of officials and secretaries comprising some 3% of this elite membership." (4)

After Stalin's death, Khrushchev set out to pre-empt this Party as his own instrument of power. He enlarged its membership and undertook to provide himself with a "permanent army of occupation" by planting his supporters in every key post, small and large, within the vast complex of the Soviet government, economy, and society. By the end of five years, he had built the CPSU into the most gigantic bureaucracy ever to exist on earth.

This entrenched bureaucracy still claims for itself—and Khrushchev claims for it—the "vanguard" role and dictatorial power which Lenin bestowed upon his handful of zealots. But its traits are chiefly and increasingly those of a privileged bureaucracy; and because of its size, its ideological arrogance, and its meddling penetration of every phase of life, it has these traits to the nth degree.

Khrushchev has shown himself to be concerned about the extent to which the apparatus has become infected by inertia, corruption, buck-passing, jealousy, personal ambition, intrigue, and sheer red-tape ponderosity. It is significant that he has encouraged writers to criticize bureaucratic excesses. Equally significant, however, is the fact that he firmly clamps down on such criticism at the point where it begins to be relevant to the basic problem: namely, where it begins to show the connection between bureaucratic excesses and the system itself.

Against this unwieldy colossus *which he cannot do without,* he has pitted minor efforts to decentralize administration and to "democratize" various processes. But these have made no real dent on the problem. They have even magnified it. For Khrushchev has had to stop short of letting any fraction of basic authority slip from Party control or "guidance." Thus, both decentralization and "democratization" have come to mean, in practice, that more Party members have had to be located in more places to keep the upper hand of more situations.

A further type of effort in which Khrushchev has seemed to invest a quite astonishing measure of hope would appear, on the face of it, to be the world's number one exercise in futility. Against the inertia and self-serving corruption of bureaucracy, he has pitted a vast propaganda drive—implemented by the same bureaucracy.

In this Khrushchev era, in short, the high cost of "monolithic unity" is becoming ever more clear. What the Soviet Union most needs at its present stage of size and complexity is what it cannot allow itself to have: namely, a loyal opposition. What it gets instead, therefore, is bureaucracy *unlimited.*

Khrushchev, eager to drive ahead toward that world con-

quest which would lift to a climax the Lenin-Stalin-Khrushchev sequence of power, keeps trying to infuse the Party
with revolutionary fervor. The Communist press, strident
with propaganda, reports the urgency of his effort. But the
time-worn slogans and stereotypes—for which there can be
no orthodox substitutes—appear to have about as much
animating effect on the bureaucracy as a pinprick would have
on an elephant. Most Party members—like most members of
the Soviet public—are tired of *endemic emergency.* They
want to settle down.

The plain fact is that Party members, today, have no sufficient reason to feel revolutionary fervor. Lenin's Bolsheviks,
each on his own, hated the Tsarism that had confined and
distorted his own life. But each member of Khrushchev's
bureaucratic Party is asked to find in self-congratulation with
respect to the system that surrounds his daily life a moving
cause for self-commitment to "socialist internationalism." At
the same time, he is asked to feel "irreconcilable hatred" for
a system—"capitalist imperialism"—which scarcely impinges
upon his own life.

The average member of the CPSU—as of the Soviet public
—encounters this "class enemy" chiefly through propaganda
stereotypes; a controlled press that he knows is controlled;
and a few fruits of capitalism which he has seen with his own
eyes and which, for the most part, he would not at all mind
having his own system deliver to him. Even if he feels a solid,
reasonable pride in the Soviet Union's advance, this does not
automatically make him a full-time hater of a remote, officially designated "enemy."

There seems no doubt that Khrushchev himself is genuinely fired by the drama of planting the Red flag everywhere
on earth. There is a good deal of the native agitator about
him. Also, unlike the rank-and-file Party members whom he
tries to infect with revolutionary fervor, he has the ego-

magnifying role of being top manipulator.

Yet the Party which he has constructed as his chosen instrument of power is, by its intrinsic make-up, nonrevolutionary. It is bureaucratic. Further, it is becoming more and more largely composed of a generation for whom the Bolshevik *coup d'état* is "far away and long ago." Within the present membership, moreover, there is a growing body of trained specialists whose interest, like that of specialists elsewhere, tends to focus on explicit tasks rather than to spread embracingly over the concept of "socialist internationalism."

If Khrushchev's absorbing concern were to build a strong Soviet Union *for the benefit of the people,* he would have, now, the makings of abundant success. But, on the testimony of his conduct both at home and abroad, he is, first of all, a *Communist.* Therefore, he cannot let an atmosphere of normal well-being replace that of *endemic emergency:* his trumped-up, virulent anti-American campaign of the Summer and Fall of 1960 testifies to this fact. And he cannot let his bureaucrats stop being a revolutionary force. Yet neither can he make them feel what he wants them to feel. As Merle Fainsod has noted, "the shrill demands of the party press for ideological commitment reveal undertones of concern at the lack of ardor and militancy in party ranks." (5)

This would seem to be one of the points at which time is working against Khrushchev's hopes. He talks about the Communist system as young and vital. But actually, on two counts, it is showing signs of premature age. A genuinely young and vital system is always marked by a creative freshness of language; by the presence of new vivid words to match new searchings for truth. But the vocabulary of Communism is already tired and old. Again, in a genuinely vital system the "aging" effect of bureaucracy is tempered by many crisscrossing influences. But where Communism takes over, the very structure of "democratic centralism" imposes bureaucracy at once; and since its power is unchecked, no limits are set upon its growth. The native vitality of the Russian people is very far from being expended; but the system that controls their lives, and that advertises itself to the world as "progressive," appears to be growing old—without growing up.

Khrushchev's third problem stems from his ongoing need to insure a safe measure of conformity and to commandeer for Party purposes the full productive capacity of the people. To this end, he needs to find a substitute for terror.

Even before Stalin's death, terrorism had reached the point of diminishing returns. A resort to it now could easily spark resistance rather than compliance. Moreover, it would quickly "deneutralize" a number of key neutralist countries and commit to anti-Communism myriad uncommitted persons and groups.

The very processes of production would, in fact, make it inexpedient. These have been rapidly going through the change-over from ancient crudity to modern precision; and no one, not even a dictator, has found a way to make a constant intensity of fear pay off in accurate scientific research or precision work in a machine economy. It seems fairly safe to say that if a return to crass terrorism is ever staged in the Soviet Union, it will be as a political resort— to defend the totalitarian system; not as a preferred economic policy.

All this is not to say that Khrushchev has scrapped either the machinery of terror or the ideological justification of it. In the Summer of 1957, the Soviet Procurator General, discussing Khrushchev's legal reforms, stated bluntly, "If it becomes necessary we will restore the old methods. But I think it will not be necessary." (6) This would seem to state the essence of the matter. What remains ambiguous is Khrushchev's definition of *necessary*.

Even this is not altogether ambiguous. Soviet intervention in Hungary made plain one kind of meaning that he attaches to the word. A more recent event within the Soviet Union itself has further defined it. In October 1959, young workers in a huge industrial complex near Karaganda struck against their working conditions—and were subdued by tanks and regular army units. (7)

We are reminded of Eugene O'Neill's play, *Lazarus Laughed,* in which Caligula boasts to Lazarus, ". . . there shall be death while I am Caesar"; and Lazarus replies with terrible truth, "Caesar must believe in death." So must a Communist dictator; for at any point where totalitarianism is threatened by any form of resistance that might start a chain reaction of anger or skepticism, he must be able to instill fear.

Khrushchev has been a killer many times over. There is no reason to think that he would hesitate to become one again. But as a practical man, he prefers to get what he wants, at home and abroad, by "peaceful" means. What he wants above all else, now, at home, is fulfillment of the Seven Year Plan. To this end, he must either apply coercion or persuade the Soviet people to "selfless" energizing. He prefers to persuade them.

To this end, he is urging them to regard all improvements to date in their standard of living as a mere "sample package." If they will forgo "whimful" and "bourgeois" desires—as these are defined by the Party—and devote themselves unstintingly to the Plan's fulfillment, they can have more of the same. Moreover, since their effort will underwrite Khrushchev's economic diplomacy, they will be doing their "international duty."

The Soviet people, by all evidence, want more consumer goods and are reasonably willing to work for them. But there is increasing doubt that Khrushchev can get from them by propaganda a "selfless dedication" to his plan for economic take-over on the world front. His Seven Year Plan, as adopted, still gave orthodox priority to heavy industry; but twice since its adoption he has felt obliged to raise target figures in the field of consumer goods. Also, as a sign that coercion may be staging a "necessary" return, he has resorted to a raising of production norms.

This is merely one phase of a problem which we shall take up in a later chapter: namely, that the type of response which the Party demands from the people it rules is such that it can never be other than at war with them—though the war may, for a shorter or longer period, take the form of "peaceful co-existence."

We turn, now, to a problem implicit in Khrushchev's foreign policy. He has made it plain, in Cuba and the Congo, that he is on the alert to move in and give aid to any "progressive" element that seizes power in any country. Because such a policy, however, must be carried out in the glare of world-wide publicity, what Khrushchev does in any one under-developed country, and how he does it, will be watched by other countries that he has marked as targets.

The Communists can always move in most easily where hoodlumism, violence, and mass hatred are on the rampage. Their opportunity lies in their exploiting these to prevent the return of law and order until Communist control can be imposed. This means that the leader or faction most likely to win their support will be the one most given to extremism. Khrushchev's problem is to make his support of such elements look convincingly like an effort to help a new nation find its way to a just, stable, and creative independence. The fate of his intervention in the Congo points up the nature of his problem.

Where he can penetrate a country by "peaceful" means—by economic diplomacy, for example—he can, for a time, be the soul of discretion. But if the point is reached where the Communists can bid for decisive power, there seems no way in which they can avoid showing their hand. At this point, in East Europe, Stalin moved in for the kill by armed force. But Khrushchev must kill the national independence of the underdeveloped countries by "friendship." How to do this in even one country without losing his chance to establish "friendship" with other watching countries is his problem—and no easy one.

What happened in Kerala, in India, is relevant here—though it may seem to have little to do with Khrushchev. In that impoverished, restless province, the Communists had an experience which they have never had in any total country: they won in a free election the right to organize the government. And they lost this right in the next election.

How did they fumble this unique chance to "sell" Communism to other watching provinces of India? We ourselves put this question to a man who had followed the developments in Kerala. What did the Communists do, we asked, to lose so quickly the support they had gained? The man looked surprised at our even asking: "Why, they acted like Communists."

They had tried to turn *elective authority* into *totalitarian power*. They had made a grab for the educational system; and had moved to suppress their opponents. But theirs was only a provisional, not a national, government; and no Red Army was on hand to seize power for them and maintain it as a *fait accompli*. Therefore, the people could vote them out as they had voted them in.

The Kerala story points up the curious fatality under which the Communists labor. No matter how "peaceful" their first approach may be, they cannot achieve their purpose *without acting like Communists:* which is to say, without trying to gain coercive control. This holds true where they infiltrate an organization in the United States, just as it held true in Kerala. For they act, always, under the Leninist edict that while they can form temporary alliances and united fronts, they cannot permanently *share power with anyone.*

A Communist minority can exert an exaggerated influence where its presence is not known or its motives are not recognized. Such a minority can also exert total control wherever it can get its hands on the machinery of coercion and make terror its weapon. But between these two conditions lies Communism's danger zone: the zone in which the Party can be *found out* before its power is total. It has thus been found out in myriad free-world institutions which it has infiltrated —in the CIO, for example; and it was thus found out in Kerala. As its tactics become better and better known to people everywhere, the danger of its being found out steadily increases.

Khrushchev's problem is to keep it from being found out in any single underdeveloped country—under the watchful eyes of other countries that did not struggle for independence in order to lose it—until he has so altered the balance of power that he can move in by armed force.

His effort, at the General Assembly, either to dominate the United Nations or to wreck it seemed to go to self-defeating extremes. But it was understandable as an effort put forth by a man in a hurry: an effort to shift the balance of power fast enough to make good a gain that has to be made good soon, or not at all. Khrushchev, in short, acted like a Communist who found himself in a situation where he had no choice other than to act like a Communist.

Finally, there is the problem of Sino-Soviet relations; and no solution to this is in sight. We do not think that any open break between the Soviet Union and Red China is in sight, either—because of what both have to gain by "socialist

solidarity." A state of unresolved tension and unacknowledged competition can, however, pose an ongoing problem—
and more for Khrushchev than for Mao. Such is the stage of
Soviet development that Khrushchev needs "peaceful coexistence" as a cover for his expansionist drive; and the
nature of this drive requires his being able to command the
services of Parties around the world.

"In the totalitarian movements," writes Leopold Labedz,
"ideological differences, though real, are bound to be over-
shadowed ultimately by the question of who is to have the
last word about them. The accusations of 'dogmatism' and
'revisionism' can be resolved only when it is clear who has
the authority to interpret the dogma and to say what 'a
creative development of Marxism' is . . ." (8)

Within the Soviet Union, Khrushchev became not only
head of the Party and State, but also leading ideologist and
theoretician, by "defeating his opponents and assuming the
mantle of authority." But China does not have to accept his
ideological guidance; for there is no such thing as an *institutionalized* headship of the Communist orbit. Neither is there
an *institutionalized* headship of the world Communist movement.

Khrushchev, unlike Lenin or Stalin, belongs to the era
when this fact is beginning to have practical consequences.
He can still hold the satellites in line because no Communist
regime in East Europe could long maintain itself without
Soviet support. But the Communist regime in China—like
that in Yugoslavia—is self-maintaining. As for Parties around
the world, they now have, for the first time in their history, a
choice between two leaderships. Khrushchev is still able to
dominate them; but what the future may hold is indicated by
the fact that the Communist Party of India is already deeply
split into pro-Soviet and pro-Chinese factions.

" 'Proletarian internationalism,' " Labedz points out, "is no substitute for authority in the system of national Communist states, and therefore the Sino-Soviet alliance is bound to be increasingly uneasy." And Khrushchev is bound to be a man in so great a hurry that he could easily, by hurrying, make the basic character of Communism all too obvious to target countries before he can consolidate his hold over them.

The "moral" of this chapter is a double one: first, that Khrushchev's table-thumping brashness does not mean that he has the upper hand of all his problems; and second, that it is no mark of "rigidity" on the part of the West to hold the line against his current expansionist drive. It is a mark of knowledgeable common sense and moral sense to give his problems time to become more and more insoluble within the frame of Marxist-Leninist ideology and totalitarian practice.

PART TWO

STRANGE WEAPONS

SIX

THE BODY AND
SPIRIT OF A PLAN

KHRUSHCHEV'S Seven Year Plan was first publicized, in December 1958, in the form of *Theses*, which were widely "discussed" throughout the Soviet Union. That is to say, Party cadres—on collective and state farms, in youth groups, in industrial plants, and wherever they could assemble an audience—were given the task of so interpreting the *Theses* as to win an "enthusiastic" response from the "masses."

The cadres were supposed, also, to elicit from the various groups "constructive suggestions." When Khrushchev presented his Plan, some weeks later, to the Twenty-First Congress of the CPSU, he read and "weighed" a sampling of these suggestions. Thus he gave a Communist type of validation to a key paragraph in the *Theses*:

"Drawing up the great plans of communist construction, the Party draws on the inexhaustible sources of the people's creative energy. . . . The task of the Party and its local organisations is to continue indefatigably . . . to expand and consolidate their contacts with the people, to educate and organise them, and, at the same time, constantly to learn from the people . . ." (1)

The unanimous and enthusiastic adoption of the Plan by the Congress was a foregone conclusion. It simply put the official stamp on Khrushchev's "package" of next tasks on the Soviet agenda—and on that of the world Communist movement.

Pravda, meanwhile, in a series of editorials which spanned the dates of the Congress meetings, testified to the "selfless" enthusiasm of the Soviet people for the Plan. Thus, it stated on January 27, 1959, that in "all the speeches of tens of millions of Soviet people, workers, collective farmers, and intelligentsia who discussed with tremendous patriotic enthusiasm the target figures of the seven-year plan, one and only one thought is revealed, one wish and one striving, to fulfill and to overfulfill the seven-year plan target figures."

On January 30, its editorial was given over to statements by workers and collective farmers. A worker in the Lihacheva automobile works in Moscow, identified as Comrade Nikitin, is reported, for example, as having said at a mass meeting of the factory staff, "The 21st Congress of the CPSU will enter world history as a great landmark signifying a new stage in the life of mankind. Our hearts beat with joy when we think that we have entered the period of the all-out building of communism."

And a collective farmer named Mikhailichanko, of Strana Sovetov farm, Rubtsovsky Raion, Altai Krai, is said in the same editorial to have voiced the thoughts of all collective farmers: "I give thanks to the Communist Party for its daily motherly care to improve our life. I, an ordinary peasant, want to say with all my heart: 'Grow strong and live long, our own party, our strength, our wisdom, our honor, and our pride and glory.' "

When we study the text of the Plan, we soon find that it is a strange amalgam—though our attention is caught and held at first by figures and percentages that declare economic goals. Thus, for the 1959–1965 period—as compared with 1952–1958—the chemical industry, the Plan indicates, is to be expanded by more than 500 percent. Such a projected gain may seem like sheer propaganda. As late as May 1958, however, Khrushchev, addressing the Plenary Session of the Central Committee of the CPSU, emphasized both the vital importance of the chemical industry and its dismal lag in the Soviet economy. From a low starting-point, a 500 percent increase could be a realistic goal.

The iron and steel output is to go up by 245 percent; that of oil and gas by 235–240 percent. In the field of consumer goods, a rise of 179–182 percent is set for building and building materials; 200–212 percent for food production and other light industries. Meat and fruit are marked for an increase of 100 percent over 1958; milk for an increase of 70–80 percent. In the housing field, 15,000,000 new flats are called for: "more than all the housing built to date since the Revolution."

As measured by these target figures, actual achievements in the Soviet economy in the period since the Plan's adoption have varied greatly from field to field. But regardless of whether or not all the projected goals were realistic, the matters represented by these figures and percentages have a proper place within a nation's economic plan. It is precisely because such elements in the Khrushchev Plan are normal that other elements, obtrusively intermixed with them, seem grossly abnormal.

It is one thing to read, for example, of the need "to expand considerably the non-ferrous metal industry in Kazakhstan

. . . on the basis of the rich raw-material resources." (2) But it is different *in kind* to read that "the decline and decay of the countries of capitalism are an irrefutable proof of the reactionary nature and doom of the capitalist order. . . . The seven-year plan is a staggering blow to bourgeois ideology . . ." (3)

It is one thing to read that the number of persons "with a higher or secondary specialized education, employed in economy is about 7½ million, or thirty-nine times more than in 1913." (4) It is different *in kind* to read that "under conditions of capitalism an increase in production leads to the enrichment of a handful of exploiters and is accompanied by relative and absolute impoverishment of the working people . . ." (5)

It is one thing to read that more than "1600 food and light-industry factories will be built . . ." (6) It is different *in kind* to read—as part of a long diatribe against revisionism —that the Yugoslavs "deny the need for international class solidarity. . . . They are trying to tell the world that there are . . . two military camps. Yet everybody knows that the Socialist camp . . . is not a military camp but a community of equal nations striving for peace.

"The other camp is the imperialist camp, which seeks at any price to maintain its system of oppression and violence and threatens humanity with war." (7)

How does this latter kind of material—which occupies a sizable part of the text—fit into a plan for a nation's economy? How does it fit into a Soviet plan adopted *in 1959:* the year when Khrushchev was most fervently urging "friendship" and "peaceful coexistence"? To get perspective on these questions, we can turn from the Soviet Plan to India's *Second Five Year Plan* and its *Draft Outline of the Third Five Year Plan;* and to Pakistan's *Outline of the Second Five Year Plan*

(1960–1965). At once, we are in a different territory of mind, spirit, and purpose.

The Government of India Planning Commission states simply, "The central objective . . . in India since Independence has been the promotion of rapid and balanced economic development." Seeking "the balanced development of all parts of the country," the *Second Five Year Plan* specifies the need both "to rebuild rural India" and "to lay the foundation of industrial progress." (8)

The *Draft Outline* of the *Third Five Year Plan* holds to the theme of balanced development and notes some of the problems involved: "In the short run, there may sometimes be a conflict between the economic and social objectives of developmental planning. The claims of economic and social equality and those of increased employment may have to be reconciled with the requirements of production. Experience of the working of the first two Plans suggests that on the whole the most satisfactory results are likely to be achieved by a balanced advance in all these directions" and "the processes of democracy and freedom of choice should be capable of throwing up the optimum to be aimed at in a given context." (9)

The Planning Commission of Pakistan expresses itself in like vein: "The economic objectives of Pakistan are long-range goals. . . . The nation aspires to a standard of living for all its people as high as can be achieved with the resources available to it . . ." (10) This aspiration means that effort must focus on the production of enough food, shelter, and clothing to meet "at least minimum standards"; on the expansion of educational and health facilities; on the opening up of more opportunities for "gainful employment"; and on "the securing of social justice."

Holding in mind these aims, and the tone of their expression, we turn back to Khrushchev's *Theses* and read, "The international significance of the Seven Year Plan lies in the fact that its fulfillment means a further consolidation of the might of the world system of socialism"; and that "the main economic task of the USSR" is "to overtake and surpass, in the shortest possible time, the most highly developed capitalist countries in output per head of population." (11)

It is to this end—this furthering of the world Communist movement—that all Party members are urged to be "active fighters for the fulfillment and overfulfillment of target figures." It is to this end that they are urged to "link ideological work ever more closely with practical problems" and to conduct "an irreconcilable struggle against bourgeois ideology." (12)

The planning commissions of India and Pakistan alike assume that the role of government is to serve the needs of the nation and its people. But the Soviet Plan makes the role of the people that of serving a government which defines its "main economic task" as that of expansionism on a world scale; and that of overcoming the "ideological enemy" of Marxism-Leninism.

Khrushchev's Plan states that "of course" the role of the Soviet Union is determined by its being "the most powerful country in the world Socialist system." (13)

It is not that Khrushchev is unconcerned about the Soviet standard of living. He predicts *with pleasure* that, before too long, all Soviet citizens will enjoy full satisfaction of their requirements for food, housing, and clothing "within necessary and reasonable bounds"; and he happily forecasts a time when the Soviet standard of living will be the highest in the world.

But there is a curious triple catch in his attitude. What constantly shows through his words is the fact that he values a high standard of living chiefly as an advertisement of Communism; that he reserves for the Party the right to define the people's needs and to brand as "whimful" and "bourgeois" any consumer desires that fall outside the specified pattern; and that living standards are to be raised only at a rate that will not interfere with Communism's drive on the world front.

As always, in brief, his interest is ideologically slanted. He needs to envision a happy people enthusiastically involved in the Party's vast design; for "the higher the conscious attitude of the masses, millions strong, the more successfully the plans of Communist construction will be carried out." (14)

What all this comes down to, it would appear from the text of the Plan, is an earnest wish to have the people well enough satisfied by what Communism "delivers" that they will exhibit a mass eagerness for the role which Marxism-Leninism assigns them: "By actively supporting the construction of a new society in the Soviet Union, [in] the People's Republic of China, in all socialist countries, and guarding it against the intrigue of imperialist reaction, the working people are fulfilling their international duty." (15)

It is in multiple statements of this kind that we find our clue to the nature of the Seven Year Plan. In spite of figures and percentages, and of the claim made for it in the *Theses*, it is not primarily a plan "for the development of the national economy of the USSR." It is a plan for forging *within* the USSR an economic weapon built to the specifications of "socialist internationalism" and Communism's "historic mission." This is why, in both spirit and purpose, it is far removed from such plans as those of India and Pakistan.

Khrushchev writes, for example, of "the grandiose plan of communist construction." (16) But Ahmed, Chairman of the Planning Commission of Pakistan, has no propaganda axe to grind; and can, therefore, write that "the rate of economic growth" contemplated in his country's Plan "is modest and no grandiose program is proposed." (17)

Khrushchev talks the language of infallibility: "The impressive tasks of the development and consolidation of the Soviet state and its economy have always been carried out successfully at every phase of socialist construction, because the Communist Party proceeds from the basic tenets of Marxism-Leninism . . . and correctly determines, in the state economic plans, the principal problems of socialist and communist construction and the ways and means of solving them." (18)

He does not remind his audience of the reason why a *seven* year plan had been drafted and a Congress to adopt it had been called in an off year: namely, that the *Sixth Five Year Plan* had proved so unrealistic, so far beyond the country's capacity to deliver the goods, that its scrapping had become essential well before its terminal date.

The Planning Commission of Pakistan, however, is not embarrassed to observe with respect to its own project, "Performance under the First Plan is a story of some successes and some failures; on record, the balance is one of fair progress." (19)

The Indian Commission was able to report an 18 percent increase in national income for the period of the First Five Year Plan; but it does not, in the Second Five Year Plan, play down or gloss over the problem that remains: "On the whole, the economic situation on the eve of the second plan is distinctly better than it was on the eve of the first plan. . . . These gains notwithstanding, the fact remains that living standards in India are among the lowest in the world." (20) The *Draft Outline* of the Third Five Year Plan is equally frank in talking about "the aspects of retarded development" to which planning and effort have to be directed: "low levels of productivity," for example, and "large scale underemployment."

This contrast between extravagant bombast and sober

modesty is more than a contrast between national temperaments or the temperaments of current national leaders. It
affords a clue to the peculiarity of the Khrushchev Plan. This
Plan merely gives a "local habitation" to the peculiarity of the
Communist viewpoint. Always and everywhere, the Party
sees itself as uniquely related to history. Dedicated to the
task of proving its "vanguard" role, it has no vocabulary save
that of propaganda and indoctrination.

India sees itself as part of the human community, past
and present. Therefore, its Commission can, as naturally as
breathing, acknowledge a debt: "Countries which start late
in their industrial career have some advantage in that they
have, in the main, to take over and apply techniques that
have been successfully worked in more advanced countries." (21) Also, as naturally as breathing, it can express
the hope, in the Draft Outline of the Third Five Year Plan,
that as the nation lifts itself "from a state of poverty" and
enters upon "the process of dynamic growth," it will be able
to decrease the extent of its "dependence on more advanced
countries for equipment and technical knowledge."

But even though Khrushchev has tried by every possible
means to tap the world's store of scientific and technological
knowledge, and though Stalin never hesitated either to steal
scientific secrets or to plunder the satellite economies, the
Seven Year Plan—like every other Party document—awards
sole credit for every Soviet advance to Marxism-Leninism,
the Party's unvarying "correctness," and the system of "democratic centralism." It is as though the economy of the USSR
had never drawn on any knowledge or skill save that which
the Party has called forth from original void.

If the Plan is marked Communist by the Marxist-Leninist
orthodoxy of the propaganda line which it directs against the
West, and against "revisionism," it is even more deeply

marked by one aspect of its domestic policy: its drive toward centralized gigantism.

This drive is often overlooked because Khrushchev has, on the strictly *administrative* front, taken various steps toward decentralization. His setting-up of the regional economic councils, for example, was such a step. On the *production* front, however, in both industry and agriculture, he has adhered strictly to the Marxist-Leninist view that vast projects are inherently better than small; centralized, better than decentralized.

Again, a contrast may be clarifying. In both India and Pakistan, the planners attach value to projects of many forms and sizes—rural and urban; public, co-operative, and private. India's third plan, for example, stresses the importance of thinking of the "private sector" of the economy in terms of "millions of farmers, artisans, traders and small industrialists" as well as in terms of large industrial installations.

Both plans, moreover, hope to modernize processes without uprooting any more people than need be, and without reducing the individual—hitherto an intimate member of family and village—to an anonymous unit for turning out material objects on a mass scale. Thus, the Indian Commission counts as an important factor the community's *readiness* to apply new methods. Also, at the village level, it puts the stress on *voluntary* co-operatives to replace an agricultural system in which inheritance laws have divided and subdivided family holdings until the separate plots of land have become too small for even subsistence farming. In neither country do the planners show any impulse to coerce people into a malleable mass.

While Pakistan is encouraging basic industries "where economically feasible," it hopes to take many small and middle-sized industries to *where people are* rather than to uproot people in multitude and take them to where vast installations have been established.

The traditional village, in fact—without its traditional isolation—is being given a new function in Pakistan. It is to be the laboratory of "basic democracy": a place where people still largely unreached by formal schooling can practice the unfamiliar art of the franchise within population units small enough for them to judge *as candidates* persons whom they have had a chance to know *as members of a living community.*

To turn from these plans to the Khrushchev Plan is to move out of a non-Communist into a Communist frame of reference. Khrushchev not only carries forward the Leninist-Stalinist commitment to the gigantic, but lifts it to new levels of exaggeration. Thus, he enacts a bias which runs through all Communist thinking.

The nature of this bias can be made clear by one quotation from Lenin, on a theme to which he returned again and again: "The strength of capitalism lies in the strength of small production"; for "small production *engenders* capitalism and the bourgeoisie continuously, daily, hourly, spontaneously and on a mass scale." (22) Only large-scale production, he insisted, could eradicate "the roots of capitalism"; could undermine the base of the "enemy." He made it clear that what he was talking about was the *force of habit* in human life—the italics are his; and the respective ways in which people in small-scale and large-scale units are related to property, work, and one another.

On this point, Stalin was an undeviating Leninist. The Soviet regime, he flatly declared, "could not for long rest upon two opposite foundations: on large-scale socialist industry, which *destroys* capitalist elements, and on small, individual peasant farming, which *engenders* capitalist elements." (23)

For both Lenin and Stalin, we must note, the issue is not

the relative capacity of small-scale and large-scale units to produce goods. Much less is it an issue of their relative capacity to provide for individual development and the satisfactions of daily human experience. The sole issue is their relative capacity to produce *Communist man:* the type of man who, under the "dictatorship of the proletariat," can be organized and manipulated in the mass.

As Stalin was a Leninist, so Khrushchev, on this point, is a Leninist-Stalinist. Even before Stalin died, Khrushchev dominated agricultural planning; and his hope was lodged, as it is today, in a vast merger program and a vast program for the new lands. Early in 1950, there were 250,000 collective farms. By 1959, mergers had reduced the number to 80,000. Yet the Plan calls for further mergers of collectives into supercollectives; and, in the long run, for the absorption of these into even vaster state farms.

Intensive farming appears to leave Khrushchev cold. He seems unable to fit it into a Communist frame of reference, and views with a somewhat jaundiced eye any evidence that it delivers the goods. The vast new lands program is his kind of project. Acre for acre, the peasants' land allotments have been the most productive plots in the Soviet Union. Ideologically, however, they are all wrong; and under the Plan, they are slated for liquidation: gradually, on the collective farms; within the next two or three years on the state farms.

In the industrial field, the traditional Communist bias in favor of heavy industry is not only maintained but is being supplemented, now, by an almost intoxicated stress on automation. In Khrushchev's mind, these two seem to fuse into an image of mammoth installations for every type of productive process, with the human beings within these explicitly routinized. They are promised benefits of many kinds from socialized services which are themselves planned on a gigantic scale. Also, they are promised more goods, a shorter working day, and "ample time for study, art, literature, sport and so on." But even their use of leisure, Khrushchev holds, must not be "whimful." It must, therefore, also be planned *in the large* and guided by the Party.

Certainly, Khrushchev wishes the Soviet people no ill. But because his thinking takes place within the frame of *democratic centralism* and *historical materialism,* with a taste for automation thrown in, the kind of good which he wishes for them seems to come straight out of Orwell's *1984.* Thus, in the Plan, he warns against a "vulgarized conception of Communist society" as loose and unorganized. When Communism —the terminal goal of the historic process—truly arrives, it will be a "highly organized and closely co-ordinated commonwealth of men and women; and its rhythm will be set by machine industry."

Lest any misconception remain, the rationale of this society is spelled out: "For the machine to be properly operated, every worker will have to perform his production job and his social functions in a definite time and according to the definite system." (24)

It is as though Lenin, by declaring bourgeois minds to be the chief product of small plants and small land holdings, had set going a drive toward vastness which has become, now, a form of perpetual motion—far beyond the reach of any check-up on whether or not size has passed the point of diminishing returns.

Within the frame of vastness, limited reforms can take place—have taken place. Khrushchev has provided greater economic incentives to the peasants and has made the price structure of the state procurement system more rational. But the reforms can only be *limited*—for they are hedged about by the ideology. Just as every non-Communist country is, in Communist thought, marked for liquidation, so is every aspect of the Soviet economy and every plot of land within the Soviet Union which still constitutes a "standing place" for the individual.

"It should be perfectly clear," states the Plan, "that in future the collective farm Co-operative and the State forms of property will merge into an integral Communist property." (25) Khrushchev says, of course, that all this property belongs to *the people;* and to prove this, he claims to be "democratizing" many processes. But for property to belong to *the people* in the Communist sense, is a very different thing from its belonging to *a person.* A person who owns property can make decisions with respect to it. But if the Soviet Union develops according to the Khrushchev Plan, the individual will, in one basic respect, come to share the fate which Marx assigned to the propertyless worker under fully developed capitalism: *he will have no means of production to call his own.*

This brings us to the ideological basis of centralized gigantism. Communism cannot tolerate any of three elements on which the free world relies: the individual who has his own stake in the social-economic order and who can stand on his own feet; voluntary associations of free individuals; and a middle class which, in contradiction to Marxist dogma, draws into itself more and more persons from the two economic extremes, instead of being drawn off into these, and chiefly into the "exploited" class.

For Communists, the stock way to guard against the emergence of these elements—and to insure "monolithic unity" under Party control—is to create conditions in which people work in masses, play in masses, are indoctrinated in masses, and applaud in masses. The very type of uprooted person whom the planners of India and Pakistan are trying not to bring into being as a by-product of industrial growth is Marxism-Leninism's preferred material for the making of

Communist man. No document, past or present, makes this fact more clear and explicit than does the Seven Year Plan.

This Plan, as we have noted, is to be Khrushchev's instrument of success. It is designed to lift to a climax the Lenin-Stalin-Khrushchev sequence of power. More than this, its fulfillment is crucial to his war called peace. Will the Plan be fulfilled?

At this writing, the chances are against its being fulfilled on schedule. In setting target figures, Khrushchev, the propagandist, seems not always to have consulted Khrushchev, the realist. To give himself a "grandiose plan of communist construction" from which to operate *ideologically,* he has set goals which call for his having an incredible number of good breaks. They could be met, also, only by his winning from the people a far more "selfless" dedication to the Plan than he has yet been able to secure. So far, things have not all gone his way.

They have not gone his way on the agricultural front; and this front has always been Communism's Number One problem. On it, the ideology is confronted by four exasperating and resistant factors: weather; the peasant mind; processes of organic growth that take their own time; and the fact that not even the fitting of human beings into a pattern of centralized and mechanized gigantism can prevent their being organisms instead of machines, and individuals instead of cogs in machines. These factors plague Khrushchev even as they plagued his predecessors.

On two counts, Khrushchev almost invited failure for the agricultural part of his Plan. He staked a disproportionate amount of hope on the virgin-lands program—which is highly vulnerable to "uncooperative" weather. And in setting his target figures, he used as the basis from which to project future gains the 1958 production level—which was far above

average. That was a year when good breaks and unprecedent-
edly good weather netted him bumper crops from the virgin
lands. But his luck did not hold. Worse, it turned: 1959,
the first year of the Plan, witnessed a decline in these crops
of almost 25 percent—to a below-average level. Bad weather
was one cause. But bad organization of the farm-machinery
program was another. Goals, in brief, which called for a
steep upward curve from a high starting point were virtually
doomed within the first year by a downward swoop of
the curve. At the meeting of the Supreme Soviet, in December 1959—less than eleven months after the Plan's adoption—
Khrushchev had to acknowledge that the agricultural sector
of it was in trouble.

On the industrial front, also, he is having problems that
range from labor shortages to labor inertia. He is tackling
the labor shortage by that educational "reform" which greatly
reduces educational opportunities for all save a gifted minority and by a cut in the armed forces. He is tackling the
problem of inertia by the most extensive and intensive program of indoctrination ever launched in the Soviet Union;
and also by offering such limited types of incentive as can
be offered within the framework of Communist orthodoxy.
How close these measures will bring him to the fulfillment of
his goals by 1965 remains to be seen.

The lessons which we ourselves have to learn from the
Seven Year Plan remain the same, however, whether the
target figures are reached by 1965—or by 1975. It is doubtful,
in fact, whether these lessons would be more than superficially changed by Khrushchev's disappearance from the
scene. They are no more likely to be rendered obsolete by
the passing of a particular dictator than are the lessons inherent in the writings of Marx, Lenin, and Stalin.

The Plan spells out once more—in terms familiar and unfamiliar—the ideological and strategic essence of Communism. Moreover, it gives us a preview of what can be expected from the Communist hierarchy, on the home front and the world front, as it becomes increasingly able to operate from strength.

Aware, as we all are today, of the world's urgent need to produce goods and services in new abundance, we would like to be able to rejoice when any nation puts forth a plan that calls for 15,000,000 new residence units and a vastly increased output of shoes and milk and meat, steel and chemicals and electrical power. But we would be unwise to let our plain, decent hopes for the human future make us misread this Plan. It is no normal plan for a nation's development nor for increasing the world's supply of necessary goods. It is a blueprint for economic warfare—against all free nations and against the free spirit of man, inside and outside the Soviet Union.

SEVEN

HISTORY AS A WEAPON

IN MARCH 1953, Stalin died. With him died his *Short History of the Communist Party of the Soviet Union.* For fifteen years, this had been the indispensable textbook of Communists everywhere. It contained all they needed to know about the events and personalities of a violent half century. Armed with its word, they were safeguarded against error.

Then Stalin, the towering hero of the book, died; and the *History* ceased to be history. The 50,000,000 copies had to be scrapped; and myriad devotees learned, by stages, that their "knowledge" had best be scrapped, too.

Abruptly, in a land where the history of the Communist Party is the history of the nation, there was no history. For no two official histories of the Party ever "coexist" in the Soviet Union; and no unofficial history is tolerated. Thus, the demise of Stalin's book meant that the past simply vanished into a limbo of silence. The prudent did not break that silence for fear of saying what the future would brand as heresy.

Words, of course, poured in their accustomed volume from Communist presses and gatherings. A system made out of words cannot abandon their utterance. But the verbiage was suddenly so infected with the caution of noncommitment that it became a container empty of meaning.

Some four months after Stalin's death, on July 26, 1953, *Pravda* published a sterile, stopgap substitute for history. All that had happened since the turn of the century was compressed into 7500 words—some twenty-five average pages. This next-to-nothing document, issued by *Agitprop*, was titled, "Theses on Fifty Years of the Communist Party of the Soviet Union." Its style had a calculated flatness. To eliminate the risk of misplacing praise and blame, it mentioned no living person. Only three persons were mentioned out of the teeming past.

Yet the flat words reverberated with the news that an era had ended. For while the name of Lenin appeared eighty-three times, that of Stalin appeared only four times. The only other person mentioned—once—was Plekhanov, Lenin's chief intellectual adversary at the time when the course of Russian Marxism was first being determined.

The CPSU and Parties around the world still discussed all requisite Marxist-Leninist subjects. But their strained effort to take a stand without standing on anything reflected the fact that Stalin's *History* had been far more than a slanted version of the past. It had been his prime instrument of indoctrination; and his aim, so far as indoctrination was concerned, had been "neither to convince nor even to persuade, but to produce a uniform pattern of public utterance in which the first trace of unorthodox thought" would reveal itself "as a jarring dissonance." (1)

Now, abruptly, there was no orthodox thought—and hence no safe way to avoid the unorthodox. "Still worse, the

'Theses' gave no clue as to whom it was now necessary to cheer. . . . To the initiated, this was a sign that a new time of uncertainty had begun, and that no living name was mentioned because no successor had yet emerged." (2)

For six years, "the much chronicled Communist Party was without any history, except the 7,500 words of depersonalized historyless history of the Department of Agitation and Propaganda." (3) Then, in the Summer of 1959, a new *History of the Soviet Communist Party* came to occupy the empty field.

Why did six years have to elapse between the death of Stalin's *History* and the birth of its successor? It was proclaimed, at first, that a new one would be out within a year. Why, then, did the post-Stalin "collective leadership" have to go on saying *for six years*, "History is dead. Long live . . . that which will appear if you wait long enough."

Non-Communist scholars might have theorized that it would take that long for even a dedicated "writers' collective" to free the Communist past from the fabrications imposed upon it by Stalin. For as far back as 1931, Bertram D. Wolfe reminds us, Stalin had described as "archive rats" those historians who prized careful research; and in 1938 —the year when Stalin's *History* gave the past its "permanent" mold—the Politburo secretly decided that "no one was to be permitted to remember anything new about Lenin or publish any memoir concerning him." (4)

Stalin's successors, therefore, could have claimed, with the warm approbation of scholars everywhere, that it would take time for them to separate the good wheat of truth from the tares of falsehood. Unfortunately, however, they cared no more about patient scholarship and accurate research than Stalin had. Khrushchev is on record as having said in 1956 that historians "are capable of upsetting everything.

They have to be directed."

Here we come to the reason for the six-year hiatus: historians could not be directed until the post-Stalin era had found its direction. As Wolfe has put the matter, the "dictatorship had to beget its new dictator; infallible doctrine its infallible expounder; authoritarianism its authority; a totally militarized society its supreme commander."

Nor was this all: "Before a new history could be published, Stalin's ghost had to be wrestled with and its size determined." It was one thing for the interim "collective leadership" to rid itself of the incubus of Stalin's excesses. It was quite another for the emerging dictator to decide what to say about all the extensions of Soviet and Communist power that were now at his own disposal solely because of Stalin's ruthlessness.

Still further, "where power is knowledge . . . the emergent authority on all things must have time to lay down the line on all problems, persons and events likely to find their way into history." (5)

In short, the new *History* did not mark a return to truth after the falsifications of the Stalin era. It was simply Khrushchev's slanted version of the past. Khrushchev does not claim authorship of it. He credits a "collective." But the volume did not appear until he was in a position to decide what the past should be permitted to reveal, required to hide, and commanded to prove.

In some respects, Khrushchev's distortion of the past is more glaring than Stalin's. Stalin demanded only that he be the hero at the center of history's stage; and that indoctrination be so formalized that even the mildest dissent would be noted by his agents of coercion. Khrushchev's *History*—which emphasizes that Marxism "enables us to know the present and foresee the future"—has a larger aim. It is a workbook designed to tell Communists everywhere how to put into effect, today and tomorrow, in diversified theaters of war, a more complex policy than any that Stalin ever conceived.

One key to the character of this *History* is to be found in Khrushchev's shifting attitude toward Stalin. On February 25, 1956, at a closed session of the Twentieth Congress of the CPSU, Khrushchev, we recall, spearheaded the attack on Stalin. It was not long, however, before he began retreating from the position he took at that time. The new *History* can be taken as a report that he had, by mid-1959, carried this retreat to what he took to be a feasible standing place. Also, the *History* has enabled him, as heir to the gains which Stalinism netted for Communism, to refashion Stalin into a man from whom one need not be embarrassed to receive a legacy.

If we return to the Twentieth Congress, to remind our-selves of what Khrushchev actually said about Stalin, we can, from that point, "look before and after." He denounced Stalin for having practiced the "cult of personality" to such an extent that, even as far back as 1934, and progressively through the years, he had ignored that primacy of the Party which Leninism requires. Further, he portrayed him as monstrous in deceit and brutality; and he offered in evidence the rigged trials of the 1930's.

Khrushchev reported that "of the 139 members and candi-dates of the Party's Central Committee who were elected at the XVIIth Congress, 98 persons, i.e., 70 percent were ar-rested and shot (mostly in 1937–1938)."

Having given this figure, he analyzed the make-up of that Congress, in 1934. Eighty percent of the voting participants at it, he said, were persons who had joined the Party "before the Revolution and during the Civil War; this means before 1921." Yet on "fabricated charges," Stalin had branded these

Old Bolsheviks as "spies" and "saboteurs." Moreover: "Confessions of guilt . . . were gained with the help of cruel and inhuman tortures."

Stalin had not submitted to the Central Committee the evidence on which he based his charges. The past records of the Old Bolsheviks were, however, known to all. Therefore, said Khrushchev, in 1956, "it was inconceivable that a Congress so composed would have elected a Central Committee, the majority of whom would be enemies of the Party."

It was so inconceivable, indeed, that at "the February–March Central Plenum in 1937 many members actually questioned the rightness of the established course regarding mass repressions. . . . Comrade Postyshev most ably expressed these doubts. He said: '. . . I personally do not believe that in 1934 an honest Party member who had trod the long road of unrelenting fight against enemies for the Party and for Socialism, would now be in the camp of the enemies. I do not believe it.'" (6)

That, said Khrushchev, *in 1956*, was what Postyshev had said in *February 1937*, in the face of Stalin's tyranny. But what had Khrushchev himself said at that time about the men whom Postyshev defended; the men who could not "conceivably" have been guilty of the crimes with which Stalin charged them?

At a public meeting, on *January 30, 1937*, Khrushchev said of these same men, "These miserable nonentities wanted to destroy the unity of the Party and the Soviet State. . . . They raised their treacherous hands against Comrade Stalin . . . Stalin—our hope, Stalin—our desire, Stalin—the light of advanced and progressive humanity, Stalin—our will, Stalin—our victory." (7)

Two years after that, moreover, at the Eighteenth Congress, in 1939—after he had played his own part in the frightful purges of 1937–1938, and had been made First Secretary

of the Ukrainian Party in place of the ousted Postyshev—
Khrushchev said: "The successful and victorious destruction of fascist agents, and of all those contemptible Trotsky-
ites, Bukharinites and bourgeois nationalists, we owe, first
of all and personally, to our leader, the great Stalin." (8)

This extending to Stalin, in 1939, of warm *credit* for the
purges is interesting. For in 1956, he went all out to show
that no one but Stalin could have been to blame for them.
True, Yezhov, head of the NKVD—the secret police—had
been the conspicuous executioner. But: ". . . it would be a
display of naivete to consider this the work of Yezhov alone.
It is clear that these matters were decided by Stalin, and
that without his orders and his sanction Yezhov could not
have done this." (9)

Now, let us come back to the new *History*, published three
years later, in 1959—to take stock of one of those miracles in
which Communist history abounds. In July 1938, it was
reported in the Soviet press that L. P. Beria—who had previously functioned only in the Republic of Georgia—had
been appointed as an assistant to Yezhov. On December
8 of that year—*at the end of the great purges*—the press
reported that Beria had replaced Yezhov. But in the new
History Beria is made to *precede* Yezhov in order that he,
a "rogue and political adventurer," can be made to take the
chief blame for the purges: "Not stopping at anything and
exploiting the personal shortcomings of J. V. Stalin for his
criminal purposes, he slandered and liquidated many honest
persons devoted to the Party and the people." (10)

Here, in one phrase, is the key to the whole elaborate
method by which Stalin, in the new *History*, is reprocessed
to become a "positive hero." The key phrase is "personal
shortcomings." These the *History* attributes to Stalin in calculated measure; but it asserts that these did not detract from

his public stature—except in so far as his "cult of personality" made him exploitable by villains like Beria. A multitude of the very high-handed edicts which Khrushchev denounced, in 1956, are now dismissed in one sentence: "Many important problems were decided by Stalin personally."

After all, only three years had elapsed between 1956 and 1959. What had happened to make necessary the burial of Stalin in the role of brutal egomaniac and his resurrection as a "positive hero" with some personal shortcomings? The answer can be simply given: *Khrushchev had become dictator.*

When Khrushchev spoke at the Twentieth Congress, he was intent to re-establish the primacy of the Party over the State and to make it his own chosen instrument of power. Stalin's long downgrading of it had therefore to be denounced. Stalin, he said, had usurped total power. Often he had not bothered even to ask the opinion of the Central Committee or its Political Bureau. Often, "he did not inform them about his personal decisions concerning very important Party and government matters." (11)

But when Khrushchev approved the *History*, in 1959, he was intent to tell a multitude of target peoples and countries that the CPSU had always been the firm, successful initiator of Soviet policies; and that it could both offer guidance and serve as an example. A Party that had been under the thumb of a personal tyrant from at least 1934 to 1953, and that had, for the most part, played sycophant to that tyrant, would scarcely have fitted the image.

Hence, another retroactive miracle: in the *History*, all rumors to the effect that Stalin's "cult of personality" had diminished the status of the Party are transmuted into "fabrications of the enemies of socialism." In truth, the *History* assures the world, such mistakes as did stem from Stalin's tendency to exaggerate his own role "could not and did not alter the profoundly democratic, genuinely popular character of the Soviet system. The policy carried out by the Party was correct, it expressed the interests of the people." (12)

Taking Khrushchev at his own shifting word, this amounts to saying that it was in "the interests of the people" that the Party, with its authority intact, refrained from putting an end to a reign of terror in which ninety-eight out of a hundred and thirty-nine members of the Central Committee were executed on the basis of trumped-up charges and confessions secured by means of torture.

Khrushchev, we must assume, is laying his bet that those whom he most cares about reaching as targets will not know enough about the past, when they read the *History*, and will not know enough about what he himself said in 1956, to join together statements which he prefers to keep asunder. Since, however, he is currently turning the whole world into his forum audience on every possible occasion, we do well to remind ourselves of how tenuously his words, down through the years, have been related to truth; and of how closely they have been related to his own ambitions and his own policies.

Quite apart from his need to prove the strong correctness of the Party at all past times, Khrushchev has had to make Stalin into a man whose methods and successes need not be repudiated. The *History*, therefore, commends him for annihilating rival parties; forcing collectivization; forcing industrialization; conquering the Baltic Republics; "liberating" East Europe; and helping to Communize China, North Korea, and North Vietnam. No one of these activities, we must note, downgraded the Party; and all of them enhanced Soviet and Communist power. Hence, nothing is "wrong" with them; and all is "right."

Here, too, we can note the manner in which the *History* deals with Stalin's persecution, in the late 1940's, of writers, artists, intellectuals, and scientists. That was the period when Zhdanov, Stalin's cultural commissar, set out to terrorize the human mind into "useful" service—with the backing of two Resolutions which the Central Committee passed in 1946 and 1948.

After Stalin's death, we recall, his successors instituted that "liberalization" known as the "thaw"; and then found themselves having to deal with such explosive results that they reinstituted a "freeze." Khrushchev's policy toward the mind has, ever since, been a kind of alternation between "thaw" and "freeze." The *History* reflects his failure to find a "correct" policy in this area by its cautiously ambiguous attitude toward the Stalin-Zhdanov tyranny.

Admitting extremism, it again—as in the case of the trials and purges of the 1930's—makes Stalin a villain *once removed*. The real villains, according to this text, were Beria and Malenkov, who exerted a "harmful" influence over Stalin. Thus, his part in the unsavory excesses of the period becomes nothing worse than susceptibility to evil influence.

The two enabling resolutions of the Central Committee —which made unlimited coercion legal—are justified by the fact that, during the war, millions of Soviet people were exposed to contact with the West. As a result, "Some citizens revealed ideological instability, had an uncritical attitude toward capitalist procedures." The Party, therefore, was "correct" in directing a decisive blow "against a retreat from Marxism-Leninism in science, literature, and art." (13)

If the *History's* handling of the Stalin-Zhdanov period tells us anything, it would seem to be, first, that Khrushchev has not found the answer to the question of how to deal with writers, artists, and intellectuals within the frame of Communist coercion; and, second, that he will have few

qualms about resorting to Stalin's methods if he ever decides
that they are necessary to defend the ideology and the system.

The most decisive reason, however, for Khrushchev's having to play down those very aspects of Stalinism which
he stressed in 1956 is that the *History* is a workbook for the
future. What has been done in the Soviet Union, it asserts,
will "inevitably" have to be repeated in all its basic features
in all countries sooner or later.

It would hardly do, then, for this workbook to give other
than an expurgated version of the brutal Soviet past. Hard-
core Party members can be trusted to read between the lines;
and they can always be briefed, at Party Congresses, as they
were briefed at the Twenty-First Congress on the meaning
of "peaceful coexistence." But Khrushchev could hardly tell
the *whole* past to that *whole* new range of peoples and
governments that he wants to "guide."

The picture of Stalinism which he drew at the Twentieth
Congress recalls certain lines which Edwin Arlington Robinson wrote in behalf of a victim of an older, non-Communist
tyranny:

> Prisons have tongues, and this will all be told;
> And it will not sound well when men remember. (14)

Khrushchev did not tell "all," even in 1956; and he ad-
dressed himself to the Party elite in closed session. When
what he had said became known to the world, however, he
had ample proof that it did not sound well. The *History*
is a masterpiece of dictatorial prudence: *everything* is made
to sound well, at whatever cost to truth.

These manifold wrestlings with Stalin's ghost tell us that
the *History*'s basic aim is to make the Soviet Union a
"worthy" friend of any country that stands in drastic need

of change; and to make the CPSU a wise and respectable guide for such a country.

Because Khrushchev's foreign policy calls for an all-out exploitation of the nationalist hopes and prides of newly independent and transitional countries, the *History*—with a fine disregard for facts—"proves" that the Party has, *from the beginning,* been the sponsor of national integrity.

One of the most bald-faced lies in the book serves this purpose. It was during World War I, we recall, that both Russian revolutions took place: the first in the Spring of 1917 led to the abdication of the Tsar and the setting up of the Provisional Government under Prince Lvov; second, the Bolshevik revolution, involved the overthrow of this Government and the setting up of the Communist regime.

Tsarist Russia entered the first World War as an ally of the West against Germany. Between the first and second revolutions, after the Tsar had abdicated, one of the most bitter bones of contention between the Provisional Government and the Bolsheviks was the proper attitude to take toward the Tsar's international commitments. The Provisional Government was determined to abide by Russia's commitment to the Western Allies. The Bolsheviks were equally determined to get Russia out of the war by means of a separate peace with Germany.

This part of the record is plainly set down in both Communist and non-Communist documents. German state papers, moreover, that came into Western hands after World War II, seem to prove that Lenin's return to Russia from exile in Switzerland, in April 1917, across German territory, was permitted because he had agreed to deliver what the Germans wanted: Russia's withdrawal from the war.

In any case, Lenin's own writings tell what his stand was. Upon his arrival in Russia, he directed the Bolsheviks to undermine the Provisional Government and demoralize the armed forces by any means that would not bring too much public disfavor upon themselves before a "revolutionary situation" could be prepared. He explicitly denounced the Provisional Government because it stood "for the continuance of the imperialist war, a war waged in concert with the imperialist powers, Great Britain, France, and others . . ." (15) Speaking with the italics of anger, he said that, instead of repudiating treaties made by the Tsar, it had "*confirmed* these treaties."

Now we come to Khrushchev's retroactive miracle. His *History* accepts Lenin's description of the war as imperialistic. But there its likeness to the original writings—and to Lenin's report—comes to an end. The April 1917 conference of Bolsheviks, it states, "protested against the slander spread by the capitalists that the Bolsheviks sympathized with the idea of a separate peace with Germany." (16)

The *History* continues: "The Russian counterrevolution had agreed to conclude a separate peace with Germany. . . . This was a clear indication of the antipatriotism of the bourgeoisie, its treacherous role in relation to the homeland. The real patriots were Bolsheviks who saved Russia from defeat by German imperialism, from enslavement by foreign states." The next sentence gives a reason for the October *coup d'état* which has certainly never been set down before—least of all, by Lenin: "The treacherous plan of the bourgeoisie could only be disrupted by the overthrow of the government of betrayal." (17)

On Lenin's own testimony, the Bolsheviks, in 1917, were unabashed revolutionaries and agents of overthrow. But Khrushchev has incorporated these Bolsheviks into the apparatus of his own foreign policy. He has simply made them over into heroes of the kind of *nationalism* that now characterizes those underdeveloped target countries which he is setting himself to exploit.

After this handling of what took place in 1917, we are not surprised to read in the *History* that when Stalin's forces occupied East Europe, at the end of World War II, the "Soviet government stressed that it was not intent on seizing foreign lands or altering the existing social order in other countries. . . . As soon as the liberated regions ceased to be a zone of direct military hostilities all control of affairs of civil administration was transferred from the Soviet command to the local national authorities." (18) In short—*on the testimony of this History*—the Soviet Union's past record of dealings with weaker countries is impeccable.

It is a matter of documented fact that the Soviet Union plundered both the Satellites and the East zone of Germany of whatever would help to build up the Soviet economy. Whole factories were dismantled and shipped off. Stalin scarcely bothered to disguise this operation. But "benevolence" has become a tactical part of Khrushchev's foreign policy. Therefore, the Soviet Union's past is made benevolent: "The Soviet Union supplied the liberated countries with foodstuffs and other aid."

This remaking of history, we must emphasize again, is *a projecting into the past of Khrushchev's present foreign policy*. Once such a remaking process has been undertaken by a "directed" body of historians, there is no limit to the number of recorded facts that can be subdued. Thus, the October *coup d'état* becomes "the first revolution in the world which gave a people not only political rights, but also the material conditions for a prosperous life." (19)

This, we might say, is the "sweetness and light" theme of Communism's new workbook. But it is not the only theme. The world, clearly, is still a wide open field for the application of Lenin's "science of conspiracy."

The *History* does not *advocate* that Parties in non-Communist countries should, today, practice subversion and exploit parliamentary processes while pretending to support them. Since not merely "progressive elements" but also new independent governments are now targets for Soviet "friendship," it would not "sound well" to advocate overthrow. The approach, therefore, is oblique.

First, by the process we have noted above, the Parties and "fronts" out in the field are provided with a Soviet Union and a CPSU that have "sales appeal." The Soviet Union has *always* identified itself with the nationalist struggles of countries exploited by imperialism. The Communist Party of the Soviet Union, by virtue of its command of the "science of Marxism-Leninism," has *always* made "correct" analyses of situations and has responded to them with appropriate action. Hence, the striking success of the Soviet Union in pulling itself up by its own bootstraps. Hence, also, its usefulness as a "guide" to other countries that want to advance themselves.

Once this image has been established, it becomes easy for the history of the Party to be turned into a disguised set of directives. *This is how it was done* becomes, for Communists everywhere, equivalent to an imperative: *This is what you must do.* By this process, all the tactics of conspiracy, subversion, and violence—as part of a "success story"—can be made to sound well.

Of particular interest, here, is the detailed account of Lenin's decision, in 1906, that Bolshevik ends could not be achieved by open revolutionary methods alone. The very diversity of situations in which the Party would have to operate would require, Lenin stated, its expedient use of legal, semi-legal, and illegal means: "The only correct type of organizational structure was recognized to be the illegal party as a sum of illegal cells, surrounded by a network of legal and semi-legal workers' societies." (20)

All this, we must note, is set down simply as part of the successful *history* of the CPSU at the stage where it had to operate under the conditions of Tsarism. But the situations which call for each type of method—legal, semi-legal, and illegal—are so minutely described that Party members and all "progressive elements" can match them to situations in countries slated for Communist take-over today.

Many other directives are similarly set down in the guise of *recorded history*. Thus, Lenin's Party is said to have learned the importance of training a "*new type of revolutionary parliamentarian*" that could function within bourgeois institutions as a "genuine representative of the working class . . . combining legal and illegal work." (21)

Through the years, the *History* reports, the Party has "correctly" analyzed and responded to situations that have called for united-front action. It has "correctly" exploited tensions between "capitalist imperialist" nations and between different elements within each of them. Under Stalin, at the end of World War II, it "correctly" analyzed the world's readiness for a "peace offensive." Under Khrushchev, it has recognized more clearly than ever the wisdom of uniting under its leadership "all patriotic forces," all "anti-imperialist" forces, and all "progressive elements" that are dedicated to "peace."

As the world was moving into the nineteenth century, Frederick von Schlegel defined the historian as a prophet with his face turned backward. Those who wrote this new *History of the Soviet Communist Party* have turned their faces backward in order to tell Communists and pro-Communists everywhere how most effectively to turn *their* faces forward and, under Khrushchev's guidance, to produce a "correct" future.

EIGHT

COMMUNISM'S PRINTING PRESS

W E START this chapter surrounded by a sampling of items which have, through the years, come from Communism's printing press. It is only a sampling. In Europe and Asia, last year, we were shown Communist newspapers, pamphlets, and books of which we have no copies. We add these remembered items to those on our desk.

Turning to those we do have, however, we begin with the oldest among them—to indicate how soon after their take-over in Russia the Communists launched their international propaganda program by means of the printed word. This oldest item is René Marchand's *Why I Support Bolshevism,* datelined Petrograd, March and April 1919, printed in Glasgow, distributed by the Communist Party in London.

Above all else, this slender booklet is a tragic reminder of the skill with which the Communists have, decade after decade, exploited human decency and idealism. The document seems a product, not of Bolshevism at all, but of that will, described by Shelley in *Prometheus Unbound,*

To love, and bear; to hope till Hope creates
From its own wreck the thing it contemplates.

Marchand, correspondent for *Le Figaro* and *Le Petit Parisien,*
saw with his own eyes the horrors of brutality, deprivation,
and colossal disorganization suffered by the armies of the
Tsar and the Russian people during World War I. He was
on sick leave in Petrograd when the Revolution of March
1917 broke out; and he watched, from that vantage point,
the desperate unfolding of events during the months that followed. Having given devoted support to the Provisional
Government of Kerensky, he witnessed with dismay the
Bolshevik *coup d'état* of October; and wrote in November
1917, "The revolution had become dear to me: the energy,
the vitality of Russia seemed inseparably associated with
the revolution. But now the revolution seemed to me to be
in danger."

It was not until mid-1918 that his wrecked hopes recreated
themselves as an all-or-nothing commitment to Bolshevism:
"Whatever happens, whatever we may have to suffer . . .
I can without fear cry aloud in the ardour of my faith. It
springs from a brain and from a heart that are wounded
and tortured by the hideous reality; but it wells up with a
force which will remain unabated while life endures!"

Thus, as so often in the years since then, a man who
would not have lasted long in the hard-core Bolshevik Party
became spokesman on the world front for a "Bolshevism"
that he created in his own mind, out of his own need to
believe.

Our second document is of a very different order: Maxim
Litvinoff's *The Bolshevik Revolution: Its Rise and Meaning.*
The text, here, is older than Marchand's. It is dated Stock-
holm, December 24, 1918. But the paperback itself was pub-
lished in Chicago, in 1920, the year when the Communist
Party of the United States, like its fellow Parties around the

world, accepted Lenin's conditions of affiliation with the *Comintern*—thereby subordinating its will to that of the Soviet Union.

"It is not often," says the *Foreword,* "that contemporaries have the opportunity of getting the story and the justification of great events from prime movers in those events. . . .

"Such a work we have here."

The work in question is a hard-core Bolshevik version of what took place in Russia in 1917–1918; and Parties, wherever they had then been formed, undertook to make it the "true" version for Communists and non-Communists alike. Hence, this booklet can be taken as the forerunner of a long line of publications of which Khrushchev's *History* might be called the latest: publications designed to make the past prove the "correctness" of Soviet totalitarianism.

We can trace, also, a second unbroken line: that of the Communist effort to exploit the problems of non-Communist countries and to prevent their solution by moderate or "reformist" means.

During Lenin's lifetime and the first part of the Stalin era, the Communist assault upon all capitalist countries, as reported in the printed word, was openly revolutionary. The hammer and sickle were on the masthead of the *Daily Worker* and of equivalent papers elsewhere; and the approved slogan was *Workers of the World, Unite!*

The effort to spark a Marxist revolution by open advocacy reached its climax during the depression. The Communists were certain that capitalism could not survive that economic crisis. Hence, they virtually flaunted their intent to make the depression the parent of overthrow. If we study the materials which they published or distributed in the United States alone between 1932 and 1935, we give ourselves an education that helps us to understand Khrushchevism. For the manner in which CPUSA then exploited unemployment and hunger in the United States is strikingly parallel to the manner in which Khrushchev is today exploiting poverty and economic and political unrest in the underdeveloped countries.

We can refer, here, to only the barest sampling of materials; but they remind us of various perennial types. There were, for example, the Marxist Study Courses: printed in London, distributed by International Publishers, New York. *Wages and the Accumulation of Capital* came out in this pamphlet series in 1932, *Economic Crisis* in 1933. Both represent the same enterprise in which Khrushchev is engaged today: namely, that of putting a Marxist-Leninist interpretation upon the unsolved problems of non-Communist countries.

In 1932, the Communist expectation was made clear in the very title of William Z. Foster's book, *Toward Soviet America*. The blueprint of this expectation was given in the simplest possible form in M. J. Olgin's pamphlet, *Why Communism?*—published in 1935, by the Workers Library Publishers, New York, and priced at five cents.

But the most striking venture of the Communist press, in the United States, during that period was the International Publishers' putting-out of Stalin's *Foundations of Leninism* in a 10-cent edition of 100,000 copies. This "classic of Marxism" had already, by then, been translated into twenty-six languages, and ten million copies had been printed in the Soviet Union. The CPUSA undertook to make it a working textbook for overthrow in the United States.

There could scarcely have been a better selection for the Party's purposes in a depression era. Rarely have the precise Leninist procedures for exploiting the problems, angers, and miseries of human beings been more explicitly stated. Together with these procedures, moreover, we find all of Stalin's key revisions of Marxism-Leninism and his analysis of the strategic aims at different revolutionary stages.

The aim which he assigned to the stage that began with the Bolshevik revolution was the "consolidation of the dictatorship of the proletariat in one country, using it as a stronghold for the overthrow of imperialism in all countries . . ." And he recommended an "alliance of the proletarian revolution with the liberation movement of the colonies and the dependent countries." If we substitute, in the above, "one orbit" for "one country," and "newly independent countries" for "dependent countries," we have a fair working version of Khrushchev's foreign policy. (1)

This issuance of Stalin's *Foundations of Leninism* marked the apex, we might say, of the Party's hope for prompt revolution in the United States; and the decline of that hope dates from the same year—1934. At the Eighth Convention of the CPSU, in April, there was expressed a bitter awareness that the "inevitable" overthrow might be warded off by reform. One sentence from a pamphlet, *The Way Out: A Program for American Labor,* which gave the proceedings of the convention, reports the nature of the Party's growing anxiety: "The 'New Deal' of Roosevelt is the aggressive effort of the bankers and trusts to find a way out of the crisis at the expense of millions of toilers."

The revolution did not come; and before the end of 1935, Moscow had directed all Parties to adopt the tactic of the united front, under the label of "The People's Front Against Fascism." This swing to the united front, with violent overthrow no longer advocated in the leading capitalist countries, ushered in a new era for the Communist press. It settled down to the business—never since abandoned—of designing "verbal packages" in which revolutionary contents could be sold to unsuspecting "customers": most notably, to those who could be relied upon to respond to the word *peace* in almost any context.

Some aspiring Ph.D. candidate might well undertake a documented study of the peculiar exploitation of language which dates from Communism's swing, in 1935, from open advocacy of revolution to the "verbal packaging" of Soviet policy for sale to non-Communist minds. By the time he had worked his way up to—and through—Khrushchev's speeches at the General Assembly of the United Nations, in September–October 1960, he would know a great deal about the moral vacuum around which the practices of Communism are constructed.

Thus, his search would take him through a welter of pamphlets, paperbacks, mimeographed materials, and magazine articles that date from the era of the Stalin-Hitler mutual non-aggression pact: August 1939 to June 1941. One of his prize exhibits, here, might be the leaflet featuring the slogan *The Yanks Are NOT Coming;* for around this slogan was built a nationwide drive to keep America out of a war that was being branded as a product of British-French imperialism. In view of Khrushchev's charges of "imperialism," today, it is salutary to recall that Stalin, under cover of his pact with Hitler and of his denunciations of Western imperialism, took over by armed force the Baltic states and part of Poland.

The research scholar would certainly want to include, also, Wilhelm Pieck's booklet, *International Solidarity against Imperialist War.* Put out by the Workers Library Publishers, New York, in April 1941, this is a veritable compendium of the anti-imperialist slogans, arguments, and denunciations that had to be scrapped, *just two months later,* when Hitler invaded the Soviet Union. Abruptly, on June 22, 1941, the "imperialist war foisted upon the world by British-French profiteers" became the Great Patriotic War, the anti-imperialist war; and the earlier slogan *The Yanks Are NOT Coming* was reconstituted to read *The Yanks Are NOT Coming Too Late.*

Thus, the materials have rolled from Communism's printing press: through the years of the "United Front to Win the War"; Stalin's postwar take-over in East Europe; the Party's attack on the Truman Doctrine, the Marshall Plan, and NATO; Stalin's launching of the cold war under the label of a "peace offensive"; the Korean War; the confusions and cross-purposes after Stalin's death; "collective leadership"; the emergence of Khrushchev's policy.

We have before us as we write a copy of *International Affairs,* Moscow, dated July 15, 1955. It contains an article by A. Denisov, entitled "International Cultural Bonds of the Soviet People," which foreshadows Khrushchev's policy of "peaceful coexistence." Also—like that *History* which we analyzed in Chapter Seven—it makes what Khrushchev *intends to do* a continuance of what the Soviet Union has *always* done and what the Party has *always* stood for.

Manifesting total amnesia with respect to Stalin's use of the Iron Curtain and total disregard of Khrushchev's continued reliance upon it, Denisov states, in pedagogic tone, "A country which isolates itself from cultural life abroad, which does not seek cultural co-operation with other countries, deprives its people of the opportunity to utilize the creative achievements of other people . . ." (2)

True; and scarcely news to the free world. But what becomes "news" is his unabashed statement that the Soviet Union has *always* recognized and honored this truth: "Soviet people, consistently advocating the policy of peace, friendship and democratic cooperation among nations, want to improve their cultural bonds with all peoples. . . . One cannot become a Communist, said Lenin, the founder of the Soviet State, without endowing one's mind with the knowledge of all the values which humanity has created in the course of many centuries." (3)

Among the "values which humanity has created" are certainly those which are embodied, for example, in the philosophy of Socrates and Aristotle, and the dramas of Sophocles and Euripides; in the Hebrew-Christian tradition and that of the Buddha; in the Magna Carta; in Milton's *Areopagitica;* in the writings of John Locke, Thomas Jefferson, and a host of others. On the basis of Denisov's article, the West would have every right to ask for as much liberty to "endow" the minds of the Soviet people with these values as the Communists have taken to "endow" minds in the free world with the values of Marx, Lenin, Stalin, and Khrushchev.

Denisov, however, was not announcing an end to the Iron Curtain—any more than Khrushchev has enacted an end to it. He was simply paving the way for Khrushchev's exploitation of what he has sized up as a "novel" and profitable way of waging war. But before we take any further look at the items which have poured from the Communist press in the Khrushchev era, we need to go a long way back: to the Leninist beginnings of this Communist effort to blanket the earth with printed materials.

In 1902, Lenin found himself engaged in a curious controversy. He had published, in 1901, his *Where to Begin?* In this, he had said, "In our opinion, the starting point of all our activities, the first practical step toward creating the organization we desire . . . is the establishment of an all-Russian political newspaper."

No local paper, he made clear, could serve the purpose he had in mind. It must be an all-Russian paper. "Unless we are able to exercise united influence upon the population and upon the government with the aid of the printed word, it will be utopian to think of combining other more complex, difficult, but more determined forms of exercising influence. Our movement, intellectually as well as practically and organizationally, suffers most of all from being scattered . . ." (4)

So long as there was no all-Russian political paper, the horizon of workers would remain narrow, as would their conspiratorial training. Thus, local leaders could easily be tempted into premature acts of terror which would set back the whole movement. Expedient terror must wait upon a nation-wide readiness for action. ". . . at the present time our slogan cannot be, 'Storm the fortress,' but should be, 'Organize properly the siege of the enemy fortress.'" (5)

Only by means of the proposed all-Russian newspaper would it be possible "to concentrate all the elements of political discontent and protest, and with them fertilize the revolutionary movement of the proletariat . . ."

But ". . . the role of a paper is not confined solely to the spreading of ideas, to political education and to attracting political allies. . . .

"If we unite our forces for conducting a common paper, that work will prepare and bring forward, not only the most competent propagandists, but also the most skilled organizers and the most talented political Party leaders, who will be able at the right moment to issue the call for the decisive battle, and will be capable of leading that battle." (6)

To Lenin, in May 1901, the need, character, and functions of such a paper seemed self-apparent. But they did not seem so to all his fellow revolutionaries. Suddenly, he found himself under attack, on the one hand, by those who accused him of belittling "the forward march of the drab every-day struggle in comparison with the propaganda of brilliant and complete ideas . . ."; and, on the other, by advocates of immediate terrorism, like Nadezhdin, who said, "To speak now of an organization linked up with an all-Russian newspaper means propagating armchair ideas and armchair work." (7)

Under attack, Lenin—in *What Is to Be Done?*—elaborated and fortified his position. Only a Party newspaper—and, more broadly, a Party press—would make it possible to "summarize the results of all the diverse forms of activity and thereby *stimulate* our people to march forward untiringly along *all* the innumerable paths which lead to revolution . . ." (8) The newspaper "would become a part of an enormous pair of smith's bellows that would blow every spark of class struggle and popular indignation into a general conflagration. . . . This is what we ought to be dreaming about!" (9)

Most important of all, in a sense, would be the fact that as Party members became conditioned to think of the whole country as their field of action, they would cease being impulsive, local-minded agitators and would become professionals. There was too much waste in having persons "shed their blood in the cause of restricted local work." What was needed was nationwide thinking that would make it practical to send "a capable agitator or organizer from one end of the country to the other. Beginning with short journeys on Party business at the Party's expense, our people would become accustomed to being maintained by the Party, would become professional revolutionaries . . ." (10)

In addition to an all-Russian newspaper, Lenin specified that there must be a "trade union press that would suit the conditions of our illegal work." It could put out pamphlets to interest workers in special fields and could accumulate, from the data associated with concrete struggles, materials out of which to compile an "excellent handbook for agitators . . ." (11)

From 1902 on, there was no doubt that if Lenin became master of the revolutionary situation—as he later did—the Party would be integrated and trained by its own press; that this press would constantly link theory and practice; and that the territory covered by it would be as wide as that within

which the Party could contrive to carry on organized activities.

After the *coup d'état* of 1917, Lenin quickly moved to implement in new ways his respect for the printed word; and
now he had to make that word his servant and his weapon
on two different fronts. Within the Soviet Union, it must
help him to consolidate the "dictatorship of the proletariat."
Everywhere else, it must help to foment revolution. Thus, the
controlled press was added to the *conspiratorial press*—both
of them equally Communist in character.

The controlled press, throughout the years, has served a
double purpose: to prevent the impact upon the mind of the
Soviet citizen of all unwanted news and ideas from the outside world; and to insure the impact upon that mind of the
official line on every subject. Censorship and propaganda
have been two sides of a single coin.

On the propaganda side, Lenin himself never concealed
the fact that his vast literacy program was designed to create
a public that could be indoctrinated by means of the printed
word. As George S. Counts has pointed out in *The Challenge
of Soviet Education,* a revolution that antedated the radio
had to depend on newspapers, magazines, and books for a
good part of the spadework of developing Soviet man: "A
person who could not read was beyond the easy reach of
Communist propaganda." (12) The very slogans that Lenin
shaped up to dramatize the literacy program were political
rather than educational: "Illiteracy is the reserve of counterrevolution," for example; and "Literacy is the road to Communism."

On the censorship side, literacy had to be prevented from
performing its normal function of opening minds up to all
sorts of new ideas: "If the people were permitted to read
books containing materials subversive of the system, literacy

itself could scarcely be tolerated." (13) Not only the daily
and periodical press, and not only classroom materials, but
also library materials had, therefore, to be brought under control: "The library, being a component part of the Soviet
system for the education of the people, is a political weapon.
. . . It must always be held tightly in the hands of the
Party." (14)

But if Lenin's "all-Russian newspaper" was, after 1917,
supplanted on the home front by Communism's controlled
press, it was extended, on the world front, into an international conspiratorial press. With the forming of the *Comintern*, in 1919, it became a matter of simple logic that there
must be a publication which would unify, organize, and train
revolutionary forces throughout the world precisely as the
"all-Russian newspaper" had unified, organized, and trained
them within Tsarist Russia. Out of this logic came the
Communist International.

Just as the old "trade union press" had been designed, in
Tsarist Russia, to serve the needs and orient the minds of
local revolutionary groups, so the newspapers and magazines
issued by each member Party of the *Comintern* served both
to channel to national audiences the international Communist
viewpoint and to stimulate "correct" words and actions on
the local and national scene. The pamphleteers went to work,
also. Publishing houses were established to turn out books
by Communists native to each country and to reprint Soviet
books. And everywhere the mimeographing machines rolled
out leaflets, teaching manuals, guides for speakers, petitions
for mass circulation, and one "excellent handbook for agitators" after another.

So far as the Communist press is concerned, nothing has
changed in essence since the time of Lenin. We might almost
say that nothing has changed in essence since he first ana-

lyzed the functions of a Party newspaper in *Where to Begin?* and *What Is to Be Done?* The output of materials has increased enormously. So has the variety. So has the subtlety of appeal. But the pattern holds.

The Party has never abandoned the concept of having one publication to unify and direct the whole movement. Throughout the lifetime of the *Comintern* this was the *Communist International*. In 1943, Stalin dissolved the *Comintern* —because he found it inexpedient to keep his Western allies in World War II reminded of his revolutionary aims; and the *Communist International* ceased publication. In 1947, however, when he was ready to launch the cold war and call it a "peace offensive," he established his own new unifying organization, the *Cominform;* and immediately it undertook to publish, for the world movement, a newspaper called *For a Lasting Peace, for a People's Democracy.*

By 1956, Khrushchev was ready to scrap both the *Cominform* and its newspaper; for neither was appropriate to his "novel" way of defining the problems of peace and war "under present day conditions." He did not give up, however, the idea of one publication for the whole world movement. This, today, is the *World Marxist Review.* By mid-1959, it was being issued in Russian, Chinese, Dutch, French, English, Spanish, German, Italian, Swedish, Czech, Polish, Rumanian, Bulgarian, Hungarian, Japanese, Mongolian, Korean, Albanian, and Vietnamese.

If we look at any issue of this magazine, we are made aware of the wide range of subjects on which all Communists around the world are expected to be *of one mind.* Thus, for example, the issue of July 1959 lays down the Party line on "the Negro question" in the United States; praises the struggle of the Italian Party against the Common Market; uses the occasion of the thirtieth anniversary of the First Conference of the Communist Parties of Latin America to specify the "correct" manner in which to talk about American "imperialism"; praises the reorganization of Czech industry; holds up as an example the ideological work of the Communist Party of Indonesia; and makes clear, by means of an obviously "loaded" letter, that political education must never be thought of as something that an individual can adequately plan for himself, without Party guidance.

A second magazine, published in the Soviet Union but available around the world, and clearly intended to keep the world Communist movement well lined up with Khrushchev's policy, is *International Affairs*—which we have already mentioned in connection with the Denisov article. Emanating from the Soviet Society for the Popularization of Political and Scientific Knowledge, this monthly magazine could well be studied throughout the free world as an indicator of how Khrushchev intends to present to target minds everywhere the viewpoints and issues which he rates as most vital to the success of his expansionist program. (15)

Again, a single issue can be made to tell the story. That of March 1960, for example, contains articles on "International Relations and the Battle of Ideologies," "The Foreign Policy of People's Hungary," "Some Economic Aspects of Disarmament," "The Economy of Capitalist Countries in 1959," and "West Germany and European Peace." One way not to be caught off guard by what Khrushchev "suddenly" says on these subjects or a multitude of others is to warn ourselves in advance by reading *International Affairs*.

It is still true, also, as in Lenin's day, that the Communist Party in each non-Communist country has its own press. In the United States, *Political Affairs* is the monthly theoretical journal, which undertakes to give the international line a national specificity. If we want to know precisely what Marxist-Leninist interpretation the Communists are putting upon events and issues in our own country, and how they are exploiting our problems, this magazine is our best source of that information. *Mainstream* is the monthly literary journal of the Party. Most recent of all is a new monthly magazine directed at young people, called *New Horizons for Youth.* Then, of course, there is the weekly paper, *The Worker.*

If a person looks at a single issue of *The Worker*—as we have just been looking at that of July 31, 1960—it does not seem like anything to get too excited about. It simply serves up the news of the week with the expected Communist slant. Thus, one headline reads *Africans Unite Behind Congo's Struggle;* and the *Editorial* "proves" that the Nixon-Kennedy campaign can lead to no good end, no matter how it comes out.

But there are two points for our minds to grapple with. The first can be put in the form of a question: by what peculiar process have the peoples of the world been brought to feel that the regular publication among them of magazines and papers retailing the official line laid down by the Soviet Union is to be *expected?* The second point can be put as a statement: this issue of *The Worker,* so seemingly unimportant in its isolation, is one minute part of the daily, weekly, monthly, yearly output of Communism's printing press.

We pick up, for example, the English *Daily Worker* of August 5, 1960—and find it reporting that Khrushchev has given in *Pravda* a "crushing retort" to a letter from Macmillan; and that Cuba's Defense Minister, Raul Castro, has declared that "a large number of rockets" would hit the United States if it attacked Cuba. And this *Daily Worker* is but another minute portion of the total output.

On the other side of the world, Burma, late in 1959, felt impelled to put a ban on all imported foreign publications— magazines and books alike; for the Soviet illustrated magazine *USSR* and its counterpart, *China Pictorial,* were bidding for an ever larger circulation, and between three and four million copies of Sino-Soviet books were on sale. The ban does not apply to the *Soviet Daily Bulletin* or the magazine *Soviet Union*, since both are locally printed.

In Djakarta, Indonesia, the total newspaper circulation is between 400,000 and 500,000; and it was estimated in 1959 that out of this total, Communist and pro-Communist papers had a circulation of 200,000. On August 10, 1960, a Reuters dispatch reported that the bi-weekly Communist publication, *Suara Ibukota* (Voice of the Capital) had been banned because of its effort to disturb public order and encourage security violations. More embracing measures of control have since been enacted. The double tragedy is, however, that these tend to rule out even those forms of dissent that are a legitimate part of freedom and that they do not succeed in ruling out many pro-Communist papers that operate in disguise. The leading Chinese-operated newspaper, for example, formerly called *Sin Po*, has taken a native name, *Pantijawarta*, and continues to retail the Party line in thinly veiled language; and *Harian Fudjur* renders a similar "service" while posing as a legitimate paper for a Moslem audience.

There is no way to give the total picture. It would have to include Communist youth publications in Latin America; the intensely anti-American paper, *Pracheachon*, in Cambodia; the papers and magazines smuggled out of North Vietnam into South Vietnam; the covertly circulated mimeographed newspapers that spread the Party line in Malaya.

As we study this flood of materials, what hits hardest is the terrible unanimity of viewpoint on every subject: the contrived, made-in-Moscow—or, sometimes, made-in-Peking—unanimity. We Americans become rightly concerned when we hear that in some one of our communities two newspapers, hitherto competitive, have been brought under one ownership. We feel that it is not healthy for the public mind to be thus made subject to a single unchallenged interpretation of what is going on in the locality or the world. But how, then, can we be *unconcerned* about Khrushchev's editorial dominion over a planetary empire of publications? That of which the "harmless" copy of *The Worker* on a New York newsstand is a tiny but integral part is an apparatus of mind-control without precedent in history.

Earlier in this chapter, we made a distinction between the *conspiratorial press* which operates outside the Communist orbit and the *controlled press* which operates within it. Never for a moment, however, do the two contradict each other. They simply serve one purpose in two different environments. Both are designed to identify Communist totalitarianism with "peace" and "progress," and to identify our own system with "war" and "reaction." As we noted in Chapter One, the Party divides the world into Communist territory and future Communist territory; and through its printing press, it sets itself to manipulate the human mind within both.

In the Philippines, for example—where the Communist Party has been outlawed since 1957—the assault upon the public mind is carried on both by the underground and by "fronts" that stay within the law. The line is that of an intensive anti-Americanism which portrays our country as engaged in economic and military exploitation of the islands—and which makes us responsible for every injustice and deprivation suffered by the people. To offset the government's pro-Western policies, the Communists encourage neutralism and an exaggerated nationalism.

What equivalent to this line do we encounter in the controlled press of the Soviet Union and the bloc? We all know, of course, that *Pravda, Kommunist,* and a host of other publications continue to brand us, day in and day out, as "imperialists" and "warmongers." But Khrushchev has found more uses for a controlled press than most of us have dreamed of in our simplicity. We will give here just two examples of the sort of thing we have in mind.

For the first, we are indebted to a man whom we cannot name. He made a trip to the Soviet Union at the time when "the spirit of Camp David" was being hailed by Khrushchev as the order of the day and the promise of the future. Talking with a woman who was studying English, he asked if he might look at her textbook; when he had glanced into it at random, he borrowed it for a longer look—and copied down a page from which we quote the following:

We Do Not Want War

We do not want war. We want peace. We want peaceful work. Our policy is peace. . . .

Workers in capitalist countries want peaceful work too. They do not want war. Only capitalists want war. They want profits. War gives them large profits. Their policy is war.

The progressive people all over the world struggle for peace.

Capitalists struggle for war . . .

By "peaceful coexistence," in brief, Khrushchev means a conflict so relentless that not even a language textbook can be other than a weapon.

Our second example is from a book called *Face to Face with America*, which was put out by the State Publishing House of Political Literature, Moscow, in 1959—in an edition of 250,000 copies. This book reports the "impressions" gained by a dozen persons who accompanied Khrushchev on his "good will" visit to the United States in the Fall of 1959. It claims to give eye-witness portrayals of one American city after another on Khrushchev's route. What it actually does is to reduce each city to a simple contrast between absolute wealth and absolute poverty. By means of unalleviated portrayal of crime, degradation, gangsterism, drug addiction, delinquency, and moral depravity, it arrives at the "conclusion" that "the much lauded standard of living of the Americans belongs to the field of statistics rather than reality." (16)

Like a host of similarly slanted reports, moreover, this book is loaded with facts and figures about what things cost in the United States with no report on wages and incomes. Thus, the Soviet reader is invited to think of these costs *in terms of his own earnings* and to visualize most of the products of our American economy as beyond the reach of all save the wealthy and exploitative few: those capitalists who "want war" in order to increase their profits.

We can best end this chapter, perhaps, by taking stock of the April 1960 issue of *USSR*, which celebrated the 90th anniversary of Lenin's birth. Khrushchev never tires of calling himself a Leninist. But here, suddenly, in this magazine, Lenin is converted into a Khrushchevist: every statement about him, every picture, every incident told to portray his character, every quote from his works is selected to make him a faithful spokesman for Khrushchev's foreign policy.

We see him engaged in personal conversations, now smiling, now seriously intent. We see him addressing enthusiastic crowds, talking with children, walking on the street as a plain man among equals, and standing alone at a window, absorbed in thought. We read the words that report him to have been *always* a man of benevolence; a man of peace; one who detested violence and terrorism; and, specifically, an advocate of "peaceful coexistence."

The articles and pictures celebrating Lenin's life end on page 15 of the magazine. We turn the page—and are confronted by an article, built on precisely parallel lines, about Communism's new man of "peace." Written by Shalva Sanakoyev, Assistant Editor in Chief of *International Affairs*, Moscow, it is entitled, "Visit of Good Will and Friendship."

Here, it is Khrushchev who is talking with farmers and children around the world, giving his autograph to an engineer in India, addressing crowds, talking with Sukarno, with Nehru, with the King of Afghanistan.

This article, in turn, is followed by one called "Soviet Statesmen Tour the United States." We see them in factories and supermarkets, amiable and interested. We see them standing at the tomb of Abraham Lincoln in Springfield, Illinois.

In the presence of this calculated display of "good will," it seems almost ungracious to remember that in *What Is to Be Done?*—the same article in which he elaborated the functions of the Party press—Lenin recommended expedient "temporary alliances," even with bourgeois democrats, to further Communist ends. Yet this fact is worth remembering as we turn the pages of a magazine in which the original author of Communism's printing press and the current master of it are presented as seeing eye to eye.

NINE

SPEAKING IN TONGUES

O NE CONSTANT danger in which we stand with respect to Communism has to do with the use of words. When Khrushchev speaks, we hear what he says; and we think he is saying what his words mean to us. Instead, he is saying what they mean to him; and, knowing that we misunderstand, he does nothing to set us straight, because he intends us to misunderstand.

Yet even though he knows that he is deceiving us, he is not, in the ordinary sense, lying. He is speaking with *Communist sincerity*. The "class morality" by which all Communists are guided does, to be sure, make lying legitimate when it is expedient. But Khrushchev—like Stalin before him —is most deceptive and persuasive when his words sound exactly as they do in our common discourse, and when they have the ring of sincerity, but when their meanings are dictated by the "science of Marxism-Leninism."

This is the kind of double-talk that has enabled him again and again to evoke from the non-Communist world a response to fit his own purposes. This, therefore, is the kind of double-talk that we must learn to decode. He will not do the decoding for us. When he comes to the United Nations or to a meeting of the heads of state, he brings an interpreter to translate his Russian language into English or French or whatever; but he does not provide for any translation of his Marxist-Leninist language into the language of our common discourse.

In his first Epistle to the Corinthians, Paul pointed out that those who speak in tongues, and who do not translate their words into the language familiar to their listeners, become authors of confusion rather than of understanding: "Wherefore let him that speaketh in an *unknown* tongue pray that he may interpret." But Paul was not a Communist. His frame of reference obligated men, in their relations to one another, to strive for mutuality of understanding. He did not inhabit a "two-camp" world. The struggle to which he was committed was not a "class struggle." His morality was not "class morality."

Khrushchev is a Communist. In his "two-camp" world, we are the "enemy." He profits by our confusion. He profits even more by his power to make and remake our moods to suit his own ends. His double-talk is deliberate. When he speaks, therefore, in an "unknown tongue," we have not only to distinguish this from the known tongue that it resembles but also to decode his Marxist-Leninist meanings.

A good case study of double-talk and its consequences is provided by Khrushchev's performance at the General Assembly of the United Nations; or, rather, by his two performances there—in September 1959, when he was a visitor to the United States; and in September–October 1960, when he headed up the Soviet delegation to the U.N.

After one of his most ferocious attacks upon the United

States from the Assembly platform, in September 1960, a woman in New York put a wistful query to a reporter: "What have we done to make him hate us so much? He was so friendly last year."

Pressed to say more about what was on her mind, she recalled the speech which Khrushchev had made just a year before, in September 1959, from the same platform from which he now shouted threats and denunciations. His earlier speech, she said, had been so friendly and reasonable. "He wasn't angry at us at all, then. What have we done? Was it the U-2 flight?"

Much had, indeed, taken place during the twelve months that lay between Khrushchev's two appearances at the United Nations. We have referred in earlier chapters to the events of that year and to the change *in Communist strategy* which they induced. But this New York woman was not thinking of a change in strategy. The only way that her non-Communist mind could "make sense" out of the contrast between the "friendly and reasonable" Khrushchev of 1959 and the vituperative, desk-thumping Khrushchev of 1960 was to assume that we had done something to change his attitude toward us: to make him, in effect, a changed man.

Yet there has been no time since Khrushchev joined the Party in 1921 when he has not been an inhabitant of the Communist "camp" in a "two-camp" world and when he has not regarded us as a chief enemy slated for liquidation. What, then, shall we say about the "friendly" character of his speech in 1959?

Certainly, the woman whom we have quoted was not alone in regarding it as friendly and reasonable. Her estimate of it would seem justified by the words he spoke—if these words are taken at face value, in their normal non-Communist sense. By and large, they were thus taken. The version of this 1959 speech which was published in the Soviet Union indicates that it was received with "stormy applause"; and there seems no doubt that it was applauded by myriad minds across America and around the world.

A small minority of the applauding delegates at the General Assembly were Communists. The vast majority were non-Communists. They represented countries which Khrushchev regards as *future Communist territory:* countries whose present regimes and present social, political, and economic forms he intends, by one means or another, to wipe off the face of the earth. Why, then, the "stormy applause"? How did he induce this into being?

When we study the speech itself, decoding its Marxist-Leninist language, the answer becomes clear. He conveyed two different meanings to two different audiences *in the same words.* He said what most of his non-Communist listeners, putting their own interpretation upon his words, wanted to hear. At the same time, he said what, to his fellow Communists in front of him and throughout the world, would mean something quite different—and something which they, too, wanted to hear. In short, he spoke a two-direction language.

On that "stormy applause" occasion, Khrushchev told the General Assembly: "Everything indicates that the time has come to open a period of international negotiations, conferences and meetings of statesmen in order that the pressing international problems may one after another be solved." (1)

His non-Communist listeners—or those not accustomed to decoding Communist double-talk—thought that he meant those problems could be *solved.* Also, they thought that he meant by "negotiations" what they themselves would mean. (2) Therefore, they applauded. His Communist listeners knew precisely what he meant. Therefore, they applauded.

For both non-Communists and Communists, of course,

negotiating means trying to reach an agreement; but they attach different meanings to the word *agreement*. Lenin made this fact plain in 1924. For "non-Party people," he indicated, an *agreement* is a resolution or policy framed during a conference between opposed groups. It is, in brief, a product of give-and-take. But said Lenin, speaking for the Communists, "we have Party decisions on all the important questions" and —with these decisions already made—"we shall never recede from these decisions." Thus: "For Party people, an agreement is an attempt to *enlist* others for the purpose of carrying out the Party policy." (3)

By this Leninist definition, "coming to an agreement" with non-Communists means "*enlisting* them on our side, *convincing* them that we are right . . ." It does not mean entering into a process of give and take. It cannot mean this; for "Party decisions," arrived at in advance, must be kept inviolate.

We must assume that Khrushchev spoke as a Communist—as a Leninist—when he called for "meetings of statesmen" to effect a solution of "pressing international problems." For his 1959 speech belongs to the period when he was betting that he could, by "friendly" and "peaceful" means, persuade the West to grant him one-sided concessions with respect to Berlin and to accept his plan for disarmament without inspection.

By September 1960, not having been able to get these concessions, he *demanded* what he had previously sought as a free gift. He still called for "meetings of statesmen" and for "negotiations." But his peculiar Communist use of these terms was made plain by his threat to wreck the United Nations if he did not get his own unqualified way. He proposed negotiations, in brief, with his decisions already reached "on all the important questions." This fact was more evident in 1960 than it had been in 1959; but, significantly, the results he intended to get—first, by "friendliness," and then by brow-beating truculence—had not changed one atom.

Another of the words which gave Khrushchev's 1959 speech the sound of reasonableness was *self-determination*. We know what the word means to us. It means the right of peoples to choose their own forms of government, and not to be subject to outside coercion. This was what Khrushchev seemed to mean, also. He said, "I deem it necessary to say here, from the rostrum of the United Nations, that the Soviet Union has the sincerest sympathy and the profoundest understanding for all people who, on different continents, are upholding their freedom and national independence. It is my opinion that this position of ours fully accords with the principles of the United Nations Charter, which is predicated on recognition of the right of the peoples to a free and independent existence and development." (4)

Non-Communists applauded these words for what they thought they meant. Lest we again be taken in, however—as we were at Yalta—it is important to recall an ingenious, little-publicized, Communist interpretation of the term *self-determination*. First worked out by Lenin, and then elaborated by Stalin, it takes the word out of the vocabulary of our normal exchange and makes it part of Communism's "class" language, effective for double-talk.

Long before the Bolshevik *coup d'état* of 1917, Lenin had made up his mind about self-determination. He could not throw out the word: it carried too much of an emotional charge and was tactically useful. But neither could he keep it without altering its meaning to comport with Communism's design for world conquest.

Therefore, he wrote, in 1903, that "our unqualified recognition of the right of self-determination does not commit us to supporting every demand for national self-determination." Why this qualifying of the "unqualified"? The revolutionary task of the Bolsheviks, he said, was "to advance the self-determination of the working class within each nationality rather than the self-determination of peoples and nationalities." (5)

When we put together with this statement the fact that he had already, in 1901–1902, defined the working class as incapable of knowing its own best interests unless instructed and guided by the "revolutionary vanguard," the Bolshevik Party, we see that what the "unqualified recognition of self-determination" comes down to is the unqualified right of the Bolshevik Party to determine for peoples and nations the "correct" form of government.

Stalin, we recall, agreed at Yalta, readily and amiably, to future "self-determination" for Germany; and then—to the bewilderment of those who had trusted his word—settled down to the business of blocking free elections in that country. In summing up the result of the verbal deception he had practiced, he said, "Thus the old bourgeois interpretation of self-determination became a fiction." (6)

What did Khrushchev mean when he spoke at the United Nations in 1959? Did he mean, in the commonly accepted sense, the self-determination of *peoples?* Or did he, like Stalin at Yalta, mean the self-determination of the *working class* as defined and guided by the Communist Party? He did not say; and no one rose to ask him whether he was using the word in the customary sense or in the peculiar Leninist-Stalinist sense.

The vigor with which he has rejected all bids for free elections in Germany would seem, however, to indicate what he had in mind. Also, we know that at the 1960 meeting of the General Assembly he was, several times over, moved to fury by the suggestion that the peoples of East Europe should be permitted to exercise the right of self-determination in the commonly accepted sense.

All of this gives point to Kohout-Dolnobransky's statement that "tactical manipulations with the concept of the peoples' rights are a decisive part of the bolshevik plan for world dominion." Thus: "In all places where Communism wishes to gain influence in the play of forces between east and west— that is, primarily in the Afro-Asian developing countries—it acts the part of the most fervent champion of self-determination, while it not only refuses the right of self-determination to the countries within its own sphere of power, but even suppresses it with brutal force of arms—as happened in Hungary in November 1956, and in the Soviet-occupied zone of Germany on June 17, 1953." (7)

Communists, in short, make the word seem to mean what they want it to seem to mean in places and at times where that meaning best serves their purposes. And, deliberately speaking "in an unknown tongue," they are careful not to interpret.

Another word which the Communists freely employ—without specifying their own peculiar definition of it— is the word *people*. We recall, for example, that when Khrushchev arrived in New York on the *Baltika,* in September 1960, he made a short speech on the pier to those who had greeted him. Then he spoke over their heads, as it were, to the "people" of the United States: "I would like to voice the profound respect I feel toward the entire American people, and to wish them success."

Whom did he mean by the "people"? He has denounced, many times over, American "capitalists"; and by Marxist-Leninist definition, this term covers not only the "exploitative" owners of big businesses and industries but also the owners of small businesses and private farms, big or little. He has, again, denounced the legal trade unions as "lackeys of capitalism." He has denounced the American government as "imperialist"; and he has labeled as "warmongers" all Americans, officials or otherwise, who have not accepted his brand of "peaceful coexistence" as signifying peace. For all these groups he has expressed contempt, not once, but many times over; so that they must be subtracted from that "entire" body of Americans for whom he feels "profound respect." Who, then, does constitute the *people* in his sense of the word?

In a long letter to Bertrand Russell, dated March 5, 1958, Khrushchev undertook to show how highly he and the Soviet Union value the "people." He was writing to refute a letter by John Foster Dulles which had appeared in the *New States-man* a month earlier, on February 8: a letter in which Dulles had said that the Communists impose their will upon the peoples they dominate—as in East Europe—and that political power should be exercised only when it reflected "the freely given consent of the governed."

"This," Khrushchev protested, "is precisely the stand we Communists take, and we fight for this, for it is the people who are the determining force, their will is sacred, it is their interests that the governments should express if they are really worth anything." (8) Then he added a sentence that would seem to mean exactly what we mean by "the people" in our democracy: "In our opinion, it is not the people who must serve the government, but the government which must serve the people."

It is only when we study Communist writings on a far broader base, and also the institutionalized practices of Communist totalitarianism, that we equip ourselves to do a swift job of mental decoding whenever we hear Khrushchev speak of the "people," and of the Soviet government—or of one or another East European government—as serving the interests of the "people." It is easy for our minds to be deceived by a single document—like this letter to Russell—or by a single speech in which Khrushchev, with Communist sincerity, professes his "profound respect" for the American people. But a broader study makes clear two distinctions between what we normally mean by the term "the people" and what the Communists—including Khrushchev—mean by it.

First, no Communist ever means *all* the people when he speaks of those who have rights. He means those whom the Communist Party designates as "the workers" or "the proletariat." The very terms of the "class struggle" ordain that the population of a country can never, in its entirety, be thought of as "the people." It must be thought of as divided against itself; as made up of exploiters and exploited; of those slated for liquidation and those who are to do the liquidating.

The very fact that no Communist country will tolerate a "loyal opposition" tells us how far removed Khrushchev's concept of "the people" is from a democratic concept. Khrushchev, for example, has hailed Kadar as the leader of the Hungarian "people"; and he was instrumental in bringing Kadar to that same General Assembly of the United Nations for which he himself was on hand when he expressed his "profound respect" for the American people.

Kadar, however, at the Seventh Congress of the Hungarian Communist Party, declared, "It has been proved here in the period of counterrevolution that the multi-party system fanned the counterrevolution . . . therefore we have rejected the multi-party system." (9)

Further than this, the *United Nations' Report of the Special Committee on the Problems of Hungary*—drawn up by representatives of Denmark, Australia, Ceylon, Tunisia, and Uruguay—does not portray Kadar as in any legitimate sense the leader of the people. This Report, unanimously adopted by the Committee, overwhelmingly approved by the General Assembly, and published by the United Nations in 1957, indicates that the Committee was unable to find any evidence of popular support for Kadar. It indicates further that Kadar has repeatedly broken his promises to the people—particularly with respect to the withdrawal of Soviet troops from

Hungary; has stripped the Workers' Councils of their power; has distorted the processes of law; and has repressed the writers and intellectuals.

The leader who could rightly claim to have popular support in Hungary was Nagy—whom the Kadar regime, with the full approval of Khrushchev, proceeded to execute after guaranteeing his safety. Facts of this sort, well-lodged in mind, exert a restraining effect upon our impulse to applaud when Khrushchev talks about *any* Communist regime as reflecting "the freely given consent of the people." The Communist tactic, today as always, is that of designating as "the people" whatever minority of a population will give unqualified consent to the totalitarian rule exercised by the Communist Party.

In the second place, no Communist ever supports or tolerates government *of* and *by* the people. Instead, he defends government *for* the people—as their interests are defined by the Party. In a later chapter, we shall examine in detail the type of "free" election by means of which the Soviet hierarchy manages to perpetuate itself in office as the "people's choice." Here, we will simply note that whenever Khrushchev talks about the government as serving the people's interests, he always means that it is the *caretaker* of the people—endowed with full authority to decide what is best for them and with full coercive power to enforce its decisions and to punish all deviations from ideological correctness."

Carl Sandburg wrote, *The People, Yes.* Khrushchev benignly proclaims, "The people, yes." But if we have any respect at all for the accuracies of language and the actualities of human freedom we do well to hold in mind the fact that the two meanings expressed in identical words are poles apart.

Now for the tricky word *democracy*. During the Second World War, writes David J. Dallin in his *The Changing World of Soviet Russia,* "the Soviet press had preached the 'alliance of democracies' against fascism." But when the war ended, the Soviet Union began, once more, to emphasize the division of the world—and to make a sharp distinction between "capitalist democracy" and "Soviet democracy," which was proclaimed to be the only "real" kind of democracy.

This use of words, Dallin reports, was repeatedly challenged by non-Communist newspapermen: "But isn't your system a dictatorship," the foreign press kept asking. "Yes," Moscow replied, "we are a dictatorship and democracy at the same time; ours is a 'dictatorial democracy.' " (10)

We come, now, to one of the most confusing of the double-talk words: *interference.* To understand the Communist usage of this word, we must remind ourselves of the Leninist principle, analyzed in Chapter I, of *penetrating without being penetrated.* It is never "interference" for the Communists to denounce the policies of a non-Communist government. Neither is it "interference" for them to extend their influence, by any expedient means, into that non-Communist orbit which they rate as future Communist territory. Neither is it "interference" for the Soviet Union to support any Communist regime anywhere against non-Communist or "revisionist" resistance. It is "interference," however, for any non-Communist government even to question the rightness of Soviet policy on the domestic front or within the orbit.

On April 7, 1958, for example—a short year and a half after the Soviet Union's armed suppression of the popular uprising in Hungary—Khrushchev made a speech in that country, at Cegléd: "Comrades, believe us. . . . By helping the Hungarian people smash the counterrevolution we performed our internationalist duty. . . . We came to you as your most loyal friends and brothers. . . . We do not interfere." (11)

The United Nations Report to which we have already referred tells a different story. What took place in Hungary in 1956, this Report indicates, was a spontaneous national uprising, due to long-standing grievances. The claim that it was fomented by reactionary circles (counterrevolutionary) was completely unsupported by evidence. The uprising was not even planned. There was evidence, however, that plans were made by the Soviet authorities, *before any uprising occurred,* to quell by armed intervention any uprising that might result from the mounting dissatisfaction of the people with the regime. Moreover, while the Soviet Union has insisted that it was asked to come to the aid of the Hungarian government, Nagy—who alone, at that time, had the legitimate authority to take such a step—denied that he had ever issued to the Soviet Union any invitation to move into Hungary to quell the revolution.

The few days of freedom enjoyed by the Hungarian people, the Report continues, offered abundant evidence of the popular nature of the uprising. A free press and free radio came to life. The AVH—secret police—was disbanded. Workers' Councils were formed. Then came the Soviet tanks; and the people's revolution was crushed. In its wake, moreover, basic human rights were again violated—by the Kadar regime.

"We do not interfere," said Khrushchev. But, he told a mass meeting in Budapest, on April 4, 1958, *others* interfere. The Soviet Union, he said, had been making earnest efforts to bring about a conference of Heads of Government to deal with "a series of urgent problems" and to seek ways of relieving international tensions.

"But they say to us that they want to discuss the situation in the countries of Eastern Europe. What exactly do they want to discuss, and, generally, what right has anyone to discuss the internal development of other countries? No, good sirs, keep your nose out of other people's affairs. The peoples of Eastern Europe have already made up their minds. They are masters of their ship and will let no one meddle in their domestic affairs." (12)

At the General Assembly of the United Nations, in September–October 1960, he did not hesitate to demand an investigation of what he called "imperialist" interference in the Congo. But he and his fellow Communists fought to the last ditch the resolution that called for an investigation of post-1956 abuses in Hungary and of Red China's armed take-over of Tibet. Such an investigation, he proclaimed, would constitute interference in the internal affairs of other countries.

Now to that much used—and abused—word *international*. In his September 1959 speech to the General Assembly, Khrushchev used this word thirty-four times. He used it with warmth, even with passion, calling for a "new spirit in international relations." He spoke warningly against those who "obstruct a relaxation of international tensions and sow seeds of new conflicts." All international issues, he said, could be resolved "by peaceful means." Thus the world would enter upon "a new state of international life."

But in no one of his thirty-four uses of the word did he define *what it meant to him*. His Communist hearers needed no definition; and if most of his non-Communist hearers did not know that they needed one, he showed no urge to point out their need.

From the time of Lenin on, however, the Party has attached a very special meaning to this word. In 1920, the *Comintern* made a distinction which the Communists have never since abandoned: "Petty-bourgeois nationalism considers internationalism to mean the mere recognition of the rights of national equality, and preserves intact national egotism. . . . Proletarian internationalism, on the other hand, demands: (1) subordination of the interests of the proletarian struggle in one country to the interests of the struggle on an international scale; (2) the capability and readiness on the part of one nation which has gained a victory over the bourgeoisie, of making the greatest national sacrifices for the overthrow of international capitalism." (13)

Thirty-nine years elapsed between the formulating of this definition by the *Comintern* (the Communist International) and the Twenty-First Congress of the Communist Party of the Soviet Union. Yet at this Twenty-First Congress, Khrushchev still spoke the language of the *Comintern*. He called for the wider "education of the working people in the spirit of proletarian internationalism." And, as we have noted in Chapter VI, he said that by fulfilling and overfulfilling the goals of the Seven Year Plan, thus helping the "world camp of socialism" to outstrip the capitalist nations, the Soviet people would be doing "their international duty."

Once we take into our minds this peculiar Communist definition of *international,* we are able to see precisely what he meant when he said that the Soviet Union did not *interfere* in Hungary, when it moved in to smash the popular uprising, but merely performed its "international duty."

And finally *peace*—a word which we have discussed so many times over, in earlier chapters, in connection with Khrushchev's concept of "peaceful coexistence," that we can here pass over it with a swift reminder.

The ancient Psalmist said of certain persons: ". . . they speak not peace; but they devise deceitful matters against them that are quiet in the land." Khrushchev has learned that it pays to speak peace. But his talk of a peace that is to be achieved without a final climactic war between the two "camps" has not diminished his effort to "devise deceitful matters against them that are quiet in the land"—and, even more ingeniously, against those whose unquietness he can turn to his advantage.

Engels "blamed the liberal, democratic bourgeois leaders of the revolution of 1848 for dangling before people a vision of world order which, he insisted, could only issue from a world proletarian revolution." (14) Khrushchev's stand, today, is only superficially—and tactically—different from that of Engels, just as it is, on the basic issue of war and peace, only tactically different from that of Mao.

When he talks of "peaceful coexistence," we remind ourselves once more, he merely maps out a battle strategy for the nuclear age. He, too, when he talks to his fellow Communists, makes it very clear that there is to be no cessation of the "class struggle" except on Communist terms. The only peace that he counts as durable is still the "proletarian peace" that will come in the wake of Communism's total victory.

How did it all begin—this strange imposition of unfamiliar meanings upon familiar words? It began, we might say, with Marx's determination to make reality fit an oversimplified revolutionary theory: that of the "class struggle."

Marx, for example, pronounced men to be exploiters by reason of "class," not conduct. The individual capitalist, he granted, might be, and often was, a kindly man who cared about his workers and was doing his best to improve their lot. Nonetheless, because he belonged to the capitalist class, he was as much an *exploiter* as his more ruthless fellows; and, like them, he would have to be liquidated when the revolution came.

What this imposition of ideology upon language and life could mean was proved after Lenin came to power. It can be illustrated by a directive laid down by Latsis, one of the high-ranking men in Lenin's *Cheka*, his secret police. Said Latsis: "We are not waging war against particular individuals. We are exterminating the bourgeois as a class. Don't look for evidence to prove that the accused acted by *deed* or *word* against the Soviet power. The first question you should ask him is: To what class he belongs, what is his origin, his training, and his occupation. This should determine the fate of the accused. Herein lies the meaning and the essence of the Red Terror." (15)

Herein, also, lies the corruption of language: the subjugation of the words of our common exchange to a rigid "class" dogma. The Communists talk a "class language"; and unless we know this, and can decode what they say, we are dangerously at the mercy of their tactics. We are, to put the matter simply, dangerously prone to engage in "stormy applause" when that which Khrushchev is actually talking about is the doom which he intends to bring upon our value system and our civilization.

In practice, we might note, the "class language" of Communism is subdivided into several categories. First, there is the *language of accusation*. Just as Marx branded people as *exploiters* regardless of their character or conduct, and with reference only to their class, so Khrushchev, today, talks about *imperialist aggressors* and *warmongers* without having to justify these terms by reference to any action performed by those whom he condemns. They simply belong to the "wrong" class; and inhabit the "wrong" camp.

In contrast—for the benefit of the Communists themselves—there is the *language of exoneration*. Whatever the Communists do—regardless of how brutal or dishonest it may be—is redeemed by their self-proclaimed membership in the "right" class: the proletarian class. The Soviet Union, as we shall note in a later chapter, has built a colonial empire during the very decades when colonialism has been swiftly declining outside the Communist orbit. Yet, in its vocabulary, only non-Communists can be guilty of colonialism. They themselves, when they subdue peoples and nations to their "class" will, are merely serving the fated process of history. They are doing their "international duty."

In the third place, there is the *language of Communist benignity.* When, for example, Stalin imposed Communist rule upon the East European countries by armed force, he was "liberating" them: "liberating" them from "bourgeois capitalism." When the Soviet Union requires these countries to subordinate their national economies to Soviet needs, it is offering them "fraternal guidance." When Khrushchev visits various countries to begin paving the way for eventual takeover by "peaceful" means, he is on a "good will" tour.

Writing from inside the Communist orbit, the Polish poet, Antonin Slonimski, in mid-1959, called for an end to the practice of hiding sense in an ambush of words. He called for a return to the integrity of language: "A healthy semantic cure is the indispensable first step toward saving our civilization." (16)

We on the outside can probably do little to bring the "class" vocabulary of Communism back within the frame of our language of common exchange. That type of "semantic cure" must be gradually brought to pass, we would suppose, by persons like Slonimski who live within the orbit itself but whose minds nonetheless reject the subordination of sense to dogma. Meanwhile, we must expect that Khrushchev and his fellows will go on fitting to their ideological purposes such words as *negotiation, agreement, self-determination, the people, interference* and *non-interference, internationalism, imperialism, aggression, peace, peace-loving,* and *democracy.*

We need not, however, remain at the mercy, or leave the free world at the mercy, of Communism's vocabularies of *accusation, exoneration,* and *benignity.* If Khrushchev, speaking in an "unknown tongue," feels no moral obligation to interpret, then the least we can do is to learn enough to do the interpreting, or decoding, for ourselves.

T E N

BERLIN: A CASE STUDY

I F WE IN the free world were less prone to forget the passing events which we call *daily news,* we would be far less
vulnerable to Khrushchev's tactics. The Berlin story offers a
case in point.

Year after year, Khrushchev, like Stalin before him, manufactures crises with respect to West Berlin. The situation does
not create these crises. He imposes them upon the situation—
with a twofold purpose. By means of them, he recurrently
tests the strength of the Western will to resist Communist
encroachment upon that city. By means of them, also, he
works, with Communist patience, to alienate the Western
peoples from their governments and to make their minds his
allies.

So far as the latter project is concerned, our forgetfulness
serves him well. When any given crisis shows that the Western powers are still determined to stand firm, he can lower
the pressure which his puppet regime in the East Zone of
Germany has put on Berlin and can call for a Summit conference to "rectify" the "untenable situation." Thus, he can

assume the mantle of reasonableness; can implant ever more broadly the idea that Western policies are "rigid"; and can tap to his own advantage the popular feeling that if a situation is "untenable" something should be done about it. All this he can do because he is comfortably certain that most of us do not remember enough about the events of the passing years to call his bluff: that is, to indicate the precise character of his calculated deception.

Not the least part of this deception has lain in his spreading of the idea that Western policy with respect to Berlin is bankrupt: that it has been a colossal failure and that no sane reason can now be given for its continuance.

Quite the opposite is, in fact, true. The Berlin story is a success story. Out of all the agreements that Stalin signed with the Western allies at the end of World War II, the only one which the Soviet Union has not succeeded in breaking has been the four-power agreement with respect to Berlin. Within the framework of this agreement, and with the strictest adherence to the provisions of the agreement, West Berlin has become a free and prosperous city. Not the *failure* of Western policy but the *success* of it makes Berlin the site of recurrent trumped-up crises.

Stalin was able to break every agreement he made with respect to the East European countries and to get away with it—because, as we have noted earlier, the withdrawal of Western troops left an "authority vacuum" to be filled by the Red Army. By breaking these agreements, he brought one hundred million people under Communist dominion. But no "authority vacuum" has been permitted to develop in Berlin. The people who inhabit the British, French, and American sectors of the city are still free. *Therefore*, Khrushchev brands Western policy as "rigid" and the situation as "untenable"; and he continues to foist upon the city—and the world—one manufactured crisis after another.

The latest of these crises was launched on September 8, 1960; but there is no reason to think of it as the last. On that date, the Communist regime in the East Zone of Germany banned West Germans from entering East Berlin except by special permit. Some few hours earlier, Mayor Brandt, of West Berlin, had warned that the city faced another "cold war of nerves"; and Western diplomats were quick to state the nature of the issue: if the Communists could break the four-power agreement on free movement within Berlin, and could get away with it, they could also break agreements on access to *all of* Berlin from the West. Because this was the issue, the Western powers made plain their readiness to resist.

Khrushchev thereupon went through his regular routine. Obviously, the time was not yet ripe for a forcing of the issue —since the will to resist was still firm. So, having wrested all the propaganda value that he could from the crisis, he once more indicated his readiness to postpone the "rectifying" of the "untenable situation." He called for negotiations to settle the "Berlin problem."

Also, however, just as he was leaving New York after his performance at the General Assembly of the United Nations, he got in one more propaganda dig: made one more effort to divide Western public opinion from Western governmental policy. The whole problem of Berlin, he indicated, was so small and so amenable to a "reasonable" settlement that any defense of the present situation which might plunge the world into war would be "absurd" and "irresponsible": the sort of thing that only "warmongers" would even consider. He did not say that there would not be the slightest risk of war over Berlin if he himself did not elect to impose one crisis after another upon that city—in the hope of being able to save the Soviet Union from the unprecedented fate of having to abide by a treaty.

Here the matter rests as we write this chapter. But because it is not likely to rest for long, the time would seem to have come for us to put our minds through the discipline of remembering—and, further, of appraising what is at stake in the Berlin situation. Only thus will we be prepared to take a realistic view of the next crisis that Khrushchev manufactures —at a point where he thinks he detects Western division or weakness; or, simply, when he is again forced to realize that he is not going to get any one-sided concession from the West that will give him, by "peaceful" means, the free hand that he wants in Berlin.

What most of us need, perhaps, is a "refresher course" on certain relevant dates and the events attached to them. (1)

October 1, 1943: Almost two years before the end of the war, the foreign ministers of Britain, the United States, and the Soviet Union met in Moscow to discuss procedures to be followed when the war ended. At this meeting, a European Advisory Commission was appointed to work out a plan for the occupation of Germany when the fighting was over.

September 1944: The European Advisory Commission met in London and worked out the London Protocol: a set of provisions for the interim occupation of Germany after the anticipated surrender of that country.

February 1945: At the Yalta Conference, Roosevelt, Churchill, and Stalin confirmed the terms of the London Protocol; and they also agreed to include France as a fourth signatory.

Under the terms of the Yalta Agreement, Germany was to be divided into four occupation zones, with the French zone made up of sections cut from the two zones which the London Protocol had assigned to Britain and the United States. The four occupying powers were to co-operate to build a free and united Germany.

Specifically, the Yalta Agreement pledged the four powers

"to the earliest possible establishment through free elections of governments responsible to the will of the people . . ." Further, it pledged those governments to facilitate the holding of such free elections.

The City of Berlin, lying within the Soviet zone, was made a unit in itself and was divided into four sectors under a joint Kommandatura. To preserve the wholeness of the city during the period of occupation and to encourage normal daily life within it, no travel barriers were to be imposed between sectors. Access to Berlin from the British, French, and American zones of Germany was also guaranteed.

Khrushchev is determined to persuade Western public opinion, and indeed world opinion, that these occupation arrangements are obsolete, and that the Western powers are "rigidly" holding to an agreement on Berlin that was intended to apply only during the period of postwar emergency. It is true that the occupation arrangements were designed to be *temporary*. Also, however, they were designed to be *fulfilled*. No mere passage of time can be a substitute for their fulfillment.

That is to say, no mere passage of time can be a substitute for the reunification of Germany under a form of government chosen by the people in free elections. Khrushchev does not tell the world that the Soviet Union has refused to abide by its pledged word. It has never allowed free elections to be held in the Soviet zone. This is the reason, and the only reason, why West Berlin now lies deep within a communized Soviet zone of Germany instead of being the capital city of a reunified nation.

Khrushchev says that the "cancer" of West Berlin must be eliminated. But how about eliminating the "cancer" of the communized Soviet zone by holding the free elections to which Stalin pledged himself? Khrushchev calls the Berlin situation "abnormal" and "untenable" because, in that city, the Western powers continue to abide by an agreement which Stalin signed but which he quite apparently did not intend to keep—any more than he kept his word, pledged at Yalta, to let the East European countries choose their own forms of government.

What Khrushchev's contention amounts to is that the Soviet Union has, in East Europe and the East zone of Germany, gained so much by breaking its word that it should be able to gain more, that it is sheer "rigidity" on the part of the West to stand firm with respect to Berlin. His rage at not being able to add the people of West Berlin to the Soviet Union's illegitimate harvest of human beings is not unlike the rage which he directs against NATO. Both Berlin and NATO represent the West's calling of a halt to Soviet expansionism in Europe.

To see precisely what happened after Yalta, we can turn to a succession of quick events that took place in the late Spring and Summer of 1945—beginning with the occupation of Berlin by the Soviet forces on May 2, and the Soviet Command's creation, on May 17, of a Municipal Council for Greater Berlin. The makeup of this Soviet-created body held, we might say, a portent for the future; for while Soviet forces were to occupy only one sector of Greater Berlin, the Council, set up for the whole city, and set up before the arrival of the Western occupation forces, *had an overwhelming majority of Communist members.*

July 11, 1945: The Allied Command—the Joint Kommandatura—took over the administration of Greater Berlin.

July 17–August 2, 1945: The Potsdam Conference was held. At this, Truman, Churchill, and Stalin pledged themselves to carry out the provisions of the Yalta Agreement. Also, they specified that "for the duration of the occupation, all of Germany [was] to be considered as an economic unit."

In view of later developments and of Khrushchev's demands, this is a key point; for the occupation was no sooner in effect than the Soviet Union began to flout this "economic unity" provision by a drive to sovietize the East zone.

So far, we have listed dates only for the period preceding the occupation. Now we come to certain events of the first year of its operation. In the light of these, it is impossible to avoid concluding that, at Yalta, and again at Potsdam, the Soviet Union had become a signatory to agreements *the spirit of which it intended to flout and the letter of which it intended to break at its own convenience.*

July 1945: This very month of the occupation's beginning witnessed the closing of the private banks in the Soviet zone. Again, we can call this a portent; for it was simply the first in a long line of steps taken to sovietize the economy of that zone in isolation from the other three zones. Soon, the drive—never since abandoned—to socialize industry and collectivize agriculture was initiated, with an attendant confiscation of private property. By February 1946, the trade unions had been remade to serve as "fronts" for the Party. In course of time, a wholly separate monetary system was established.

October 1, 1945: The study of Russian was made compulsory in the schools of the East sector of Berlin. This may seem a small matter. But wherever the Soviet Union has extended its domain, the forced study of Russian has been a sign that the territory was regarded as Communist *for keeps.*

Akin to this sign was another. In *March 1946,* Communist youth groups—called "Free German Youth"—were organized throughout the East zone. The culture, in brief, like the economy, was being sovietized. The German people were not being prepared—or permitted—to choose their own future.

April 21, 1946: The organizational meeting of the Socialist Unity Party—the Communist Party of the East zone—was held; and two days later, the newspaper *Neues Deutschland,* still the official organ of that party, appeared for the first time. (Just two years later, on *April 16, 1948,* all Western newspapers were banned within the zone.)

Meetings of the Joint Kommandatura were not going off in a smooth-as-silk fashion during all this time. It is to the eternal credit of the Western allies that, however much they may have let their hope and faith run ahead of their judgment in their original trusting of Stalin's pledged word, they tried unceasingly to implement the terms of the Yalta and Potsdam agreements; and they were blocked at point after point by Soviet recalcitrance.

This was no random recalcitrance. It takes us back to a feature of the ideology which we noted in Chapter I: namely, that Marx's "fated" historical process is a one-way process. It calls for a progressive *expansion* of the Communist domain, but never for a *contraction* of it. Capitalism, in short, must always and everywhere be on the way out; never on the way in. This has come to mean in practice that *all Communist grabs are for keeps;* and they are no less *for keeps* simply because they have been made under cover of a treaty that proclaimed them to be temporary. For Stalin to have encouraged—or tolerated—the reunification of Germany, by free election, along non-Communist lines would have amounted to his countenancing a reversal of the "historic process."

He did not countenance it. By the Summer of 1946, the era of the barbed-wire barrier between the East and West zones of Germany was being ushered in. Also, on July 12 of that Summer, a month-long Paris conference of the foreign ministers of the four occupying powers broke up without achieving its aim. That aim is important to recall in view of Khrushchev's effort to make it appear that the Western allies have held back from consideration of any peace treaty for a reunified Germany.

At that Paris conference, just one year after the occupation began, the Western powers contended that the time had come to work out the terms of a peace treaty for Germany as a whole. The Soviet Union ruled out any consideration of a peace treaty except with what they called an "anti-fascist" German government. What they meant, in practical effect, was a government that would, over an indefinite period, make the whole of a reconstituted Germany into an economic vassal of the Soviet Union—to pay war reparations.

This matter of reparations became a permanent bone of contention. France and Britain, also, we must remember—particularly the latter—had suffered vast wartime damage at the hands of Hitler's forces. The prime aim of the Western allies, however, was to stabilize Central Europe by helping Germany to build a viable economy that could underwrite the development of a democratic state. The Soviet Union's prime aim appeared to be to take, and take, and take—and, in the process, to render Germany permanently subservient.

To get ahead of our story, two later conferences, in July and December 1947, broke up on the same issue. The Soviet Union demanded control of the Ruhr and also reparations from the emerging economy of the West zone in an amount that would have crippled its growth.

The character and extent of the Soviet Union's voraciousness are established by its conduct in the East zone. There, it simply dismantled whole industrial installations and shipped them off to be reassembled in the Soviet Union—thereby providing for a significant part of that swift build-up of the productive plant by means of which Khrushchev "proves" the superiority of Communism. In appraising his boast, we must take account, however, of that retarded economic development in the *Communist* zone of Germany which has resulted from its vassalage to the Soviet Union.

It was shortly after the break-up of the Paris conference in July 1946 that an event occurred which underscored Soviet intentions and deepened the cleavage between East and West. On August 1, 1946—one year after the Potsdam conference—the Soviet Union announced that it had created *by decree*, not by free elections, an East zone government for internal affairs.

October 20, 1946: This is one of the most dramatic dates in the Berlin story. Apparently, Stalin was convinced that propaganda and pressure had got results enough to make safe the holding of free elections for the Berlin Municipal Council. In any event, such free elections were held under four-power auspices.

This was the same Council for Greater Berlin which the Soviet Union had set up some sixteen months before, when first occupying the city, and which had been "loaded" with an overwhelming Communist majority. In this free election of October 1946, the Communists won only 26 seats out of a total of 130.

Having thus suffered defeat, the Communist members settled down, under Soviet direction, to make the Council *theirs* by conspiratorial means; and the Soviet Command, by use of the veto, overruled the Council's election of Ernst Reuter as Mayor. The Council, with no choice but to bow to the veto, elected an "acceptable" Mayor. The Communist members, however, so persistently blocked the work of the Council and so patently tried to maneuver themselves into key posts—particularly that of the chief of police—that the Mayor eventually resigned. The Council then re-elected Reuter. The Soviet Command again vetoed his election. An acting Mayor took interim charge.

We rate this election as one of the most dramatic parts of the Berlin story for two reasons. First, after their defeat at the polls, the Soviets scrapped all pretense of adhering to the terms of the Yalta Agreement: they countenanced no more free elections in their sector of Berlin and none in their zone of Germany.

The second reason is the unmistakable parallel between what happened in Berlin in 1946 and what happened in Russia, by Lenin's instigation, in 1917–1918. From April 1917 to the *coup d'état* in October, Lenin vociferously demanded that the Provisional Government arrange for the election of a Constituent Assembly by popular vote; and such an election was already scheduled when the Bolshevik *coup d'état* was staged. Confident of victory at the polls, Lenin went ahead with the election. Had his Bolsheviks won in this election, his regime would have entered history as *legitimate*. But they lost. They secured only 9,000,000 votes out of the 36,000,000 that were cast.

How did Lenin respond to defeat? When the duly elected Constituent Assembly met, in January 1918, he and his Bolsheviks broke it up—and plunged the nation into civil war. That was Russia's last free election. The *illegitimate* regime was established by force; and it has, by now, spawned its multiple illegitimate offspring, in East Europe and in the East zone of Germany.

"They imagine," wrote Lenin contemptuously, "that serious political questions can be decided by voting. As a matter of fact, such questions, when they have been rendered critical by the struggle, are decided by civil war." (2) During the intervening years, they have many times been decided, also, by the Soviet Union's exploitation of its veto power and by its breaking of its pledged word.

From this point on, the record is one of a constantly widening gap between Western and Soviet policies; and, we must note, between original agreements and Soviet infractions of these agreements.

December 2, 1946: The Western powers, finding themselves unable to make any progress toward fulfilling the Yalta and Potsdam agreements, decided to do what lay within their own power to end the fractionated condition of Germany: they united their three zones—an act which Stalin denounced as a violation of the agreements.

December 15, 1947: The Soviet military administration instituted permits for automobile traffic between Berlin and the East zone of Germany, where no permits had been required before.

January 18, 1948: The commandant of the Soviet sector of Berlin issued an order forbidding transfer of property between that sector and the Western sectors.

March 20, 1948: Marshal Sokolovsky, Soviet representative on the Allied Control Council, staged a walk-out—and thus put a virtual end to the effort to work out problems on a joint basis.

March 29, 1948: The Soviet military administration ruled that even military travel and communication between East and West zones would be restricted, and that permits would be required.

June 18, 1948: The Soviet blockade of West Berlin was begun: that blockade which the Western powers, under the leadership of General Lucius Clay, challenged by the airlift —and challenged successfully. After almost a year, on May 12, 1949, the blockade was lifted: West Berlin had not been starved or frozen into compliance.

June 20, 1949: A Paris conference of the Council of Foreign Ministers broke up over the Soviet demand that an all-German government be created, not by free elections, but by a merging of the governments of the so-called "two Germanies" —a "myth" that had just been invented—and that a peace treaty with this all-German government be signed, one clause of it requiring the withdrawal of all Allied forces from Germany a year later.

When we recall how a Communist minority in the Municipal Council of Greater Berlin attempted to dominate that body by conspiratorial and obstructionist means, we can imagine how much orderly progress could have been made by any government compounded of the freely elected West German regime and the Communist regime of the Soviet zone. From this effort to effect such a juncture, however, we can date the long Soviet insistence that "two Germanies" exist and must be recognized.

October 7, 1940: A government for the Soviet zone was formally established under the title of the German Democratic Republic; and a "made in Moscow" constitution was adopted.

It seems well to take time out, here, to note that these years which we have been reviewing are the same years in which the Soviet Union, in direct violation of the Yalta agreement, was building itself a satellite empire in East Europe.

For the Yalta agreement had not dealt with Germany alone. It had specified that the peoples of East Europe, freed from Hitler's domination, would have their full sovereign rights restored to them and would be free to form governments of their own choice, as indicated by the results of free elections. *One month after the Yalta conference ended,* Stalin took Rumania by a dovetailed action of local Communists and the Red Army, and set up a "puppet" government. Almost four years later, in January 1949, while the Berlin blockade was in effect, Poland fell to the Soviet Union by the same tactics. During the intervening years of stress and strain, Bulgaria, Albania, Hungary, and Czechoslovakia were brought under Soviet domination and provided with puppet regimes.

It was within this same span of years, in September 1947, that Stalin organized the *Cominform* to insure that all Communist Parties around the world would toe the Soviet line. This signalled the launching of Stalin's world-wide program of propaganda, agitation, and subversion—under the label of "peace offensive."

In brief, the type of Soviet policy by which the Western powers were confronted in Berlin, and in the larger German scene, was no isolated phenomenon. It was part and parcel of Stalin's drive for empire.

But there was a difference between the situation in Germany and that in East Europe. Allied troops had pulled out of East Europe, leaving an authority vacuum into which Stalin could pour the strength of the Red Army—to exploit a situation which the local Communist Parties had prepared against his coming. But there was no authority vacuum in Germany. The Western forces stayed on the job. The Soviet effort to get them out has been unremitting. The demand which we have noted above—that an all-German peace treaty provide for their leaving within a year—was part of this effort. Khrushchev's propaganda drive to turn Western public opinion against the "rigidity" of their staying on the job is also part of the same effort.

Before we come to Khrushchev's policies, however, we wish to take account of one date that stands out in such lonely isolation in the record that it deserves to be spotlighted.

May 24, 1953: On this date—some two and a half months after Stalin's death, and during Malenkov's brief period of power—*Pravda* came out with an unprecedented and un-repeated suggestion: namely, that the Soviet Union co-ordinate its German policy with that of the Western allies *in accordance with the Yalta and Potsdam agreements.*

Here is an interesting answer to those apologists for Stalin who say that the whole "German problem" has resulted from a misunderstanding: that Stalin, at Yalta and Potsdam, simply read into the agreements the meanings which the words conveyed to him; and that he was, therefore, as much de-ceived as deceiving.

An even more conclusive answer, we might note, is to be found in one of his own reported comments at Potsdam. Hav-ing just reconfirmed the Yalta agreement for free elections in both Germany and the East European countries, Stalin said that in all the latter, at that time, such elections would go against the Communists: ". . . and this we cannot allow."

Perhaps we should take account here of one other unique event in the long record. Just ten days after the *Pravda* article appeared, the Central Committee of the Communist Party of the Soviet Union demanded that the Communist leadership in the East zone of Germany adopt a less repres-sive internal policy.

This appears to have been an effort—too long postponed—to ease explosive tensions that were developing in that zone. One chief reason for these tensions, however, was precisely that the exorbitant economic demands which the Soviet Union was making upon East Germany required production norms that reduced the workers to a state of underpaid serfdom.

The effort of the CPSU to stave off trouble came too late:

June 17–18, 1953, witnessed mass strikes in East Berlin and other cities of the Soviet zone. In their totality, these strikes added up to a major uprising; and, just as in Hungary three years later, the uprising was subdued by Soviet armed force. This is another fact to remember when Khrushchev talks about the "independence" of the East German government and calls for its being recognized as sovereign.

The multiple occasions, through the years, when the Soviet Union has refused even to discuss plans for the holding of free elections throughout Germany, as a basis for the re-unification of that country, would make a date-list in themselves.

In August 1952, for example, it refused to take part in a conference dedicated to this problem; and on February 18, 1954, a conference of foreign ministers, which had been in session for almost a month, broke up because the Soviet Union rejected a plan to hold such free elections under international controls.

It was shortly after this—on March 25, 1954—that the Soviet Union abandoned the effort to unify Germany according to its own plan, without free elections, and declared for the first time that the relationship between the USSR and the Communist German Democratic Republic was between sovereign and independent nations.

It is from this period that we can date the effort to maneuver the West into recognizing East Germany as sovereign and thereby tacitly granting its right to control access routes to West Berlin: to issue travel permits *or to deny them*. On April 16, 1954, Soviet High Commissioner Semenov announced that the German Democratic Republic would henceforth handle its own foreign relations. A straight line of Soviet policy—and of Western rejection of this—extends from this announcement to the events of September in 1960.

When it became clear, in the late Summer of 1954, that the Western powers were moving toward the inclusion of West Germany in NATO, the Soviet government urgently proposed, in a note dated August 4, 1954, that a conference on questions of European security, including the reunification of Germany, be held. But no willingness to hold free elections was indicated. Nor was there any indication of why the Soviet Union now claimed authority to work out plans for the future of that East German government which it had, four months earlier, declared to be *sovereign*.

By the Summer of 1955, the Soviet Union was again declaring for "two Germanies." On July 26, Khrushchev stated in East Berlin that there could be no reunification of Germany at the expense of the East German regime—the subject of free elections simply being ignored. And some ten months later, he told French Prime Minister Mollet, on May 19, 1956, that he preferred 17 million Germans under Soviet control to 70 million Germans in a United Germany, even if it were neutral.

After this statement, we might say, he settled down to his propaganda drive to get Western forces out of Berlin and out of Germany; and to get American bases out of all foreign countries. In typical Khrushchev fashion, threats and professions of "friendship" made an alternating design: to intimidate those who could be intimidated; to sell the Soviet brand of "peace" to the credulous.

By late 1958, Khrushchev was ready to proclaim, on his own initiative, the scrapping of all past agreements on Germany and Berlin. On November 10, 1958, at a "Polish-Soviet Friendship Meeting" in Moscow, he flatly stated that the Soviet government intended to change the status of Berlin; and on November 27, he sent official notes to the three Western powers and to the governments of the "two Germanies" demanding that the status of Berlin be revised within six months.

At virtually the same time, he announced his intention of signing a separate peace treaty with the Communist German Democratic Republic. On December 25, 1958, he informed the Western powers and the Federal German Republic that their official notes would no longer be accepted if they referred to the German Democratic Republic as the "Soviet zone of Occupation." By March 1959, he was extending the six-month period of ultimatum on Berlin for an unspecified time.

There is abundant reason to believe that he thought, after his visit to the United States in the Fall of 1959, that "the spirit of Camp David" would insure his own way, at last, with respect to Berlin and Germany at the Summit conference which he set himself to bring into being. There is also abundant evidence, as we have noted in an earlier chapter, that his growing recognition, during the Spring of 1960, that he was not going to get what he wanted led to his so exploiting the U-2 incident that the Summit conference of May 1960 ended before it started.

Thus, we return to the Fall of 1960—and to his new policy twist: the extending of permission to the East German regime to act as a sovereign power and exert its control over the boundary between East and West Berlin, while he himself still holds in reserve both his threat to make a separate peace with the East zone and his authority to check the East German regime at any point where its policies cease to serve his ends.

We must emphasize again that Khrushchev is determined to brand as "abnormal" a state of affairs that blocks his expansionist aims; and to brand as "rigid" the West's continued adherence to pledges which the Soviet Union has, virtually since the date of signing, elected to break.

Khrushchev, we must conclude, hopes to create by an astute blend of diplomacy, propaganda, threat, and repeated crisis that "authority vacuum" in Germany which Stalin was never able to create; and which he himself has not been able, so far, to create. He keeps telling the world that the situation is "abnormal." We need to keep asking ourselves—and the world—what is *abnormal* about the West's insisting that the people of Germany, and of all Germany, should have the right, originally guaranteed in the four-power agreement, to determine their own fate through free elections?

What is *abnormal* about the Soviet Union's being held, for once, to the terms of an agreement that it freely signed? After all, Stalin was neither pressured nor hurried into accepting the terms of the Yalta agreement. Those terms were worked out, over a two-year period, to his professed satisfaction. There is nothing sacred about the Soviet Union's right to break treaties.

Again, what is *abnormal* about the West's refusal to put the people of West Berlin at the mercy of Soviet power? What is *abnormal* about a refusal to provide the Soviet Union with the conditions it needs for the take-over of that city and, later, of West Germany?

Berlin is, today, the Soviet Union's most urgently needed and most urgently wanted *point of take-off* for a new Soviet drive in Europe. If West Berlin could be brought under Soviet domination, a swallow-up of West Germany would be made far easier to accomplish. Then, "if the Soviets could control and organize West Germany as a satellite, they would have a production power so formidable as to make our position critical . . ." The adding of West Germany to the orbit would, in short, "bring the Soviet dream of world conquest close to a sure gamble. . . . The side that wins control of Germany may well control Europe and the fate of civilization." (3)

Here we would ask our readers to look at a map of the European-Asian land mass. We would ask them to compare the present relative size and position of the Communist and non-Communist orbits; and then, in their mind's eye, *to add West Germany to the Communist orbit.*

This addition would, at a single stroke, advance the Soviet's boundary line to Denmark, the Netherlands, Luxembourg, France, Switzerland, and to that narrow neck of Austria across which Italy lies; and it would provide an outlet to the North Sea. The Soviet Union's gain would be colossal; and it might well be determinative. Freedom's domain in Europe would be reduced to a narrow fringe of countries pressed upon by the enormous weight of Communism's European-Asian empire.

Thus, if the Communists, by force or concession, can gain control of West Berlin, they can add its resources to their own; eliminate it as a Western outpost; and ready themselves to make West Germany their next target. If they can, then, swiftly, or simply by a wearing-down process, take over West Germany, they will be in a position to make their pressure upon the residue of Europe well-nigh irresistible. And beyond Europe lies a Western Hemisphere in which they have already, in effect, established a Cuban beachhead; in which their Parties, "fronts," and agents are exploiting every tension and discontent; and in which only the United States is highly industrialized and defensively equipped.

Khrushchev does not talk in these terms. He talks of his readiness to guarantee the status of Berlin as a "free city." But the whole Soviet record in Germany and East Europe is a reminder that no Soviet "guarantee" is worth the paper it is written on: it is simply a means of bringing to pass a condition favorable for take-over. More than this, Khrushchev's pressure on Berlin cannot be separated from his attacks on NATO and on American bases; and from his bids for total disarmament without inspection.

It is in the light of this total picture that we must look at that dot on the map which is Berlin. It is in the light of this total picture, also, that we must understand the stiff resistance of the West to the Soviet Union's flouting—once more —in September 1960, the four-power agreement on Berlin.

What the puppet regime in the East zone of Germany did on that September day can be made to sound too trivial to justify a world crisis. All it did was to issue an edict that, for an unspecified period, all persons from West Germany who wanted to go from West to East Berlin would have to apply for special passes. This "trivial" act, however, represented a new kind of infringement of the four-power agreement: "Even during the 1948–1949 blockade, people within the city could move freely regardless of their status." (4) Now such freedom was unilaterally withdrawn.

Few individuals were, in point of fact, affected by the edict of September 8; for it applied only to persons from West Germany, and not to residents of West Berlin. But the West was concerned lest it be a first step toward a closing of the inner-city border between East and West Berlin.

This concern proved to be well founded. By September 13, the edict had been extended. Residents of West Berlin, it was announced, "could no longer travel in or through East Germany on West German passports, although no other passports are available to them." (5) Meanwhile, Zaharov, the Soviet commandant in the city, backed up the East German regime in a statement ambiguous enough to leave open the question of whether or not Moscow had turned over its legal powers within the four-power city to the East Germans.

Therefore, American, British, and French officials in Bonn agreed that immediate steps must be taken to resist this latest Soviet dodge. Again, resistance had its effect: by the time he left New York, in mid-October, Khrushchev was calling for negotiations in the Spring of 1961. But a host of American, British, and French people—having forgotten the record of the years—were left wondering why the "Berlin problem" has to remain as a perennial source of trouble.

"East German leaders have long been chagrined by the fact that though East Germany officially dates its existence from October 7, 1949, not one non-Communist government has extended diplomatic recognition to the so-called German Democratic Republic . . ." (6) Why has non-recognition been thus unanimous?

"1. The so-called German Democratic Republic is . . . a Communist imposed regime which is based on Soviet military strength and not on the popular consent of the East German people.

"2. The overwhelming majority of people in East Germany, Berlin, and West Germany hope for the eventual re-unification of their country. Diplomatic recognition of the East German regime would mean accepting the permanent division of Germany. . . .

"3. Virtually the entire non-Communist world recognizes the freely-elected government of the Federal Republic of Germany as the only legitimate German government." (7)

"The East Germans," states the *Manchester Guardian* of September 15, 1960, "have now started the second phase of their probing pressure on West Berlin and Western solidarity. . . . Encouraged perhaps by what they took for a

half-hearted Western reaction to this measure, they no
longer trouble to invent pretexts for their new restrictions.
They feel sure of Russian support and approval, and Moscow
itself keeps up a flow of threats and protests in Notes to
Bonn. They know that their restrictions are illegal and contrary to the four-power agreements. . . . But they have
already said that these agreements were signed by the Russians and not by their own 'sovereign' Government. If they
can get away with this, they will most certainly impose
further restrictions. . . . For the West, more is now at stake
than illegal interference with access to Berlin and the threat
will grow unless action is taken soon."

The threat will grow, we might say, unless our own minds
are ready to see why Western action is necessary; and more
colossal nonsense has been put into our minds by Soviet
propaganda on the subjects of Germany and Berlin than
on almost any other. Insistently, year after year, Khrushchev
has tried to reduce us to puppets through whose mouths he,
the master ventriloquist, can speak. It is time for us to choose
our own words. The danger of war would be vastly decreased
by the voluntary development among us of a firm, informed
Western public opinion with which to back up the "rigid"
policies of Western governments with respect to Berlin.

Khrushchev's "clinching" argument is that the situation
which now exists in Berlin and Germany cannot go on. But
there is no reason why it cannot go on *as long as it must go
on to stave off disaster*. If Khrushchev wants to change the
situation, he can do so at any time by returning to the
terms of the Yalta agreement and allowing free elections
in the East zone of Germany. But there is no specified date
by which free people have to stop defending their freedom
by the best means which have been left to them by the
Soviet record of broken agreements.

ELEVEN

EXCHANGE PROGRAMS:
WHOSE WEAPON?

STALIN carried to the point of diminishing returns the sealing-off of the Soviet bloc behind the Iron Curtain. Khrushchev has certainly not scrapped the Iron Curtain. But he has shown himself to be aware that its use could neither prudently be pushed to further extremes nor be "settled into" as permanent policy in a changing world. Least of all could it be reconciled with his own appraisal of what comes next on the agenda of Communism.

He has, therefore, been feeling his way toward a "methodology" for the next long pull; and this "methodology" has called for his establishing a wide range of non-Stalinist contacts with the world outside the curtain. Among these contacts have been those covered by scientific, technical, and cultural exchange agreements with Western nations—including the United States.

We cannot separate this phase of Khrushchevism from his all-over foreign policy. Neither can we separate it from his urgent domestic drive to produce *Communist man;* for *Communist man,* if made according to Khrushchev's specifications, could be exposed to a controlled measure of "bourgeois" influence without being dangerously infected by it.

This "new man," however, has not yet been turned out in a proper model or in sufficient numbers. The daily press of the Soviet bloc is a "textbook" from which we can learn this fact, even though all propaganda aimed at the outside world is designed to conceal it. Therefore, all exchanges with the West involve for the Communists an element of risk. Khrushchev knows this. Such satellite dictators as have followed his lead in establishing cultural exchanges also know it. Only such knowledge would account for the extreme wariness of all Communist officials who have anything to do with exchange programs.

Sometimes this awareness of risk is shown in an abrupt closing of the Iron Curtain. After the demise of the Summit conference, in May 1960, for example, the jamming of Western radio broadcasts—which had been markedly relaxed from mid-1959 on—was reinstated with a vengeance. In a split second, we might say, the Communist orbit was again sealed off; and it was kept sealed off long enough to insure the people's being fed a "correct" diet of news about certain key events. Khrushchev's press conference in Paris was given an altogether different tone for home consumption.

Repeatedly, the awareness of risk is spelled out in the Communist press with specific reference to exchange programs. We might cite as typical a warning published in *Elet Es Irodalom,* Budapest, on January 15, 1960, by the Chairman of the Hungarian Writers' Union. He warned that because "international contacts are becoming broader, the channels in which the two cultures meet will grow in number; hence, it is evident . . . that cultural and intellectual elements which are not our own will arrive regularly, and we have to be well prepared to fend them off."

To exploit and to fend off: these twin efforts comprise the Communist approach to all exchanges between the "two worlds." The will to exploit profitable contacts makes for a limited non-Stalinist venturing—and gives us a limited chance to introduce the Soviet and satellite peoples to a West very different from that which their own propagandists describe. But the urge to fend off makes for a constant muted Stalinism.

When Khrushchev is talking for world consumption, he does not stress the "fending-off" aspect of Soviet policy. He tries to give the impression that he not only welcomes all sorts of exchanges but has had to urge them upon a reluctant West.

Many persons, even in our own country, have come to accept this version. Some of them, as a result, have added their voices to Khrushchev's in reproaching the West for timidity and stand-patism. Others contend that since exchange programs are Communist inventions we should have nothing to do with them. Thus, they unwittingly help Khrushchev to "prove" to the world's non-Western millions that we are afraid of the impact of Communist "culture."

The record needs to be set straight. Between 1948 and 1953, Stalin, aided by his cultural commissar Zhdanov, virtually walled off the peoples of the Soviet bloc from all contacts with other countries. After Stalin's death, in 1953, Western diplomats decided to put an end, if they could, to this "psychological estrangement of peoples." Therefore, they put the problem of cultural exchanges on the agenda for talks with the Soviet Union.

"In July 1955 the Geneva conference of heads of state expressed the desire 'to bring about freer contacts and exchanges.' On October 31, 1955, France, Great Britain, and the United States submitted for Soviet scrutiny a proposal intended to further the development of cultural relations. In his reply of November 13, Molotov rejected the main points of the proposal, stating that they were 'an attempt to interfere in the internal affairs of the Soviet Union.'" (1) He said that what the West meant by "a free exchange of ideas" was "freedom to propagate war and hatred"—which the "peace-loving" Soviet Union could not allow.

After this rejection of diplomatic proposals, various nongovernmental groups in the West tried to establish some "exchange of ideas." The Society for European Culture, for example, induced the attendance of Soviet representatives at a meeting of writers, in Venice, in March 1956; and in September of that year, a conference of editors of literary magazines was held in Zurich.

One aftermath of this conference shows how hard it is to effect exchanges, governmental or otherwise, with a regime committed to "penetrating without being penetrated." As the sessions ended, Ignazio Silone, editor of *Tempo Presente,* gave to one of the Soviet editors—Ivan Anisimov, of *Inostrannaya literatura*—a list of questions which, he hoped, might serve as a basis for a further exchange of ideas. "It was agreed that the questions, the answers to them, and the ensuing exchange of opinions would be published in full by both sides." (2) After three months, Anisimov sent Silone partial answers to some of the questions; and Silone, by return letter, continued what he hoped might be made to grow into a fruitful exchange. But: "The questions and Silone's letter were not published in the USSR."

The Hungarian uprising and the Soviet crushing of it, in late 1956, put an abrupt temporary end to all bids for exchanges. But in mid-1957, consideration of them was resumed. The United States proposed an exchange of radio and television broadcasts. At this point, the Soviet Union reversed its policy of rejection and invited a "full dress discussion of possibilities." A meeting in Washington was scheduled for October.

From this meeting there resulted the first agreement on "Cultural, Technical, and Educational Exchanges" between the United States and the USSR: signed in Washington, on January 27, 1958, by Ambassador William S. B. Lacy, for the United States, and by Ambassador G. N. Zaroubin, for the Soviet Union. (3)

This Agreement went far beyond the setting-up of a few incidental projects. It specified the conditions for exchanges of any sort. Then it called for exchanges of radio and television broadcasts; exchanges of groups of specialists in industry, agriculture, youth and student groups; exchange visits of delegations from our Congress and the Supreme Soviet; joint conferences of various USA and USSR organizations; cooperation in the motion-picture field; exchange of theatrical, choral, and dance groups, of symphony orchestras, and of individual performers; visits by scientists; exchange of university delegations; exchange of athletes and teams; development of tourism; exchange of exhibits and publications; and establishment of direct air flights.

Obviously, if our layman's phrase, "cultural exchange," is to be used to cover all these diversified provisions, the word *cultural* must embrace far more than works and activities in the fields of literature and the arts. Our American press has tended to focus on forms of exchange that have a ready human-interest value—tours by musicians, controversial art exhibits, and so on—and thus has narrowed the public concept of what the full Agreement embodies. Caught up in small specific dramas, we have almost lost sight of the larger drama. But this Agreement was, in effect, a first set of rules for the mutual confrontation of two cultures that adhere to basically different views of man and society; that must, each in its own way, deal with matters relevant to all men and all societies; and that are involved in a fateful competition for the human future.

The basic provisions of this first Agreement were extended, in November 1959, into a second—under the title, "Scientific, Technical, Educational, and Cultural Exchanges." This second Agreement is in operation as we write this chapter. It is our only broad formal agreement with any country of the Soviet bloc. Yet it does not stand alone. Other Western countries have also instituted East-West exchanges; and we have entered into numerous agreements with certain of the satellites—most frequently, Poland—for the exchange of specific projects and teams.

In appraising the worth of this web of exchanges, we do well to recall that Ambassador Lacy himself, speaking to the National Press Club in Washington, on February 12, 1958, described our first Agreement with the USSR as "something less than a Magna Carta of East-West dealings." It might better be called, he said, "a beginning stage of the preliminary arrangements for getting our foot in the door": that door which Stalin slammed and locked, and which Khrushchev is willing partially to open only if he can keep adjusting the width of the crack; but that door behind which the Soviet and satellite citizen, not yet *Communist man,* lives and moves and has his being.

Against this background of history, and of the broad provisions of our Agreement, we can see in perspective the Soviet Union's current two-pronged effort: to claim all credit for instituting cultural exchange programs; and to secure forms of exchange profitable to itself, while fending off others.

Why did the Soviet Union, in mid-1957, reverse its previous policy of rejection? Does the change prove that Khrushchev—having disposed of Molotov *et al.*—can now be as "liberal" as he "has always wanted to be"? To accept this view, which was recently put to us as the most probable explanation, would be pleasant; but also, we believe, inaccurate and dangerous.

Something nearer the truth is suggested by a statement which G. Zhukov, Chairman of the Soviet State Committee for Cultural Relations with Foreign Countries, made, in August 1959, to André Parinaud, editor of the Parisian weekly, *Arts*. During an interview, Parinaud asked Zhukov what he meant by "coexistence."

"Our public opinion," Zhukov replied, "wants peace. . . . Furthermore, we Marxists are capable of working things out. We also have the patience given us by the conviction that the normal evolution of things will lead us to victory. Coexistence is the entr'acte. In other words, this is the moment when you talk in a friendly manner, showing yourself from the best side." (4)

Thus, Zhukov compressed into one statement most of the factors involved in the Soviet approach to "coexistence" in general and exchange programs in particular; and not the least of these factors is "public opinion." During the past few years, the Communist press has been punctuated by items which directly or indirectly acknowledge that public opinion, even though it has no chance to become an *organized* opinion, exerts a force within the orbit which it did not exert in Stalin's day; and that this public opinion wants not only peace but contact with things Western.

As a typical instance, K. Mazurov, First Secretary of the Central Committee of the Byelorussian Communist Party, made an almost desperate plea in February 1960 for a stepping-up of indoctrination to counteract the effect of

Western broadcasts: "It must be remembered that we still have persons not versed in politics, unstable persons who draw incorrect conclusions from the foreign anti-Soviet radio broadcasts and other hostile propaganda." (5)

Confronted by a new kind of public opinion and by the people's readiness to draw "incorrect conclusions" from unapproved Western materials, and confident that it can "sell" to world opinion a new "progressive" image of itself, the Soviet Union, it would appear, has decided to "seize this nettle danger": to take the initiative in exposing Soviet minds to *selected* Western materials. Certainly, this would seem to be the meaning of a further statement which Zhukov made to Parinaud: "We are offering the cultural exchange which our public opinion desires, without politics . . ." That is to say, without any of the forbidden content that might stimulate questions about the ideology or the system.

How do the Communists behave when they feel that both Soviet public opinion and the world situation call for their talking "in a friendly manner"? Khrushchev has provided an example of their approach. As reported in *Pravda,* on September 22, 1959, he said that cultural exchange comes down to the following: "We have only one regulation! Offer your goods and we shall select what we have to buy. We in return shall offer you (what we have). If you are pleased, then buy. If not, don't buy!"

This statement is well calculated to make unwary persons, the world around, say that Khrushchev really wants a fair, honest competition of cultural wares "in the open market places of the mind." Those who thus interpret his words are more ready thereafter to credit charges of Western recalcitrance: as when Ilya Ehrenburg, in *Literaturnaya gazeta,* for November 5, 1959, accuses the West of "hindering the exchange of books."

But what was Khrushchev saying *in the context of cultural reality?* When the West offers its "goods," these are widely diversified. In them are manifest all sorts of individual and group values. Among the books published in America, for example, in any given year, there are many that are critical of our culture or of specific aspects of it; and many which, because they quite legitimately deal with one or another of our unsolved problems, can have their meaning so twisted as to make our whole way of life seem like one gigantic unsolved problem. Again, motion pictures and radio and TV programs are varied enough in quality and subject matter that they can be *selectively* used to prove almost anything about us.

Furthermore, while arrangements for exchange of persons and programs under our *Agreement* are made by our State Department, they deal with free individuals, voluntary groups, and privately owned materials. The State Department, we might say, is a middleman between our system of free enterprise and the USSR.

The cultural "goods" which the Soviet Union offers, however, are State-owned or processed, and are designed to be "monolithic" in impact. Khrushchev, in short, was saying that from the full range of our privately owned, diversified wares, the Soviet Union would choose *what fitted its purposes;* and that we would have an "equal" chance to make a "free choice" of exchange materials *from among the "monolithic" wares which the Soviet Union elects to offer us.* If we look beyond these and express an interest, for example, in the novels of Dudinsev, we are accused of trying to "fan the cold war."

Are we being unfair to Khrushchev's statement of policy? Not in view of the record. Within the frame of matched item-for-item exchanges specified in the Agreement and firmly held to by our own negotiators, the Soviet negotiators persistently twist and turn to secure maximum benefits with minimum ideological risks.

To begin with, they rule out certain subject matters altogether. Neither British nor American book exhibits at the Moscow fair, in 1959, were permitted to contain any works on religious, political, and economic themes—a fact which both illumines Zhukov's remark about offering what Soviet "public opinion desires, without politics," and throws a strange light on Ehrenburg's charge than the West hinders the exchange of books.

Again, they rule out any type of people-to-people contact that would expose the Soviet public to a free exchange of ideas. While the extension of our first Agreement into a second was being negotiated, Khrushchev complained that Americans are always wanting a "so-called free spread of ideas. . . . They want to foist all sorts of rubbish on us, which would poison the minds of Soviet people. Can we agree to this? Of course not." (6)

This taboo is not limited to public discussions of forbidden ideological subjects. It applies to all materials and media that might conceivably "corrupt" public opinion. Thus, when Parinaud suggested to Zhukov that there be organized some genuine exchange of experience between Western and Soviet artists, writers, and musicians, and that Western representatives of these arts be allowed to explain and defend their views before a Soviet audience, he was told curtly, "Painting is the affair of the state and not a game for esthetes."

When Parinaud asked for at least a freer exchange of books and some relaxing of Soviet censorship of the press, Zhukov was adamant: "There must be complete supervision of the printed thought in the interests of socialism. We shall not permit the publication of one work which does not correspond in any way to our ideology." (7)

With this rigid taboo upon anything that savors of a really free exchange of ideas, how do the Soviet negotiators contrive to meet the terms of the Agreement? One answer is that the Agreement itself licenses as large a measure of censorship as Soviet law embodies; and it cannot do otherwise. It explicitly states, and would have to state for our own protection, that none of its provisions must be so applied as to transgress the law of the land where they are put into operation.

Usually, however, the Soviets manage to keep exchanges on the safe side of a "free spread of ideas" without a crude resort to legalities. As Zhukov said, "we Marxists are capable of working things out." One way of "working things out" is to let visiting experts from the West speak freely to their Soviet counterparts in closed session. Even though representatives of the press are often present, *censorship* of the press can be relied on to fend off from the public mind any "incorrect" statement that was freely made.

Thus, in June 1959, Norman Cousins was invited, on a cultural exchange basis, to speak before the Praesidium of the Soviet Peace Committee in Moscow. In the course of his talk and discussion, he stressed that "no agreements other than enforceable ones" could serve as a basis for relationships between the USA and the USSR where matters of national security were at stake. Further, he pointed to the dubious record of the Communist Party in the United States as one reason why Americans are wary of Soviet protestations of "friendship." This Party, he said, "has directed its main energies not toward the development of social progress in America—but toward the needs of a foreign government. . . . It has taken advantage of the machinery of a free society to weaken that society." (8)

Except for one "flurry of excitement"—quickly controlled —the audience was "polite and attentive." But: "The Soviet press, which was amply represented at the meeting, published nothing about the talk the next day. Moreover, the censor's office did not clear stories about [it] filed by foreign correspondents."

This type of censorship—which is a common Soviet appendage to the amenities of exchange—has the flavor of Orwell's *1984*. In that book, we recall, persons were turned into *unpersons* by the erasure of every scrap of evidence of their ever having existed. What we are describing here is comparable. When visiting experts make statements displeasing to the regime, these are simply turned into *unstatements* —by being buried in silence.

This selective ruling-out of Western offerings and Western types of free discussion is matched by an equally selective "ruling-in." Wherever possible—and particularly with respect to mass media—the Soviets try to secure two types of materials: those that are critical enough of Western culture that they can be presented to the Soviet public as expressing the viewpoint of the "exploited masses"; and those that can be used to "prove" the weakness, corruption, and decadence of the West.

Zhukov is a skilled negotiator. But his methods are not too subtle for detection by our own negotiators—who are not less skilled; and they have served, in the past few years, to add several cubits to our knowledge of Soviet tactics. Also, they keep us reminded that "coexistence" is only "the entr'acte."

In the Fall of 1959, Khrushchev, whose "benignity" was at full tide, insisted that "relations between the U.S.S.R. and the U.S.A. should be built upon the foundation of friendship and that they should fully correspond to the principles of peaceful coexistence." (9) Simultaneously, Zhukov was maneuvering to inject into the extension of our first *Agreement* a patently unfriendly provision. This provision would have left the Soviet State in full control of all persons and materials that come out of the USSR on an exchange basis, but would have let that State by-pass our government entirely, in the arranging of exchanges, and deal directly with private artists and producers. Such is the character of "the entr'acte."

The "friendly" nature of Zhukov's aim was made clear by his urgent effort to secure *West Side Story,* a vivid portrayal of delinquency in New York City. Presented in New York, to an audience that has daily contact with the manifold other sides of American life, such a production can serve to remind us that we have not finished our democratic "homework." But it becomes something else altogether when urgently sought for presentation to a Moscow audience which is calculatedly being fed the line that America is in the final throes of decadence.

Had Zhukov been able thus to have his way with the Agreement, he could have made exchange programs *all his own.* The choice of what came to us from the USSR would have been his. But so, in effect, would have been the choice of what went from our country to the USSR. By dealing directly with private artists and producers—letting expediency be his guide in the offering of money, prestige, and a chance to promote "peace"—he could have had at his disposal their uninformed good will, their natural inclination to cooperate, their pride in having their work singled out, and their financial self-interest. Thus, while he could have warded off materials not "suitable" for impingement upon the Soviet mind, by the simple expedient of not soliciting them, he could have exposed that mind to materials chosen to underscore the Party line with respect to conditions in America.

Zhukov did not secure his one-sided advantage. Our negotiators are far from being as naive as he persistently hopes they will be. But the fact that he tried to secure it, and kept on trying right up to the end of the negotiations, is a report on both Communist "friendship" and the Soviet bloc's enduring need for a practical substitute for Stalin's Iron Curtain.

In evaluating exchange agreements, we must never forget that neither Khrushchev nor the satellite dictators can risk *unguardedness*. Zhukov acknowledges this in language that makes *guardedness* an ideological virtue. When he had rejected all Parinaud's proposals for a freer exchange of ideas, the latter observed that such extreme caution argued a lack of self-trust on the part of Soviet authorities. Zhukov replied that "we are afraid of nothing, but being Marxists we cannot leave anything to the whim of fate." Thus, he gave a capsule expression to the paradox of Marxism-Leninism: namely, that what is historically "fated" to happen must never be left to "the whim of fate." At every specific point, it must be manipulated and coerced into happening.

Khrushchev prefers an expansive by-passing of the whole issue. He likes to say that the "socialist states are ruled by the people themselves, the workers and peasants, the people who themselves control all the material and spiritual values of society." (10) But his propaganda line always contains an ideological "escape clause."

One of his toughest sessions in the United States, we recall, was with a group of labor leaders: men who had learned too much about Communism at first hand to feel obligated to deal gently with Communism's dictator. Referring to Khrushchev's bid for more trade, Walter Reuther asked, "How can you oppose a free flow of ideas?" With abrupt anger Khrushchev resorted to his "escape clause": "As head of the working class, I will protect the workers from capitalist propaganda." (11)

Do the people "who themselves create all the material and spiritual values of society" wish to be thus protected? It would scarcely seem so in view of the nearly fifteen thousand books which were apparently lifted from the American exhibit at the Moscow fair and started on their surreptitious hand-to-hand circulation.

The Communists are discovering, in fact, that even when

they get the exchange items they want, the impact of these is unpredictable. *Rude Pravdo*—official organ of the Communist Party of Czechoslovakia—carried, on April 19, 1959, an illuminating article which undertook to dispel the illusion that "safe" exchange materials are safe: "The struggle against bourgeois ideologies which come to us from the capitalist countries is a more complicated problem than it would appear . . ."

To establish its point, the article told what had happened with respect to a West German motion picture, *Die Wunderkinder*. This had seemed "progressive" enough—that is, critical enough of the Western order of things—to be suitable for a Czechoslovakian audience. Yet many audience members had responded "incorrectly." Recalling what they had been told about the oppressive character of the West German regime, they "asked themselves how it was possible for such a film to be produced in Adenauer's Germany." The article concludes that even when a Western import presents its message in a "distinctly progressive manner," there is still "a good deal of explanatory work" to be done.

But this "explanatory work" cannot really be done. People throughout the Soviet bloc now talk far more freely among themselves than they did in Stalin's day. The regime can "fend off" exchange materials that would *directly* disprove the Party line about the oppression of "the masses" under capitalism. But how can they prevent people's asking, in their own minds and among their friends, how it happens that oppressive capitalism not only permits the free portrayal of its own evils but, further, permits this portrayal to go into the Communist orbit under an exchange agreement? This, as a matter of fact, is a question which Western tourists might well learn to ask when they talk with individuals whose Party-made image of the West has been confirmed by selected exchange materials. "Sometimes," says *Rude Pravdo*, "explanations are necessary . . ."

The "necessity" for such explanations was, we might say, injected into history by the fact that Marx, studying in the British Museum, failed to ask himself a question equivalent to that which members of Czechoslovakian audiences asked about *Die Wunderkinder*. Building up his image of capitalism as a system which could not reform itself, Marx spent many months studying the "Blue Books" put out *by the British government* to expose the evils which prevailed in mines and cotton mills and to bring about necessary reforms. According to Marx, this British government was merely the servant of those who owned the mines and mills. But he did not ask why, then, it published studies about the exploitation that took place in these. Had he asked this question—had he even seen that it needed to be asked—many things in today's world might have been different.

Soviet and bloc officials have learned that exchanges with "the enemy" are not all cakes and ale. But neither are they so for the free world. To quote Ambassador Lacy, the negotiating and implementing of an exchange agreement "is a grim game, a hard contest, played for ultimate stakes." (12)

What risks do we ourselves elect to run when we sign a broad exchange Agreement with the Soviet Union or, in the case of certain satellites, an agreement with respect to specific materials or projects? How have these risks been mitigated? By what potential gains are they justified? What are the "ultimate stakes"?

It can be flatly stated that no American should be scorned for recognizing that there are risks. The province of exchange is not one in which vague good will can be permitted to have a field day. Also, it can be flatly stated that no one except our most astute, tough-minded, experienced, and interminably patient diplomats should negotiate or implement this kind of agreement—or any other to which the Communists are a party. As Ambassador Lacy says, ". . . if agreements with the Soviet Union are to be successful, they must be *self-enforcing*—because no other basis, so far, has been found to work." Thus, every provision of the agreement "is based on reciprocity. What the Russians fail to deliver they do not receive in return . . ."

What does this mean in practice? "For each delegation the Soviet Union is allowed to send to this country, we must be allowed to send an equivalent delegation to the Soviet Union. If our delegation cannot go, then theirs cannot come, and that part of the agreement lapses. If ours is not provided a suitable itinerary, theirs is not allowed the requested itinerary." The Soviets never tire of trying to find loopholes. But at every point they are held to the item-for-matched-item provisions of the Agreement.

What about espionage as a by-product of exchange activities? Ambassador Lacy rates this as a question which free citizens have every right to ask—particularly in view of the Soviet Union's constant exploitation of Embassy privileges, not only in America, but around the world. Embassy personnel, however, he indicates, enjoy a freedom of movement not enjoyed by visiting delegations on planned itineraries.

Besides, he reminds us, ours is an "open" society. For decades, the Communists and their "fronts" have been gathering information. It is unlikely that persons held to planned itineraries could add much to the Soviet Union's store of "secret" knowledge. On the other hand, these delegations gain knowledge of a kind that we want them to have: that is, knowledge with which to "edit," in their own minds, what they have been told by their Party propagandists.

True, those who come from the Soviet Union have been selected for their ideological "correctness." Also, regardless of what they see, many of them, when they return home, will write accounts of their experiences that bolster the Party line: that line which Mikhail Suslov, among others, made explicit at the Twenty-First Congress. "Capitalism," said Suslov, "finds it increasingly difficult to keep its head above water. It will sink under the weight of its own crimes against mankind." (13)

Most exchange delegates, when they get back to the USSR, echo this line. If they did otherwise, they would stand no chance of ever being sent abroad a second time; and the hunger for travel is growing throughout the orbit. In the judgment of our negotiators, we stand to gain far more, in the long run, from the Party's being self-infiltrated by individuals who have seen the West with their own eyes than we stand to lose by a few more repetitions of the stereotyped propaganda line.

We stand to gain, also, from the multiplication of people within the orbit who, even if they have not been abroad, are acquiring new facts out of which to frame skepticism about the repetitive stereotypes: people who have talked with our counterpart delegations; who have had a chance to size up our exhibits; and who have been on the receiving end of our unwarlike friendliness.

This brings us to the heart of the exchange drama. What are we reaching for? And what intrinsic advantages can we believe that we have as a free people even though our Agreement is strictly reciprocal?

One basic advantage on our side is that our system exists *in its own right*. It does not have to be propped up by calculated falsehoods about other systems. Our awareness of developments in the Soviet Union since Stalin's death has certainly lagged; and many American tourists have experienced a first dizzying shock of surprise at the evidence of material progress and the absence of overt signs of police-state terrorism. But this shock is one which our own government prefers to have us experience, if need be—so that we can assimilate it, put it behind us, and settle down for a long pull. This long pull is one in which the "ultimate stakes" are those of respect for the human individual, freedom of peoples from an imposed "psychological estrangement," and freedom of nations from the threat inherent in their being regarded as future Communist territory.

Our government, in short, can afford to have us know all that we can learn about Communism. The less we are misinformed, the better. The sooner we get over our naivete, the better. But all Communist governments, in contrast, have "a good deal of explanatory work" to do at every point where objective evidence contradicts the Marxist-Leninist line. Exchange programs are one way of giving them a great many occasions to do such "explanatory work"—which can never really be done.

To an extent, moreover, that seems well-nigh incredible, exchanges are forcing upon Soviet officials themselves types of knowledge about our system that we would have supposed they already had; and that we want them to have—to reduce the risk of their making the mistake Hitler made when he saw us as too weak or divided to hold our own against him.

We would expect, for example, that a man like Mikoyan would certainly know, with his resources of information, what basic conditions prevail in America at any given time. Yet when he came here, Ambassador Lacy reports, he actually seemed surprised not to find the country in the grip of a major economic depression. As he traveled around, taking in facts about American life and productivity, the "remodeling" of his estimate was an almost visible process.

Again, those who came from the Soviet Union to negotiate the first exchange Agreement were unbelievably ignorant of how the government and the people are related in a free society. To quote Ambassador Lacy again, "they simply could not believe we were telling the truth when we said that under the American Constitution private citizens could not be compelled to carry out an exchange agreement made by their government. . . . When we finally convinced them on this point, they next doubted that the voluntary efforts of American private citizens and organizations could be relied on for carrying out the agreement. . . . The negotiations nearly broke down on this question . . ." (14)

But: "If the Soviet Union needed a demonstration of the genius of a free system, of the good will and good faith of a free people, they have had it." For in spite of Soviet incredulity, the Agreement has been consistently and precisely implemented by the voluntary support of individuals and groups.

We are so impressed, sometimes, with the Soviet Union's vast web of Parties, "fronts," and secret agents that we forget what history has taught us about the dictator's peculiar insulation against unpalatable facts: the reluctance of his agents to tell him what he does not want to hear; and his capacity to discredit what he does not want to believe.

Communism had added new thickness to this historic "insulation" by imposing the ideology upon it. What the dictator *does not want to believe* about the strength or stability of capitalist nations coincides precisely with what Marxism-Leninism declares to be *impossible*. Even if it appears to be true, therefore, he can rate it as only superficially so; and those who report it to be true are likely to find themselves branded as "unreliable": not faithful to the doctrine. If we can make realities, directly encountered, cut through this insulation and reach the minds of even a few high-ranking Communists, the world will be that much less likely to be plunged into war by their underestimation of us.

Finally, exchange programs and delegations are the best means currently at our disposal for preventing the Soviet and

Soviet bloc citizen from being made into Communist man. When we say this, we are not saying that those who go into the orbit under exchange agreements should foment trouble or try to set the people against the Party or State. The task is an altogether different one—which can be performed without in the least straining the terms of the agreement. It can be performed by individual tourists in chance conversations or by expert delegates, meeting with their counterparts. People qualify for this task simply by being free persons who value and use their freedom.

The first part of the task is to remind the Soviet or bloc citizen of that "lost part of himself" to which Communism denies a right to exist: his individuality; his will to enquire and wonder; his "cosmopolitan" urge; a friendliness that resists being harnessed to the class struggle; and a compassion that does not want to be cut down to the stunted lineaments of "class morality." Our exchange teams do not need to deliver lectures on these subjects or otherwise to infringe the taboo against a "free spread of ideas." They have only to handle every subject that comes up as a free and responsible person would handle it, and then let their Soviet or bloc counterparts respond with the relevant portions of their own minds.

One of our exchange teams of psychologists, for example, had a chance to visit and compare professional undertakings with more than a hundred Soviet psychologists. Again and again, they asked about researches in the field of individual psychology and the development of personality; and they received a stereotyped answer: that such matters, in the Soviet Union, are "ideologically determined." It would have infringed the spirit of our Agreement for our psychologists to have argued this point; and they did not do so. But they were well within their rights in asking the question and *in talking about their own work:* for they were there as experts talking to counterpart experts. It would seem a safe bet that among those who gave them the stereotyped answer there were many who knew, *as psychologists,* that their truth-seeking function was being invaded by the State.

The second part of the task is to keep people in the Soviet Union, and more particularly in the satellites, tied in with the Western heritage and reminded of stakes they had in this long before Communism took over. Not even in Stalin's day were reminders of this sort lacking. Within the orbit, for example, there have always been religious leaders who have refused to forget that the boundaries of Christendom are far wider than those of the Communist empire; and scholars who have never denied the universality of the mind's domain. Outside the orbit, Radio Free Europe, RIAS, and other broadcasting stations have done their job—penetrating the "jamming" curtain; and books have never ceased to find their way across the border. But the more variously the "reminding" task and the "binding" task can be done, the better—for the more impossible it becomes for any Communist dictator again to seal off the orbit as Stalin did.

And here, we must note, the advantage is all on our side. No Soviet or satellite delegation can, by simply presenting its exchange "goods," reanimate in Western minds deep-rooted affinities with a now forbidden Communist past. There never was such a past. Communism remains, in spite of all its material strength, what it has been from the beginning: an artificially fabricated system that has always to be protecting its own "legitimacy" by warding off contacts of one sort and another.

Developments that spontaneously took place during the post-Stalin "thaw" put one fact on record: namely, that within the orbit there are multitudes of persons, many of them "good Communists," who feel the pull of the West. In late 1957, for example, Poland's Minister of Culture complained, "Books and films from the USSR and other People's Democracies have become as rare (in Poland) as Western books and films were several years ago. Such a state of affairs is, of course, abnormal." (15)

In historical perspective, such a state of affairs is, of course, normal. It is abnormal only by Communist standards—which themselves are a strange imposition upon history. Since 1957, the Polish regime has made repeated efforts to restore a "normal" balance in the materials of cultural impact. But the pull of the West has not been weakened; and by gradual stages the regime itself is implementing a trend set by the people. Alone among Communist countries, for example, it is experimenting with letting its citizens travel outside the Curtain *as private individuals*.

As matters stand, it would be irresponsible folly for any free people to pretend that exchanges, just because their materials are intrinsically those of peace, can remove themselves from the frame of *the war called peace*, and enjoy an autonomous existence. Paradoxically, however, they may yet prove to be among our best weapons for waging this strange war; for if exchanges are allowed at all, these materials cannot be prevented from reaching through to people at the level of their humanity and at the level of their professional self-respect.

Those who have negotiated and implemented exchanges for the United States, like those who have performed similar functions for other free nations, profess a working faith that is patient and unspectacular. They do not make dramatic predictions about the future course of events. But their aim is to keep the future roomy enough for creative developments to take place within the orbit *with the individual, morally responsible human mind as a prime mover*.

TWELVE

COLONIALISM: SOVIET STYLE

IN A SPEECH at the Twenty-First Congress of the Communist Party of the Soviet Union, on January 28, 1959, Khrushchev said, "There are no people more steadfast and devoted to the cause of the struggle against colonialists than communists."

On October 5, 1960, in the General Assembly of the United Nations, Australian Prime Minister Robert G. Menzies called Premier Khrushchev a hypocrite: "I venture to say it is an act of complete hypocrisy for a Communist leader to denounce colonialism as if it were an evil characteristic of the western powers, when the facts are that the greatest colonial power now existing is the Soviet Union itself."

What does the record tell us?

Pre-communist Russia, we know, had a long history of imperialist and colonialist expansion. This began in the middle of the sixteenth century, when Ivan the Terrible took Kazan. It continued with the incorporation of large numbers of Turkic peoples. A century later, Cossack and Ukrainian peoples were brought under Russian hegemony. Peter the Great incorporated the peoples along the coast of the Baltic Sea. Catherine the Great made further additions from lands to the west, including Poland. The Caucasus was added later; and the rest of Turkestan was acquired by Alexander II before the end of his reign in 1881.

"The extraordinary territorial expansion," writes Alex Inkeles, "was estimated to have proceeded at the rate of 50 square miles a day over a period of 400 years, from the end of the 15th to the end of the 19th centuries. . . . Russia was a huge colonial empire; but in distinction to the other empires of Europe, her colonial possessions were contiguous to the homeland. Thus she *incorporated* her possessions . . . within one continuous border, with the captive nations strung around the outer limits of the solid Russian core." (1)

This geographical difference between Russian colonialism and Western colonialism must be carefully noted. The Western nations went out and conquered distant peoples, thereafter ruling them from afar. Russia, pushing out from the center, simply went on *absorbing* other nations and peoples. After these had been absorbed, the old boundary lines that had set them apart simply vanished from the average map. The color of Russia on the map simply spread out over them; and, as time passed, the eye of the world was unreminded that they had ever had a separate, independent identity. Thus, Russian colonialism was far less likely to be noted and remembered than was Western colonialism.

Ask the average Westerner to name Russia's colonies. The chances are that he has never heard of them. He merely knows of a huge land, all of it seeming to be "Russia"—with snowbound Siberia a "land of exile." But this seemingly homogeneous land mass is, in fact, a congeries of many "minority" peoples. It was this congeries which the Soviet Union inherited from the Tsars—and which it would not, and still will not, surrender.

What to do with the congeries? This became a question for the Bolsheviks when they took over. All revolutionary groups in Russia had been keenly aware of Tsarist imperialism—and opposed to it. With the fall of the Tsar, early in 1917, the right of self-determination and secession was declared. The congeries promptly showed signs of coming to life. One of the early acts of the Provisional Government, under Kerensky, was to grant Poland its independence; and this act was symptomatic of the mood of the time. Independence was in the air and was taken seriously by the minority peoples.

This fact became a problem for Lenin's Bolsheviks when they overthrew the Provisional Government and seized power in the Fall of 1917. To their embarrassment, they found that ". . . in most of the national areas of the former empire the local leaders took their right of secession quite seriously . . . and viewed themselves as equals with the former leaders in Moscow . . ." (2)

In revolutionary *theory*, there was no reason why they should not thus view themselves. The Bolsheviks, however, having no intention of letting them go, "did not hesitate to use the force of arms to meet the upsurge of independence, sending their Red Armies to regain control over most of the provinces of the former empire." (3)

We do well to remind ourselves, here, that a pattern of conquest which became familiar to the world only with Stalin's take-over in East Europe actually dates from the first years after the Bolshevik *coup d'état*. It was brought into being to prevent the national minorities that had been gobbled up by Tsarist imperialism from regaining their independence.

During the period of the Provisional Government, Bolshevik organizations had been set up in the borderlands—the national minority regions—precisely as Communist Parties were later set up in non-Communist countries; and for much the same conspiratorial purposes. Later, after the Bolsheviks had seized power, these organizations cooperated with the Red Army "to overthrow, or more often to attempt to overthrow, the newly established national governments." (4) Here, in brief, was the precedent for that cooperation which the world was to witness, after the Second World War, between the Communist Parties in East Europe and Stalin's Red Army.

Also, we might note, a "creative development of Marxism" was in the making—to rob these rim countries of their theoretical as well as their practical right to self-determination. "Theory soon began to show signs of changing to something more in accordance with practice. In January 1918 Stalin asserted that independence in any particular case would only be recognized upon the demand of the working population of that area, and that self-determination must be viewed as a method of struggling for socialism." (5)

When the Constitution of the All-Russian Federal Soviet Republic was adopted, Article Two of the Constitution described the RSFSR as a "federation of national Soviet republics." This would have seemed to mean that the RSFSR, as a "federation," was a union of equal states, each with a considerable autonomy of action. But it soon became evident that the Communist conception was far from this.

The Constitution began by reaffirming the principle of self-determination and the right of secession. Promptly, however, it qualified this right on two counts. First, it "proposed" a federal union of states built on the Soviet pattern—this union to be "one of the transitional forms on the path to complete unity"; *not,* significantly, on the path to complete independence. Then, in the second place, it stated that the question of who was to be regarded as expressing the *national will* with respect to separatism must be decided, in each instance, "according to the historical stage of development of that nation."

This verbiage, decoded, meant simply that the Communist Party would decide which nations were, and were not, to enjoy the right of independence and self-determination. "This convenient formula," as Leonard Schapiro has noted, "enabled the communists during the civil war to agitate for national self-determination in territories in which they were not yet in control"—precisely as Khrushchev, today, agitates for an ending of all non-Communist colonialism. Also, however, it enabled them, "in the case of territories where they were in control, to resist nationalist movements aimed at separatism" (6)—precisely as Khrushchev, today, refuses even to discuss the right of East European countries to determine their own fate by free elections.

The subjugated nationalities, in short, in spite of their manifest wish for independence, remained subjugated. Their destiny, formerly in control of the Tsar, was now shifted to the control of the Communist Party. And "self-determination" was redefined to mean "struggling for socialism."

A clear example of what this Communist policy meant is found in the case of four of the "rim" nationalities clustered in the region of the Caspian Sea and abutting on China and Afghanistan: Kazakhstan, Kirghizia, Tadzhikistan, and Uzbekistan. These were Muslim peoples; and they hated the Russians who, for years, had been insinuating themselves into their lands. Their similarities of language and culture might quite properly have led them, after the fall of the Tsar, to unite in some kind of federated state, and to break away from the Soviet Union.

The Bolsheviks, however, had other thoughts in mind; and they thought quickly. Realizing that they could not afford either to lose these Muslim territories or to let them erect states that might prove hostile to the Soviet Union, they acted swiftly to put the four nationalities at odds with one another. They did this by an arbitrary realignment of frontiers, so dividing among them the rich Fergana Valley that they could not become separate, independent states without being separately impoverished; and could not readily act in common.

On this question of rearranging frontiers, Khrushchev presented a characteristic, after-the-fact Communist interpretation at the Leipzig all-German Conference of trade union and plant officials, on March 7, 1959. "The question of frontiers," he told his audience, "is one of the most acute and complicated questions inherited by us from the old capitalist world. Today, old ideas about frontiers based on bourgeois legal norms still exist. Even many communists are not free from these remnants. . . . Therefore . . . we must lead the masses patiently to the understanding of this question from the point of view of communism." (7)

Lenin and Stalin, faced by the actual desire of nationalities to achieve separatism, were not so patient. They used the Red Army to subdue the "seceders." After that, they changed the frontiers to suit their own purposes.

Khrushchev, in that same Leipzig speech, made his *apologia* for "friendly" change: ". . . the borders between the [Soviet] Union and autonomous republics integrated within the Soviet borders are gradually ceasing to mean what they used to mean. As our country moved toward socialism, the borders between its individual republics were, in fact, vanishing. . . . If you ask any Russian, Ukrainian, Byelorussian today whether the administrative boundaries of their republics are of any topical interest to them, I think most of them would be puzzled by the question. Why? I think it is because all the nations and nationalities enjoy equal rights within our socialist state; life is based on a single socialist system . . ."

This statement differs only in detail from the type that he repeatedly makes with reference to the countries that comprise the Soviet bloc. All these countries—the USSR, Hungary, Poland, Rumania, Czechoslovakia, Bulgaria, and Albania—are declared to be equals "fraternally united" within the frame of "socialist solidarity"; and all are declared to be equally disinclined toward any type of national independence which they do not now enjoy.

How did Bolshevik Russia (heir to the vast Tsarist colonial empire) treat the subject peoples on her borders? In good Tsarist fashion, the Soviet Party-State "incorporated" them into a new colonial empire; and proceeded, politically, economically, and culturally, to bend them to its will.

It sent Party chiefs—proconsuls—to rule them. In each of the so-called Republics, the first or second Party secretary was non-native and usually trained in Moscow. The Soviet government—meaning, in practice, the Central Committee and the Party—took over full direction of economic planning and development. To show their serious intention of keeping these people well subjugated, they put into effect the principle of Russification. Pressures were brought to bear against the historical, religious, and linguistic traditions of the Republics. In many cases, for example, the people were taught that their national heroes had been nothing but bandits; and the new official line was that there had always been deep love between central Asia and the Russian people.

Thus, when the struggles for independence had been brought to an end by the Red Army, and when the dust had settled, what remained was a full-blown Communist-style colonialism—far more extreme in its denial of freedom than most forms of Western colonialism; and far more ingeniously *totalitarian* in remolding native cultures to fit the Russian-

Communist pattern.

When the Soviet leaders boast, today, that the Communists control one-third of the population of the earth, these "rim" territories, denied their right of secession, should be remembered. The East European satellites need also to be remembered. These two types of "controlled" populations add up to one hundred and eighty-seven million people; and they have never been given any choice about being controlled.

Remembering the determinative part which the Red Army has played in their subjugation, we must recall the *Declaration* which Lenin, as Chairman of the Soviet of People's Commissars, piously signed on October 28, 1917: "If any nation whatsoever is detained by force within the boundaries of a certain state, and if [that nation] contrary to its expressed desire . . . is not given the right to determine the form of its state life by free voting and completely free from the presence of troops of the annexing or stronger state and without the least pressure, then the adjoining of that nation by the stronger state is annexation, i.e. seizure by force and violence." (8)

It is, we can grant, precisely that: seizure by force and violence. But within a year from the time that Lenin signed this statement, his Red Armies were in action—to prevent the "rim" nations which the Tsar had annexed from achieving their independence. And an unbroken line of Communist policy connects his sending of the Red Army into these "rim" nations with Khrushchev's sending of the Red Army into Hungary in 1956.

What makes a colony a colony? Obviously, two conditions must be present: *political domination* and *economic domination*. In the case of the "rim" countries and the satellites,

there is no question about the Soviet Union's political domination. Is there also economic domination of a kind and to
a degree that would justify our calling these countries
colonies?

Economic realities with respect to these countries have
long been blurred by Communist verbiage—just as political
realities have been blurred by the use of such labels as "Republics" and "People's Democracies." But careful studies
have been making their way into print; and these report facts
and statistics which can not only be understood but accepted
as reliable.

One such study is a book by Baymirza Hayit: *Turkestan in
XX Jahrhundert* (*Turkestan in the Twentieth Century*). The
author is a native Turkestanian who has known Soviet rule
at first hand. Also, he has had personal contacts and access
to source materials unknown to Western scholars.

Hayit shows clearly that the native economic, political,
and social structures of Turkestan have been made to fit
the "Procrustean bed of the Soviet system." By nationalizing
and redistributing land and water resources, the Soviet
government has secured control over the basic means of
production and has shattered the power of the groups most
likely to resist. By collectivizing the peasants, the government has forced them to abandon their traditional crops and
to concentrate on raising cotton. Today, the role assigned
to the inhabitants of the region is simply that of producing
the raw materials that go to supply the Soviet economic
machine.

Political domination of the region was made secure by
various devices. One was its arbitrary subdivision into
separate states. A second device was the imposing of artificial
linguistic and cultural barriers. Yet another was the planting of non-natives in all top State and Party posts—even after

natives had been admitted to the lower layers of the apparatus. Again, the educational system was re-designed to remove the young generation from the politically recalcitrant influence of their elders and to mold them according to Soviet specifications. The Muslim religion was subjected to constant pressures looking toward its eventual extirpation. Finally, periodic purges have made clear the Soviet regime's demand for conformity.

In the midst of all this, the "new lands" program brought in floods of Russian and Ukrainian settlers, these to be followed by other floods of outsiders when the irrigation projects in the central "Republics" were far enough along to effect an increase in arable lands. The native inhabitants—far from being given a first go at improved lands—have been progressively reduced to a rightless minority.

This is Soviet colonialism in Turkestan. Lenin once called the Imperial Russia of the Tsars a "prison of peoples." The Russia of the Tsars is gone; but the "prison of peoples" remains.

In October 1960, Khrushchev, at the General Assembly of the United Nations in New York, called for an immediate end to all colonialism—and took refuge in a desk-thumping fury when Menzies reminded the Assembly that the Soviet Union is now the greatest colonial empire on earth.

At that time—as now—the Soviet Union ruled over forty-nine colonial and semi-colonial territories: lands and peoples that are not free to choose their own political forms or to establish their own economic systems—and that would quickly feel the onslaught of Soviet power if they tried to do so.

The colonial territories included in the USSR are as follows:

Colonial areas	*Colonies within these areas*
Central Asia (Turkestan)	Kazakhstan, Kirghizstan, Uzbekistan, Tadzhikistan, Turkministan
Caucasus	Armenia, Azerbaijan, Georgia, Dagestan; the lands of the Chetchens, Ingush, Ossets, Kabardines, Cherkessks, et cetera
Southwest portion of the European part of the Soviet Union	Moldava, Ukraine
Miscellaneous	The Baltic States—Latvia, Lithuania, and Estonia; Komi; Yakutsk; the areas inhabited by the Mongol tribes; and other areas to the east and north

All these belong in the category of "rim" countries—the "Republics"—that appear on the map as integral parts of the USSR.

To these must be added the semi-colonial countries which, although they remain at present outside the geographical boundaries of the USSR, are politically and economically dominated by that power through the machinery of puppet regimes: Poland, Hungary, Czechoslovakia, Rumania, Bulgaria, Albania, the Soviet-occupied zone of Germany, and the Asian satellite, Mongolia.

To understand the economic grounds on which the "rim" countries are designated as colonies, we need to discover the share of their production that goes to Metropolitan Russia—and that goes *on demand,* without any element of free choice with respect to deliveries, or any chance to seek more profitable markets elsewhere.

We can start with the following basic list of products: coal, oil, iron ore, manganese ore, nonferrous and rare metals, uranium ore, gold, diamonds, wool, cotton, silk, sugar as a finished product, tea, wine, southern fruit, Indian corn, wheat, vegetable oil, and pelts. (9)

The total production percentages of these which are sent to Metropolitan Russia from Central Asia, the Caucasus, and the "rim" countries of the southwestern European part of the Soviet Union range from 58 percent to 100 percent. In fact, the metropolitan area absorbs the entire or almost the entire production of such vital items as oil, manganese ore, nonferrous and rare metals, gold, cotton, silk, sugar, Indian corn, vegetable oil, and pelts.

What this means in terms of colonialism is that, within the Soviet Union, Russia exploits the "rim" countries—which she has kept by armed force—in the precise manner in which Khrushchev continually accuses the Western powers of exploiting the backward countries: those colonies for which he demands immediate freedom. These "rim" countries are treated as "backward" sources of raw materials. In many instances, these raw materials are their prime natural resource. In other instances, as in Turkestan, the local economy is twisted out of shape and made into a one-crop economy in order to satisfy Russian demands.

We have noted earlier one reason why the Communists can never relinquish any territory over which they have asserted their control: namely, the ideological reason. The "historical process" must always be in one direction: toward the extension of Communism.

But here we note a second reason: Communism's vast program of industrial expansionism depends upon raw materials from its colonial empire. "Without its colonies, the metropolitan area would play no part in the world's economy, nor in international politics and the military field.

". . . Moscow cannot give up its colonies since, without them, it would no longer be a factor looming large in world politics and the world economy." (10)

The Communists never acknowledge that they are practicing the very type of colonialism which they denounce. Yet they are not forced, in the ordinary sense of the word, to conceal the fact. Instead, they give themselves an ideological "out." When they practice colonialism it becomes "proletarian internationalism."

Let us remind ourselves of how this formula works; for if we are to be able to counter Khrushchev's exploitation of the issue of colonialism, we must know both the facts and the rationale of the Soviet Union's own colonial practices.

The Communists' ideological goal is to make the whole world one unit, operated from one center. This type of ultimate "monolithic unity" represents their ideal. Until it has been achieved, the "historic process" is incomplete; and, until then, there can be on earth only a tactical sort of "peaceful coexistence"—not genuine peace. Each step taken toward this total unifying of the world under Communist auspices is, therefore, "progress."

Most human beings, however, do not yet recognize it as progress; for their outlooks have been distorted by "bourgeois" concepts and the "exploitative" practices of "capitalist imperialism." Only the smallest fraction of the population of a country may be "progressive." It is "correct," however, to designate this fraction, however small, as "the workers"; as "the people." Also, *because it is ready to cooperate with the Communists,* this fraction is said to voice the true, legitimate aspirations of the country; and the Soviet Union, in providing leadership and support for this Communist minority, is merely doing its "international duty." This is the precise rationale in terms of which Lenin justified his holding of the "rim" countries that had been subjugated by the Tsars and that so urgently wanted their freedom, after the fall of the Tsar, that they had to be held in line by armed force. It is also the rationale by which Stalin justified his flouting of the Yalta agreement and his converting of the East European countries into Soviet satellites. Finally, it is the rationale that enables Khrushchev, with Communist sincerity, to seek out, everywhere in the world, the power elements or dissident groups that will accept Soviet "guidance"; and to proclaim these elements to be "the people."

Now we turn from the "rim" countries—the "Republics" —to the satellites: Poland, Czechoslovakia, Hungary, Rumania, Bulgaria, Albania, the Soviet-occupied zone of Germany, and Mongolia. It is certainly an open secret by now that these countries are politically subservient to the Soviet Union. In no single one of them could the Communist regime maintain itself without Soviet support. *Therefore,* Khrushchev can rely on the puppet dictators to echo his words, to come at his call, to do his bidding—without reference to the will of the people; but, always, with the claim that those who go along with the hierarchy *are* the people. If the leaders of any ex-colonial nation are friendly with the West, Khrushchev calls them "lackeys of capitalism"—a favorite Communist term. He thus designated even Nehru in the early days of India's independence—before he decided that it would better serve Communism's ends to establish "friendship" with India. But if ever there were "lackeys" on earth, these are the puppet dictators of the satellites: lackeys of the Soviet Union.

All this is generally known, now. But what is less generally known—though the facts are amply available—is the extent to which the economies of these countries have been reduced to a colonial or semi-colonial status: the extent, that is, to which they pay tribute to the Soviet Union; and to which they have to bend their economic systems to fit into the pattern of Soviet needs.

Mongolia's relation to Moscow is not untypical. Mongolia is a country of cattle-breeders "who have to pay tribute to the metropolitan area in the form of hides, leather, wool, and other animal products." (11) And here is the colonial catch. The "deliveries" go to the Soviet Union under the label, "Exports from the People's Republic of Outer Mongolia." Actually, however, they are not exports in the normal, commercial sense. They are payments of tribute made under Soviet prescription.

The point must be emphasized that these are *deliveries* which Mongolia has no choice about making; and the payment received for them is wholly a matter of Soviet, not Mongolian, decision. This is no exceptional case. It illustrates the rule which has prevailed throughout the satellite empire ever since Stalin's take-over. These countries are said to be "fraternally related" to the Soviet Union. But they have been exploited as colonies. Their economic subservience has been fivefold in nature.

First, as we have noted, the choice of what they deliver to the Soviet Union is not their own. The delivery plan for the whole "empire" is, when all pretenses are stripped away, made in Moscow.

Second, in order that they may deliver what the Soviet Union needs, or what will fit into an orbital plan, their economies have been twisted out of any normal balance. Hence, their *political* subservience is also secured: they cannot make a strike for freedom and become self-sustaining because they have no well-rounded economic system on which to rely.

Third, the Soviet Union manipulates the prices of two-way deliveries. It has consistently paid the satellites less for materials and products delivered than these countries could secure on the world market. At the same time, it has overcharged them for products delivered to them from the Soviet Union. In brief, it has collected tribute money from them, and continues to do so.

Fourth, the workers in the satellites have been both underpaid and coerced into filling production norms set in Moscow. Hence, the strikes that have so upset the regime: in East

Berlin and the Soviet zone of Germany in 1953; in Poland, Hungary, and elsewhere. These strikes are never—as in the capitalist countries—against local owners of factories, because there are none. They are against the regime that *owns all*.

Finally, the economies of these countries are being forced, today, to underwrite Khrushchev's world-wide plan for achieving Communism's victory by means of "peaceful competition." Here, because of its industrial plant, Czechoslovakia has been most conspicuously exploited. When Khrushchev sees a chance, anywhere on earth, to effect economic penetration, Czechoslovakia is supposed to do its "international duty." It is supposed, in brief, to deliver the goods in requisite type and amount—and without regard for whether or not what is thus taken out of the country is needed by the Czechoslovakian people themselves.

Various of the satellites are strikingly different from most colonies in the modern world. Both Western colonies in Asia and Africa and the "rim" colonies of the Soviet Union have been chiefly sources of raw materials. But countries like Czechoslovakia, the Soviet zone of Germany, and Hungary are valuable to the Soviet Union chiefly because they have industrial plants and precision workers. They belong "to that certain type of work colonies in which the working power and intelligence of the population are being exploited by an alien conqueror. Analogous cases of subjugation and exploitation of culturally superior countries through culturally inferior peoples are to be found frequently in history." (12)

Rome, for example, got scholars and skilled artisans, rather than raw materials, from Greece. Russia gets its telecommunications equipment from highly skilled Hungary. And that is by no means all that it gets. Khrushchev's Seven Year Plan for the economic development of the Soviet Union is supported by plans for a wide range of specified deliveries from the satellites. Thus, it is decreed that industrial exports from Hungary to the Soviet Union will increase by 60 percent for the period 1961–1965. During this span of years, the satellite is to deliver 121 ocean-going ships and river boats, 193 diesel locomotives, 5500 metal-cutting machine tools, and telecommunications equipment in the value of 785 million rubles; and these items by no means exhaust the list of what is being requisitioned to help "prove" that the Soviet Union, because it is a Communist country, can outproduce any capitalist country. What it actually proves is the ancient and tedious fact that an imperial power can grow strong at the expense of its colonies.

One further part of this story remains to be told: the story of COMECON. Established in 1949, COMECON—an all-over economic organization for the Soviet bloc—was Communism's reaction to the Marshall Plan, which was dramatically helping to revitalize the economies of Western Europe. Both Poland and Czechoslovakia had indicated their desire to join in the Marshall Plan, and had been accepted: a fact which Stalin found intolerable. He could not expediently, however, force them to renounce their association with the Plan without offering an alternative. He projected, therefore, a plan for the Soviet bloc, calling it a plan for "broad economic collaboration" and "mutual aid on a basis of equality of rights." COMECON was to organize and administer this plan.

"The stated purpose is to weld the separate nationalities of the Satellites into one commonwealth based on international cooperation and division of labor. . . . In theory at least, the Communist Eight (including the USSR) are out to secure some of the classic advantages of free trade within the framework of national economic planning." (13)

In practice, however, three obstacles have stood in the way of the success of this collaborative endeavor. The first can presumably be overcome: the ignorance and relative impotence of the planning authorities. The second is harder to overcome, because it is rooted in Marxist-Leninist theory: namely, the complete absence of the self-adjusting mechanism of free prices and flexible monetary systems. The third, which reduces collaboration to a shabby pretense, is the vested, monopolistic interests of a State ownership that centers in the USSR.

Thus, in 1956–1957, "Soviet dictation was the basic means of allocating economic tasks and the USSR was not above using the full leverage of its superior economic resources to bring the smaller countries into 'unanimous' agreement. When a country demurred at a Soviet order to undertake or to abandon a given line of production, the Soviet Union threatened to stop deliveries of vital raw materials. In one instance cited, when Poland refused to drop its automobile industry the USSR put a ban on purchases of Polish automobiles by other COMECON members." (14)

There simply is no basic resemblance between, for example, the Common Market Six and the COMECON Eight. The Common Market is a freely willed economic collaboration of free nations; COMECON is a contrived, Soviet-controlled arrangement for a bloc of nations that are elaborately proclaimed to be "sovereign" but that are never permitted to take issue with the plans of the USSR.

More recently, to ease national discontents, the Soviet Union has refined its heavy-handed methods: it is offering certain projects for competitive bidding among the satellites, the assignments to go to those who promise to complete the tasks most quickly and cheaply. But the spirit of colonialism still prevails: *such projects as no one of the satellites voluntarily chooses to undertake are simply assigned by Soviet fiat.* So much for the vaunted "equality" and "national sovereignty" that COMECON promises.

With his Humpty-Dumpty genius for making words say what he wants them to say, Khrushchev declared in Moscow, on November 6, 1957, that the "shameful [colonial] system is on the way to complete liquidation." At the General Assembly of the United Nations, in October 1960, he demanded its prompt and final ending.

But the world is learning to listen *to what he does not say.* He did not remind his hearers that, since the Second World War, the Western colonial powers have granted independence to more than 750 million people in thirty countries; and that yet other peoples are slated for independence within the next two years. What Khrushchev demands has, in brief, been brought close to fulfillment *so far as the Western powers are concerned.*

But if he did not remind his hearers of this fact, neither did he remind them of the Soviet Union's war and postwar record of empire-building. He did not recall how, during the period of the Hitler-Stalin pact, and under cover of "mutual nonaggression treaties," Stalin had added the Estonians, Latvians, and Lithuanians to that long list of subject peoples which the Soviet Union had already taken over from the Tsarist empire—and to which, by force of arms, it had denied that right of self-determination which Communists preach to the non-Communist world. Neither did he describe for his hearers Stalin's methods of take-over in East Europe or the present disguised colonial status of the satellites. He did not discuss the degree of "independence" and "national sovereignty" that are enjoyed by Outer Mongolia, North Korea, and North Vietnam.

What he did not say is, however, precisely what all free

people must learn to say—and to say with chapter and verse at their command. They must learn to specify the difference between the ex-imperialism of the West and the obdurately entrenched imperialism of the Soviet Union: an imperialism, moreover, that is committed to ever greater expansion over the face of the earth.

Khrushchev has unwittingly told the world that the Soviet Union is vulnerable on this count: that while it needs to squeeze the last possible atom of propaganda value out of Western colonialism, it needs no less to conceal the fact of Soviet colonialism. This is what was "said" by his desk-thumping response to Menzies, at the General Assembly of the United Nations. This is what was "said" by his shouting fury against the Philippine representative's reference to Soviet colonialism as among the kinds that should be eliminated.

It does not take a master psychologist to recognize that something is amiss when the only response that any Communist leader seems able to make to the charge of Soviet colonialism is desk-thumping, name-calling, and shouting. The lack of an alternative answer cannot be ascribed to Khrushchev's personal temperament. For it was not Khrushchev, but the Soviet Ambassador to Bonn, Andrei Smirnov, who screamed and waved his fists under the nose of West German Economics Minister Ludwig Erhard, on October 21, 1960. Erhard, speaking to the inaugural session of the German-African Society, had declared that there was "no worse colonialism" anywhere than that which the Soviet Union has practiced. And Smirnov's "answer," in Bonn, was identical with Khrushchev's "answer" to similar challenges at the United Nations in New York: namely, an uncontrollable—or calculated—outburst of rage.

If the Soviet record will stand examination, why do not Khrushchev, Smirnov, and their fellow Communist leaders welcome every chance to examine it in the eyes of the world? Why do they have to resort to rage and shouting as diversionary tactics?

The fact which they can in nowise escape is that the record will *not* stand examination by any save Communist minds: minds already converted to the Marxist-Leninist concept of "proletarian internationalism." And these already-converted minds are not the target of Khrushchev's anti-imperialist propaganda. He cannot afford to have the newly liberated countries of Asia and Africa, or the peoples of any other target country, know the exact processes by which Communism's domain has been extended. Neither can he afford to have them know the extent of the Soviet Union's continued political-economic domination over countries to which it claims to be "fraternally related." What he cannot afford to have these countries know is precisely what we must learn to say to them; and to say with facts enough at our command that we do not need to thump the desk and grow red in the face with angry shouting.

THIRTEEN

THE PARTY'S WAR
AGAINST THE PEOPLE

IN PRESENTING his Seven Year Plan, Khrushchev stressed, as he has on many occasions, the "boundless love" of the Soviet people for the Communist Party.

To prove the existence of this love, he said, "The elections to the U.S.S.R. Supreme Soviet in March 1958 were a most vivid manifestation of the triumph of social democracy. Over 133 million people, almost 100 percent of the total voters, cast their votes for the candidates of the people's bloc . . . The wonderful results of the elections . . . show convincingly the working people's universal support and ardent approval of the policy of our Leninist Party, the monolithic and unbreakable cohesion of all the peoples of the Soviet Union around the Communist Party." (1)

How were they conducted—these elections which "convincingly" showed so much? In his *Main Street, U.S.S.R.*, Irving R. Levine provides an eye-witness account:

"Every Soviet citizen has the right to vote, beginning at the age of eighteen. Everyone is expected to vote. To make sure that everyone does, *agitpunks* are set up in libraries, museums, hotels, concert halls, and apartment houses . . .

"On election day the polls open at 6 A.M. and close at midnight. At a polling place in the Sovietskiy district, only a short way from the Kremlin, election workers sat at tables with huge books in front of them with the names of voters in the district. As a voter entered he (or she) walked to a sign indicating the initial of his last name and presented any identification, such as a trade-union card or factory pass; the name was then checked against the residence list. The voter received one ballot for each of the two chambers elected."

This description *so far* is unremarkable. The citizen has entered the polling place and identified himself. His name has been checked, and he has received his two ballots—each of them listing the candidates for one chamber of the Supreme Soviet.

At a point comparable to this, the voter in an American election would disappear into a polling booth, there to register his private choices of candidates. And this is the point at which a free electoral system and the Soviet electoral system sharply diverge.

Levine continues: "At the far end of the room, under a silver-colored bust of Lenin and bordered by pots of flowering plants, stood two sealed ballot boxes watched over by an unsmiling, bespectacled attendant. The voter folded the ballot papers and dropped one through the slot of each of the boxes."

This, significantly, is all that he did with the ballots. "It's made just as simple as possible for the voter. He doesn't have to mark the ballot in any way. No need to write *Da*. Just take the ballot, drop it into the box, and it will be counted as a gesture of assent for the approved candidates on the list. It's explained that there's no reason for *choice* of candidates because all elements of the populace are represented in the best possible way by the candidates nominated. There's no room for opposition candidates because the people are unanimous in following the leadership of the Communist Party. This is the rationale of the Communist."

We must hark back, however, to Khrushchev's statement that "almost 100 per cent of the total voters" had cast their ballots for "the candidates of the people's bloc." How does that *almost* come in? What provision does the Soviet system make for dissent?

Levine answers this question: "Three green-curtained voting booths of telephone-booth size were available against one wall, where the voter might register disapproval of the candidate by crossing out his name or writing another name. While I watched, no one availed himself of the privilege . . ."

Khrushchev, we must suppose, would say that no one availed himself of the privilege of dissent because no one wanted to do so. All were satisfied that those Party officials *who already held power* had "selflessly" exercised the best possible judgment in making up the slate of future officeholders.

But two other reasons for the manifest "unanimity" suggest themselves. First, no alternative candidates had been given any chance to make themselves or their viewpoints known to the public. And secondly, as Levine notes, anyone who entered a booth would conspicuously brand himself as a non-conformist; and "an agitator might at the very least pay the dissident a visit to inquire into the nature of his objections to the approved candidates." (2)

Only a dissenter, in brief, casts a "secret ballot" in the Soviet Union; and the process by which he can do so is far from secret. The results of his doing so, moreover, are likely to extend far beyond the polling place and the election day. In a country where every citizen's record is on file; where any act of dissent is likely to start a broad inquiry into a person's total behavior; and where a manifest desire for privacy has become a sign that a person has something to hide, only the peculiarly naive or stouthearted voter is likely, ballot in hand, to turn aside from the straight, watched-over line that leads to the ballot box.

At best, his dissent would be only a gesture. It could not influence the outcome of the election. At worst, it could become the focal act around which other evidences of his "nonconformity" would be made to cluster—thus putting in jeopardy the whole pattern of his daily life.

Because physical terrorism has declined in the Soviet Union, we are tempted to believe that the people are on the way toward gaining an ever greater measure of genuine freedom. But the weight of evidence is to the contrary. They remain a basically unfree people because they remain a *watched* people.

Joseph Novak, in *The Future Is Ours, Comrade,* reports his findings with respect to the watched-over character of daily life in a Soviet apartment house—though today the house committee is not, as in Stalin's day, designed "simply to denounce tenants, to spy on them, to provoke them, to play off one against another. . . .

"In one apartment, where I lived longer than in most, I was told about an incident which had taken place two months before my arrival. It wasn't considered exceptional by my hosts.

" 'It concerned the B. family, who had lived two flights below us,' my hosts said. 'You couldn't imagine a quieter, more average and normal man than B., who worked in an office.' His wife was a saleswoman in a store. Their eighteen-year-old son, a member of the Lenin Young Communist League—Komsomol—worked in a garage as a mechanic and went to night school. The family occupied a tiny room in a five-room apartment. All the other tenants had to pass through it to reach their rooms."

One day B. had a private quarrel with an office colleague —who brought the matter to the attention of the trade union, charging that B. had insulted him, "a socialist citizen and union activist." The case was referred to the personnel department, which looked into B.'s record and noted that he was listed as politically "passive": as a person who "avoided social work." The record contained nothing, however, on which a valid complaint could be based.

The chief of personnel, therefore, "wrote to the house committee asking for data on the 'normal and political life of B. and his family.'

"The chairman of the house committee investigated." But "B. had the reputation of a quiet man. The committee wasn't able to dig up anything against him immediately . . ."

The word *immediately* is significant; for it points to the reason why the decline of overt terrorism has not put an end to the people's endemic uneasiness. B. was rated as politically "passive," while the charge against him was brought by an "activist." *Therefore,* the house committee kept the charge open and watched for evidence that might be counted against him.

B. realized that he was being watched, and his tension mounted accordingly—to a point where, one day, he accused a co-tenant of "hanging around" to spy on him. The co-tenant, offended, was so violent in his reaction that a brawl ensued. "A few days later a meeting of the union passed a resolution, based on the opinion of the house committee, asking the personnel department to discharge B. He was charged with 'violation of the moral unity of Soviet Society; an antagonistic attitude toward co-citizens, unworthy of a socialist citizen.'

"After some days B. received orders from the factory management transferring him to duty in a remote corner of the U.S.S.R. His wife was transferred too, to 'avoid separating a socialist family.' But their son remained in Moscow . . ." (3)

This type of story has been verified many times over. The most appalling thing about it, in fact, is that the average Soviet citizen regards it as unexceptional; and that the average Party official would see nothing about it that called for concealment. The procedure with respect to B. was "correct."

But let us suppose, now, that when the personnel department first looked into B.'s record, after his strictly private quarrel with a fellow office worker, it had turned up a report that in the elections to the U.S.S.R. Supreme Soviet, in March 1958, B. had availed himself of the privilege of casting a "secret"—that is, a dissenting—ballot.

Let us suppose, further, that when he was subsequently called upon by a "solicitous" Party agitator, who had inquired into his reasons for being dissatisfied with "the candidates of the people's bloc," he had not only criticized some of these candidates but had said that it was cynical nonsense for the Party to provide for a "secret ballot" and then investigate a citizen's use of it.

This fact, added to that of his office quarrel, would have been enough to insure his vocational exile to a remote part of the U.S.S.R. Lenin and his fellow revolutionaries bitterly denounced the Tsar's sending of political prisoners to Siberia. But the Communist Party has never abandoned the practice.

Under Stalin, virtually anyone could be branded as a political offender on any pretext and sent to a slave labor camp. Multitudes were sent, in fact, for no better reason than that Stalin wanted to rid himself of their presence. Thus, after the Red Army took over the eastern part of Poland, during the period of the Stalin-Hitler pact, more than a million and a half Poles were sent to Siberia—simply because Poland was too full of Poles to be effectively Sovietized. The efficient executioner of Stalin's order to get these million and a half human beings out of Poland and into Siberia, where they could swell the supply of expendable labor, was Khrushchev—who claims the spotlight, today, as spokesman for "peace," "anti-colonialism," and the right of all people to "self-determination."

The population of slave labor camps has now been markedly decreased. But Khrushchev has his own agricultural and industrial program for the remote areas of the U.S.S.R.; and he has his own favored way—that of the arbitrary job-transfer —of getting workers to where he needs them, and where they do not want to go. He does not call these people political prisoners—or prisoners of any sort. But to suffer an imposed "exile" they do not have to be revolutionaries, or even outright critics of the regime. It is enough for them to be politically "passive" and "non-conformist."

Here we must return to the matter of elections; for only if we understand both the process and the rationale of the Soviet electoral system can we understand the nature of either totalitarian Communism or of the Party's unremitting, undeclared war against the people.

Stalin was frank to admit, after World War II, that the Communists could not win by majority vote in any country of East Europe or in the Soviet zone of Germany. Therefore, he refused to hold any type of election that could go against them—his pledge at Yalta notwithstanding. Khrushchev has continued his policy of refusal.

To our Western minds, this has signified that the Communists, where they hold power, will not tolerate free elections unless they are sure they can win. Or, in reverse, we assume that they would gladly hold such elections—thereby validating their regime and confounding their critics—if they were sure they could win.

Two historic cases, both mentioned in earlier chapters, seem to support this view. First, Lenin, after the *coup d'état*, went ahead with the election for the Constituent Assembly which had been scheduled by the displaced Provisional Government; and, second, Stalin agreed to one free election, under the four-power Kommandatura, for members of the Municipal Council of Greater Berlin. The Communists lost disastrously in both elections and have not tolerated any other free elections within their orbit.

Does this mean that if they had won—and particularly if Lenin's Bolsheviks had won in 1917—they would have gone on holding free elections after they came to power? A victory at the polls would have let them establish a legitimate government. Would it have moved them to build into their system the machinery of free elections and to abide by the expressed will of the people—win or lose? Or to come up to date, is Khrushchev now so "liberalizing" the system as to justify hope that the Communists intend, eventually, to submit their case to the people in a free election?

The "ifs" of history remain "ifs." But nothing in Communist pronouncements or policies, past or present, encourages us to answer *Yes* to any of the above questions. There is weighty evidence to suggest that the answer is *No*.

For one thing, there is the ineradicable fact that in both cases where they countenanced the holding of free elections, they refused to abide by the outcome. Lenin's Bolsheviks broke up the duly elected Constituent Assembly at the point of the bayonet. Stalin's Communists could not thus break up the duly elected Municipal Council, because of the presence in Berlin of British, French, and American forces. But they undertook both to obstruct the work of the Council and to maneuver themselves into all strategic posts. A Party which "believes" in the rules of a political system *only when it wins under these rules* does not believe in them at all.

This is the essence of the matter. The Bolshevik-Communist Party cannot believe in free elections because it strongly *disbelieves* in the type of relationship which such elections would establish between the Party and the people. Long before the Bolshevik defeat at the polls, in 1917—as far back indeed, as 1901–1902—Lenin had made plain that the Party must never think of itself as merely equal with other parties. Its task, always and everywhere, was to organize and lead all other groups.

Under the special conditions of 1917, it would have been *expedient* for the Bolsheviks to win—as they thought they could—in a free election. It would have given them an advantageous position from which to work for the consolidation of their power. It would have postponed the civil war long enough for Lenin to organize his Red Army and his secret police—the Cheka. It would presumably have meant recognition of the Soviet regime by the Western powers. The United States, for example, after the fall of the Tsar, had been quick to recognize the Provisional Government. Even if it regretted the fall of this first revolutionary government in Russia, it would have felt bound to respect the outcome of a free election. Thus, Lenin had everything to gain and nothing to lose by trying for a victory at the polls. But when his Bolsheviks lost, he did not hesitate: he prepared to seize power by armed force.

Stalin, too, would have found it *expedient* to win control of the Municipal Council of Greater Berlin by means of an election the outcome of which the Western powers would have had to respect. With his Party thus in a position of strength, he could have postponed his break with these powers—and have given the Communists a "legal" chance to obstruct the development of a non-Communist order in the Western sectors of the city. But when the Communists lost in the election, Stalin was no more hesitant than Lenin had been about flouting the outcome of that election.

Three Leninist statements are much to the point, here. Lenin, we recall, decided to force a "Marxist" revolution in a Russia that was not, by Marx's standards, ready for it. To get over this ideological hurdle, he identified his Bolshevik Party with the working class—designating it as the "progressive element" of this class. Thereafter, whenever it suited his convenience to do so, he used the words *party* and *class* as synonymous. Stalin carried forward this semantic practice; and Khrushchev still adheres to it.

After the *coup d'état* of 1917, Lenin set forth in unequivocal terms the role of this party-called-class: "The class which took political power into its hands"—flouting the outcome of a free election—"did so knowing that it took power *alone*. This is part of the concept of the dictatorship of the proletariat. This concept has meaning only when the single class knows that it alone is taking political power in its hands, and does not deceive itself and others with talk about 'popular government elected by all, sanctified by the whole people.' " (4)

The will of "the whole people" he dismissed as irrelevant: "The question is not one of numbers, but of giving correct expression to the ideas and policy of the truly revolutionary proletariat." (5)

As for a pro-Communist majority, this was to be regarded not as a means of achieving power, but as something for the Party to create *after* seizing power: "In order to win the majority of the population to its side, the proletariat must first of all overthrow the bourgeoisie and seize state power and, secondly, it must introduce Soviet rule, smash to pieces the old state apparatus, and thus at one blow undermine the rule, authority and influence of the bourgeoisie." (6)

These Leninist definitions and injunctions serve to underscore a point that is hard for our Western minds to grasp: namely, that Khrushchev, *as a Communist,* could not hold a free election in the Soviet Union even if he could be dead sure that "the candidates of the people's bloc" would win by a landslide; and that similar lists of favored candidates would win hands down in every election throughout the foreseeable future. For more would be at stake than winning or losing in any number of elections.

Even to schedule a free election would mean granting an organized minority a right to exist. The Party might win by an overwhelming majority. But afterward it would have to take some practical account of a minority, however small, that had polled enough votes to impress upon the public mind the fact of its existence. How should it deal with such a minority? Should the Communist Party learn to live side by side with it—thereby undermining the whole system of democratic centralism, and repudiating Lenin's edict that the "class which took political power into its hands did so knowing that it took power *alone*"? Or should it liquidate the minority—thereby advertising to the Soviet people and the whole world that the free election had been a farce?

Even to schedule such an election would, in short, be *ideologically* wrong; and no victory at the polls, however sweeping, could make it ideologically "correct." The Communist Party has no concept of itself except as a "vanguard" party. It is self-designated as the most advanced element in society. It has a "duty" to perform which it cannot shirk, share, delegate, or permit to be wrested from its hands: the "duty," namely, of steadily moving the world in the one direction which "history" has set. That is, toward Communism's ultimate take-over.

For this Party to countenance, in a country in which it had once assumed power, an election in which it had to go out and argue its case against an opposition party, thus bidding for the support of the people instead of imposing its will, would be an act of irreparable "revisionism." It would introduce into the one-directional "historic process" the idea that "retrogression" could be valid. It would, in short, introduce the possibility of a "reactionary" party's winning out over the "advanced" Party: the "truly revolutionary proletariat."

Khrushchev never misses a chance to call the Communist Party a Leninist Party. As such, it has only two proper roles to perform: a conspiratorial role within non-Communist countries, where it may exploit parliamentary processes to its own ends; and a totalitarian role within Communist countries. Its own concept of itself precludes its accepting any third role or its honoring the outcome of any election that thrusts a third role upon it.

"When the Western proposal for free elections as a means of unifying Germany was under discussion at the Geneva Conference of 1955," writes Irving Levine, "Mr. Harold Macmillan, then British Foreign Secretary, is said to have countered the objection of V. Molotov, then Soviet Foreign Minister, by declaring, 'It's too bad, Mr. Molotov, that you've never had any experience with free elections. It would do you good to run for office.'

" 'Why?' demanded Molotov.

" 'Because,' said Macmillan, 'you would be defeated.' " (7)

Molotov's answer is not reported. But had he given an answer consistent with Communism's record, he would have replied, "Then I, with the support of the Red Army, would nullify the outcome of the election."

To "justify" this answer, he could have quoted a passage from Lenin to which we have referred in an earlier chapter:

"They imagine that serious political questions can be decided by voting. As a matter of fact, such questions, when they have been rendered critical by the struggle, are decided by civil war." (8)

It would not have been expedient for Molotov thus to answer Macmillan; so we can assume that he did not do so. Yet this has been, in word and act, Communism's reply to a defeat at the polls.

In view of all this, why are elections held in the Soviet Union; and why are all the people urged and prodded into voting when they are not given any choice of candidates or any real chance for dissent?

The world has had dictatorships aplenty in which the populace has been given no voice in the selection of its rulers or in the shaping of policy; and in which there has been no pretense of its having such a voice. What is it that so distinguishes a Communist regime from dictatorships of this kind that a *ritualized unanimity* must periodically be sought by means of a no-choice election? How does Khrushchev—with Communist sincerity—manage to convert the outcome of a rigged election into a "convincing" proof of the people's "boundless love" for the Party?

Anyone who studies Marxist-Leninist writings becomes aware that he has moved into a closed, impervious universe of circular reasoning. Within this universe, the Communist Party is, on its own testimony, the most "advanced" element of human society. Whatever it decides to do is, therefore, "advanced"—and cannot be otherwise, because the "advanced" Party would neither stumble into "retrogressive" action nor be deliberately guilty of it.

This type of circular reasoning has almost endless applications. A certain group, for example, in a non-Communist country is designated as "progressive" for no other reason

than *because it is pro-Communist*. Once it has been so designated, however, the Communists support it *because it is
"progressive."*

In parallel manner, a Soviet election is so set up that the
only possible outcome is a virtually unanimous vote in favor
of "the candidates of the people's bloc"; and then this inevitable outcome is hailed as proof that, on the verdict of the
people, the Party nominated exactly the right candidates.

There is no way in which normal logic can penetrate the
ideologically bounded universe of Communist discourse. But
with respect to elections, one question persists: why does the
Party bother to provide itself, every so often, with such an
elaborate "popular" confirmation of candidates and policies
which have been decided upon in advance and which the
public would not be permitted to oppose?

One reason—although one which no Communist would
give—is that the Party is a usurper and can never acknowledge this fact even to itself. In objective terms, it became a
usurper on January 18, 1918—when Lenin's Bolsheviks broke
up the Constituent Assembly. On that date, the Party took by
force what the people had denied to it at the polls. In ideological terms, however, it had become a usurper long before
that. It became so when Lenin declared his handful of zealots
to be, in effect, the working class; and when he stated that
they knew better what was good for the people than the
people themselves could know.

At that point, the Bolshevik-Communist Party undertook to
walk the path of usurpation all the way to history's ending;
but to walk it, not as mere power-seekers, but as "vanguard"
creators of "a new heaven and a new earth." In behalf of the
people, it displaced the people.

Toward what kind of ending can such a course of usurpation move? The Communists can accept no ending save one
which would prove that they never had been usurpers at all;

that they had been correct from the beginning in their claim that, even though they took power *alone*, they truly represented the people.

So far as they are concerned, therefore, not the Party but the people—first, in the Soviet Union, but eventually everywhere on earth—must bear the burden of proof. They must be brought to the point where they will voluntarily hail the Party's decision to act in their name; and where they will recognize that the only freedom worth their having is to be found in productive dedication of themselves to tasks set by the Party.

"The view of human nature held by Soviet leaders," writes Hadley Cantril, in his *Soviet Leaders and Mastery over Men,* "is an odd and dangerous blend of utopianism and cynicism. In their official utterances, Soviet leaders are optimists who seem to think that man can do anything. But in actual practice these same leaders play on all of man's weaknesses and seem to regard him as a pretty poor creature indeed." (9)

This statement sums up the two-fold character of the Marxist-Leninist tussle with the nature of man, and, therefore, with the generations of living men and women in whom this nature has been embodied.

From Marx to Khrushchev, the Communists have been optimistic in words; for words have been the pliant raw material out of which they have fashioned an order of things to meet their own specifications. While they have talked this new order of things into being, making it whole and perfect in its simplicity, and in the mutual adjustment of all its parts, they have also talked themselves into believing in it.

Convinced of its rightness, then—because how can the whole and perfect be wrong?—they have undertaken to duplicate their verbal universe in the tough, complex, resistant stuff of reality. This has brought them up against the human being who is always more than the "productive unit" for which alone they have provided in their verbal system; and, at the same time, always less than the happy, cooperative, diligent, "scientific" man of their vision.

Thus, for the Communist world-makers, *man as he is* always represents a letdown from *man as he should be*. Identifying their own neat concept of *man as he should be* with *man as he would want to be if he were not so blind and distorted,* they undertake to make him over. Setting their sights by an image which they themselves have created out of the pliant material of language, they demand that the living individual be compliant enough to let them superimpose this image upon his nature.

The Communists, as we have noted, like the word *patience.* They can afford to wait, they maintain, because history is on their side. Yet their prime characteristic is their ruthless impatience with the growth processes of organic life and the evolutionary processes of society. The model of their universe is a vast, perfectly functioning machine. The parts of a machine, however, do not become unique selves by some mysterious process of growth, some interplay between inner and outer compulsion. Rather, they are made; and they are made to fit in where they belong, and to render the service for which they are designed. If they are faulty, they are cast aside.

Even the Communists have to recognize in practice that the man they have to deal with in the real world is never the exact counterpart of that "productive unit" which their theory conceives. The respects in which he differs from this unit are not, however, taken to be as important as the respects in which he corresponds to it—or can be made to correspond to it. They are, in effect, irrelevant; and they can justifiably be liquidated by the twin methods of *coercion* and *conditioning.*

In Marxist-Leninist theory, and also in Communist practice, coercion is justified by the present distorted condition of man's being. This distortion, the Communists say, has been wrought by "capitalist imperialist exploitation." It is so great that neither "bourgeois" man nor the Soviet man who is still marred by "bourgeois remnants" in his makeup can recognize that what is being done *to him* by the Party is, in fact, being done *for him.* Until he can recognize and appreciate this, coercion must remain one instrument of his redemption. In the long run, however, coercion will be rendered obsolete by the cumulative effects of conditioning. In order that man may become Communist man, all the factors by which he is shaped must be so controlled that he is brought to share that vision of the good which is presently in the Party's keeping.

"If the word 'freedom' is looked up in the standard Soviet dictionary," Cantril reminds us, "the definition is given as *'the recognition of necessity.'*" (10) By virtue of its "advanced" insight, the Communist Party must assert and defend its right to define what is necessary. This is the basic respect in which it must take power *alone.* "A person is free, then, to the extent that he understands why the Party line is right." (11) He becomes more nearly "free" whenever he performs an act that makes him identify his own good with the Party line. He manifests his "freedom" whenever he indicates in any approved fashion—from diligence on the job to the casting of a vote—that such identification has taken place.

The ballots, therefore, properly folded, are dropped into the boxes by one hundred and thirty-three million persons who take the straight, watched-over course that is marked out for them: one hundred and thirty-three million individuals who are presumed to signal by this act that they are on the way to becoming Communist man. And what Khrushchev draws forth from the ballot boxes which have thus been ritualistically filled is "convincing" evidence of the people's "boundless love" for the Party.

FOURTEEN

THE MAKING OF COMMUNIST MAN

IF MAN IS simply a material object in a material universe, there is no logical reason why a new model should not be turned out from time to time: a more efficient model, to keep pace with the efficiencies of science and technology in other fields.

The belief in such new human models has, from the beginning, been implicit in Communist thought. Marx saw capitalism as the agent of change for the modern period. As it matured, it would automatically produce the class-conscious proletarian. Having been mass-produced by the system, not "custom made" by individual experience, this new type would be remarkably standardized. No matter how many units were turned out, they would all be sufficiently *of one mind* to exert mass pressure for revolution. Revolution would change the mode of production, from capitalism to Communism. The new mode of production would thereupon turn out yet another human type: Communist man.

Lenin accepted this basic pattern of "fated" advance. But

he introduced, as we have noted, a new coercive agent of change: the elite Party. This Party was presumed to know both the model of man that should come next on the agenda of history and how to turn out this model on a mass scale.

For Lenin, as for Marx and Engels, the actual process of transformation, for man and society alike, was incredibly simple. It was, in fact, so simple when viewed in his mind's eye that he expected the earth and the inhabitants thereof to be remade in a few years' time. Lenin's era was that in which the Communist dogma first collided with the practicalities of psycho-social-economic life; and, significantly, it became an era, not of dogma re-examined, but of *utopia postponed.*

Again and again, Lenin had reluctantly to extend the time that would be required to put the human scene in order. For nothing in the world of economic processes and man's behavior turned out to be as simple as everything was in his vision and that of his fellow Bolsheviks.

The prime necessity, in Lenin's view, was to get hold of the means of production. The next step would be to eliminate the capitalist "anarchy" of competing plans and to shape up one all-embracing plan—first, for the Soviet Union, but soon for the whole world: "the more *comprehensive* the plan, the *easier* it would be to operate." (1)

With this much accomplished, the rest would be child's play. It would almost literally be child's play; for Lenin contended that *anyone* could operate an economic order that was correctly set up. The entire plan could be directed from one center; and this center would be primarily concerned with the statistics of material resources, needs to be satisfied, and the allocation of tasks.

Capitalism had already brought large-scale production into being. Therefore, said Lenin—before the Bolshevik *coup d'état* brought him up against the problem of actually making an economic system work—"the great majority of the functions of the old 'state power' have become so simplified and can be reduced to such simple operations of registration, filing, and checking that they will be quite within the reach of every literate person." (2)

In view of the fact that one of the most difficult problems for a Communist system to handle has turned out to be the allocation and flow of capital, it is interesting to recall that Lenin viewed this problem as simplicity itself. Capitalism had brought large banks into being. The Communists, therefore, had only to take over the banking system *"ready-made* from capitalism." They could then *"chop off* that which capitalistically disfigures this otherwise excellent apparatus and make it even *larger* . . . as huge as possible." (3)

The all-embracing plan, in short, once it had been correctly designed, would do the real work. So little managerial skill would be required, according to Lenin, that the workers would take turns operating the system. They would take turns, in fact, at all the tasks required by the system; and in this process, "bourgeois" man would be transmuted into Communist man.

This new man would have two prime characteristics. First, by both education and job experience, he would be *omnicompetent.* Division of labor, said Lenin, would be abolished. Schools, aiming at the *"all-around* development" of students, would produce "people *able to do everything."* (4) In the second place, because of his experience of taking turns on all kinds of jobs, managerial and productive alike, Communist man would have a thorough understanding of the all-over plan and would ask for no higher form of satisfaction than to do what it required of him.

Elliot R. Goodman, in *The Soviet Design for a World State,* recalls the manner in which Bukharin, one of Lenin's chief co-thinkers about the Communist future, viewed the relation-

THE MAKING OF COMMUNIST MAN

ship of plan to worker: "Everyone would become accustomed 'from childhood onward' to live according to this plan, would understand that 'life goes easier when everything is done according to a prearranged plan,' so that the social order moved 'like a well-oiled machine.' In 'the entire mechanism of social production there will no longer be anything mysterious, incomprehensible, or unexpected.' " (5)

Lenin found out that both the "mechanism of social production" and the nature of man contained a great deal that was "unexpected"—and also obdurate. The consequences of what he did, and what he did not do, as a result of this discovery are with us still. They were carried forward into the Stalin era; and they are, today, embedded in Khrushchev's Communism.

He took account of the unanticipated complexity of things in three ways. As we have noted, he postponed the coming of world revolution, and the resultant coming of the perfect order, far beyond the date he had hopefully set; and he established the apparatus of power and conspiracy for continuing the struggle against "capitalist imperialism" for as long a time as might prove necessary. Second, he undertook to effect in man by coercion and conditioning the type of change which, in theory, was to be produced by the Communist mode of production after this was established. And third, he made whatever adjustments to economic expediency he felt to be called for—introducing state capitalism, for example, under the NEP, and employing the services of those trained managers whose role he had deprecated.

What he did not do, however, is equally important. He did not re-examine the dogma, to see whether or not it had, in fact, any correspondence to reality. He did not temper his antagonism to the capitalist order from which he borrowed the skilled know-how that he had thought unnecessary. He did not modify his edict that the Party must exercise power *alone,* nor question its aptitude for this role. He did not forsake his idolatry of the all-embracing plan and the huge enterprise: the bigger the better. And he did not question the Party's right to make over the human being to fit its own conception of Communist man.

All his adjustments to unexpected complexity, in brief, were merely expedient. The dogma remained intact—and "infallible." In spite of all the miscalculations that marked his own record and that of his fellow Bolsheviks, the Party remained uninfected by self-doubt or humility. It was still assigned the "vanguard" role of organizing and leading all other groups. Its design for the human future was still rated as correct enough to justify its liquidating—by violence, if need be; by propaganda and conditioning, if possible—all opposing elements.

The world has had evidence aplenty of what the Communists are willing to do to man in order to seize and consolidate their power. From Moscow to Peking, this part of the record has been written in blood. But Khrushchev has become specific about the planned nature of man when, in theory at least, the blood-letting is over: when the Party has made good its hold on the total human situation. Compared with his portrait of Communist man, the descriptions left by Lenin and Bukharin are mere sketches.

Khrushchev's becoming thus specific must be counted a matter of necessity rather than of choice. For strategic reasons, he has announced that the historic changeover from Socialism to Communism is actually taking place, now, in the Soviet Union. Thus, he has both put the Communism of his own era on a "higher" plane than that of the Stalin era and has kept the Soviet Union ahead of Red China's "big leap forward."

Also, however, he has "announced himself" into a position where he must safeguard the system against false hopes in the public mind: hopes associated with such Marxian phrases as "to each according to his need" and "the withering away of the state"; and less utopian hopes for some easing of Party controls.

Since, on the testimony of his Seven Year Plan, he does not intend to countenance even the slightest change in the basic structure of power, he has had some explaining to do. If we follow where his explanations lead, we find ourselves in the presence of *Communist man.*

Khrushchev's first precaution, it would appear, was to make plain that Communism has both arrived and not arrived in the Soviet Union. The present transitional form of it, he explained to the delegates at the Twenty-First Congress of the CPSU, is by no means the "higher phase of Communism"; and the period between the two will be of indefinite duration: "There is no set date for our entry into Communism. . . . There must be no undue haste, no hurried introduction of measures for which the time is not ripe. That would lead to distortion and would discredit our cause . . ." (6)

Thus, while proclaiming change of historic moment, he has left unchanged one permanent aspect of the system: namely, that it is always at a *preparatory* stage, so that there can always be a further postponement of such benefits as cannot conveniently be delivered and a further urging of the people to energize mightily in behalf of a distant goal. As a second precaution, he made the prerequisites of Communism such that, in practical terms, the distant goal remains very distant indeed.

The material prerequisites are demanding enough: "a highly developed, modern industry, total electrification, scientific and technical progress in every branch of industry, comprehensive mechanization and automation in all productive processes . . ." (7)

Even more demanding, however, are the psychological prerequisites: "The realization of the grandiose plan of communist construction" calls for the forming of "a new man in the spirit of collectivism and diligence . . . in the spirit of socialist internationalism and patriotism . . ." (8)

It will take a long time, Khrushchev indicates, to complete the "irreconcilable struggle against bourgeois ideology" and to overcome "the survivals of capitalism in the consciousness of the people." It will take a long time to instill in all Soviet citizens "a Communist approach to labour": an "ingrained urge to work in accordance with their abilities" and yet not to seek any reward that smacks of "bourgeois" individualism. A long time.

Meanwhile: "Every step we take toward communism will increase the role of conviction, public influence, communist education and conscious discipline of the members of socialist society and diminish the means of compulsion." (9)

The diminishing of compulsion is, however, *conditional.* The people cannot demand it, but can induce it by giving the Party less and less reason to coerce them. On the domestic front, in brief, as on the world front, "peaceful coexistence" can be insured by the voluntary submission of those whom the Party is appointed to control.

While compulsion may thus diminish—if no "unreasonable" resistance is offered—Party control will not: "All the experience gained in the battle for the triumph of Socialism and Communism . . . confirms one of the key principles of Leninism, namely, that in the process of building Communist society the role of the Party must increase, not decrease, as the latter-day revisionists maintain." (10)

Moreover, the Party's alter ego, the State, is not to "wither away" within the foreseeable future. To clinch this point, Khrushchev quotes Lenin: "Until we reach the 'higher' phase of Communism, Socialists demand the most *stringent* control of society and by *the State* over the amount of labour and the amount of consumption." (11)

Where does all this leave the people of the Soviet Union? It leaves them lodged within a system which does not intend to change in any basic respect, except to intensify its control, but which promises that they can enjoy both material benefits and a lessening of coercion to the extent that they, on a mass scale, undergo change: from the pre-Communist model of human being to the Communist model.

What, then, is he to be like: this made-to-order "new man" for whom Communist society will be a natural habitat? He will have one thing in common with Marx's class-conscious proletarian: he will be mass-produced by a system, and more inclined to mass action than to individual action. But here the resemblance virtually ends. For Marx's proletarian, brought into being by a matured capitalism, was to constitute a force for revolution. Communist man, brought into being by Lenin's Party, is to be compliant man: dedicated not to the overthrow but to the service of the force that has produced him.

To be thus compliant in any "efficient" sense, he must be a standard product. The whole fabric of Communist thought and practice is permeated by *idolatry of the standardized*— the standardized and predictable. It can be wrought into monolithic unity and made subject to the machinery of power. That which poses a threat to the Party is the unique, the individuated, the private, the spontaneous, the "different."

It is no accident that so many Communist terms of derogation—revisionist, subjectivist, deviationist—are aimed at persons who, in one or another respect, stand apart from the category into which they are supposed to fit. They are square pegs within a system which has ordained that only round holes are "correct."

We encounter this idolatry of the standardized in the grim uniformity of Soviet architecture; in the denunciation of a poem that expresses "private emotion"; in the fury with which the CPSU has lashed out at the Yugoslavs because they "deny the need for working class solidarity"; even in the ordained rhythm that marks the "spontaneous" applause of a Communist audience.

Each of these represents a coming to the surface of one underlying tenet of Leninism: that what is standardized can be controlled, but that the diverse is always potentially anarchic. That which has been most successfully standardized is the machine. That which has been most stubbornly diverse is human nature. To condition this into the semblance of the machine is, therefore, "progressive."

It is significant that Soviet psychology, in its development, reports this urge to control. Those branches of psychology are stressed which help the Party to get predictable results on a mass scale and to fit people into categories. There is no tolerance for those which stress individual differences of the factors involved in self-actualizing.

One practical result of this, among many, is that Soviet educators set a *chronological* age by which students must prove themselves to be good material for a higher education if they are to have a chance at this on more than a part-time basis. It would be "incorrect" for educators to take account of the fact that some children mature more slowly than others; for this would introduce an indeterminate element into planning.

The stress which Communists put upon mass production of material goods is an old story. But here we can appraise it as one phase of this idolatry of the standardized. When Khrushchev visited Indonesia, early in 1960, he was reported as having made one bad break. He showed all too plainly his lack of interest in a carefully chosen gift of native handcraft which was presented to him. He can scarcely have wanted to offend his hosts. His response was a *Communist* response. In the most profound sense, the Indonesian gift was foreign matter in his hands; and he looked upon it as that.

A hand-made object, like an individuated human being, lacks ideological function. It is more like a relic of the "bourgeois" past than a forecast of the Communist future. If it is spectacular—like the Tsarist crown jewels—it belongs in a museum. Otherwise, it belongs nowhere. It has no role to perform with respect to the class struggle; no value as a symbol of power; no worth as a model to be put into mass production; no contribution to make to the overtaking of capitalism. It is simply itself; and what can a Communist do with that which is simply itself?

We can count it, perhaps, a mark of boorishness or provincialism that Khrushchev underestimated what handcraft means to the Indonesians. But it must be counted a mark of shrewdness, Communist style, that he never underestimates what standardized mass production means to the Party. It means the power to control. His shrewdness appears to be telling him, now, that a new urgency attends the mass production of *Communist man:* a man who can be relied upon to want what the Party wants him to want, and against whom, therefore, no inexpedient measure of coercion need be applied.

To judge by the current stress on indoctrination, this "new man" is still in the blueprint stage rather than in that of mass output. His traits, however, have been made so specific—in speeches, resolutions, articles in the press, and in the Seven

Year Plan—that they can be ticked off, one after another.

First, he does not think of himself as having inviolable rights as an individual or as "housing" any form of reality that lies beyond the Party's jurisdiction. Neither does he think of himself as having aptitudes which should be developed and expressed in ways marked by individuality.

"People of the individualist bent who have the bourgeois conception of the interests of the individual cannot understand the new moral traits of the Soviet people . . ." (12)

To the extent that these "new moral traits" are established in a person, he has the merits of a standard product. He and his fellows—all who are covered by such terms as *the workers* and *the masses*—have been shaped by the concentrated impact of a controlled environment from which the normal diversity of crisscrossing influences has been eliminated.

Thus conditioned, he is strongly marked by "the spirit of collectivism." He has little taste for privacy. Organized groups have become his element. From "collective" experiences within these he derives all the sense of identity and of personal significance that is appropriate to Communist man.

His work life is "collective" in both its physical aspects and its goals. Rarely does he work alone. Never does he invent a job for himself. He may be a specialist. But this does not make him *stand out*. It simply determines where he *fits in*.

His life of recreation is "collective." Its being so is doubly insured: by the almost complete absence of places where he can be alone, and by the insistent presence of places where he is encouraged to join in group activities. If, moreover, he were to show a conspicuous wish for privacy, this would invite the "solicitous" attention of a Party cadre: was there some special reason for his being unhappy in the group?

For the most part, he does nothing to invite this question. By the unalleviated experience of being a unit, not a self-motivated individual, he has become "collective" in his habits and expectations. His powers of self-direction and self-entertainment have atrophied from disuse. Thus, he "freely" confirms the Party's dictum—expressed in the Seven Year Plan —that because man is a "social being," his life "outside the collective" is inconceivable.

The life of his mind, we must note, is as "collective" as the life of his muscles. He is at the furthest remove from the solitary thinker—and that is where the Party wants him to be. The Party, like Caesar, views as dangerous the man who walks alone and "thinks too much."

The "new man" poses no problem on this score. What thinking he does, he likes to do with others—in a class, study circle, discussion group, lecture hall, seminar. His own mind is not to him a "kingdom." He is not "subjective"; not given to wondering. What he likes is to get facts straight. He has learned that the organized group is the right place for that. The people in charge do not leave him with a sense of being all mixed up about things.

This "new man's" relationship to Marxism-Leninism is "sound." The ideology is important to him. It gives purpose to his "diligence." But he is willing to leave the interpretation of it to the ideologists. After all, his position is not that of the "bourgeois" individual who is always having to probe into this question and that, in search of the truth. For Communist man, the truth is already in; and nothing is added to truth by poking at it all the time. He simply does not feel, in short, that the Party's pre-emptive control of the ideology limits his own intellectual freedom.

Even if his work is in an intellectual field, if he is, for example, a social scientist, the domain which he takes to be proper for his research is that which the Party maps out: "the social sciences can fulfill their tasks only if they are organically linked with the practice of communist construction . . .

with the topical requirements of party propaganda." (13)

Communist man believes with the Party that it raises "the role of the social sciences" for them to take on the task of enriching propaganda "by inquisitive and investigative thought." If he is told in advance what his "inquisitive and investigative thought" should prove—as, for example, that present-day capitalism is in a general stage of crisis and decay —he does not boggle at this. Why should he? He is *Communist man:* the most triumphant product of the Party's historic, "Let there be . . ."

The Communist Party's attitude toward the mind of man is one of the most peculiar and deceptive phenomena on earth. Yet it has its own logic. Marx was an angry intellectual. Lenin was another. Both regarded ideas as weapons; minds, as targets. In the domain of thought, both were military strategists.

Only if we understand the military strategist as an expert sensitized to what certain types of weapons can be made to accomplish—in his own hands, but likewise in enemy hands —can we understand the Communist Party's preoccupation with the dual task of subverting minds in non-Communist countries and controlling the mind of the Soviet and Soviet-bloc citizen.

Emerson wrote: "Beware when the great God lets loose a thinker on this planet. Then all things are at risk. It is as when a conflagration has broken out in a great city, and no man knows what is safe, or where it will end." (14)

Emerson, however, was that solitary thinker who stands at the furthest remove from Communist man. He delighted in the very sort of risk against which he warned. It put zest into life and made freedom a spacious thing.

The keepers of Marxism-Leninism know the explosive character of thought quite as well as Emerson ever did. But they want none of it *in areas where they have taken control*. They want it to be put to use only to dynamite the "enemy camp." Khrushchev spoke as a true Party member when he said to a French delegation, in 1956, "Historians are dangerous people. They are capable of upsetting everything. They must be directed." For the word *historians*, he might have substituted *writers, journalists, social scientists, psychologists, philosophers* . . .

Countless persons around the world have been impressed by the Soviet Union's investment in research centers and educational institutions; the huge editions of books which come from its presses; the high salaries it pays to professors and scientists; the provision it makes for museums, libraries, and cultural centers.

In spite of its rigid control of the press, its fabricating of history, and its interminable harassment of novelists and poets, many persons are ready to say that, whatever their other faults may be, the Communists at least attach a proper value to the human intellect.

They do—in their own Marxist-Leninist way. As military strategists, they do not stint on the most vital of weapons. "Education," said Stalin, in a conversation with H. G. Wells, in 1934, "is a weapon whose effect depends on who holds it in his hands and who is struck with it." (15)

The Central Committee of the CPSU, in the Resolution on Propaganda which it adopted on January 10, 1960, goes into specifics: ". . . houses of culture, clubs, libraries, reading rooms, museums, parks, and other culture and educational establishments must become true centers of agitation and propaganda work." (16)

They must, in brief, become "true centers" for making Communist man. This diligent, useful private in a war where ideas are weapons must never be permitted to grow to his full stature as *homo sapiens*. But, more than this, he must be persuaded to like the measures by which his growth is expediently stunted. To put the matter bluntly, the Communist Party has staged, and is currently staging with urgent vigor, the most colossal trespass upon the human mind that the world has ever witnessed.

Now we come to a different but related trait. Just as he feels no need for privacy, and no need to call his mind his own, so the "new man" has no taste for private property. His indifference to it goes far beyond a belief in the public ownership of the major means of production. It makes him attach little or no importance to having things that are his own: things so related to his own tastes, plans, memories, skills, and interests that they become a kind of extension of the self.

Tools of his own, for example, made doubly his by long and intimate use, still have for Communist man only the "objective" worth which their function gives them: a worth equally lodged in tools owned by the collective or the State. And if he happens to be a poet, it would not occur to him to write:

> —I am all alone in the room.
> The books and the pictures peer,
> Dumb old friends, from the dark.
> The wind goes high on the hills,
> And my fire leaps up, being proud . . . (17)

If he did, in a "regressive" moment, write such lines, he would certainly be called to account for "subjectivism."

There is no ideological reason, we must understand, for a Communist society to remain a materially deprived society —not after the priority claims of heavy industry, economic diplomacy, and the military have been met. Marxism-Leninism stresses the role of man as a material being with material needs. Khrushchev proclaims that a high standard of living is to be one of the prime factors by which the Soviet Union advertises Communism to the world.

Access to material goods, within bounds deemed "reasonable" by the Party, is considered right and necessary—however long it has been subordinated to the consolidation of power. But, states the Seven Year Plan, there is "a really Communist way of raising the well-being of the people . . ." (18)

This "really Communist way" is to incorporate so much into the collective and public system of goods and services that private property becomes a shrinking, vestigial appendage to public property. Thus, the Party hopes to raise the material standard of living and yet rule out the danger which it takes to be inherent in ownership—not merely of *the means of production* but also of *the means of experience.* The Party seems always to fear that private ownership may put the individual, or some private corner of his mind, beyond the reach of the "collective."

It may give him a feeling of security, however limited, which does not derive from Party or State. It may make him divert some measure of energy from collective and public enterprises to the tending of that which is his own. The peasants have thus stubbornly diverted their energies to the cultivation of their "household land allotments"; and these, in the Seven Year Plan, are slated for liquidation. Again, private property may tie in so closely with the development of unique aptitudes that it encourages "bourgeois" individualism.

For good Communist reasons, then, the Party is going all out to sell the idea that people in capitalist countries want to own property only because they are constantly aware of impending privation, and because they have false standards of prestige: "It is well known that in capitalist countries man withdraws into his shell, holds aloof from others and depends only on his own strength, because he has no one else to depend on. . . .

"Here each man feels the solicitude of society, of the State. That is why the urge for self-aggrandizement, for private property, is disappearing from the mind of the Soviet citizen . . ." (19)

In plain fact, it is *not* disappearing from the mind of the Soviet citizen. On the best available evidence, the contrary is true. The State, moreover, during recent years, has made a major concession to the citizens' "bourgeois" taste for ownership. Within controlled limits, and under edicts that are subject to change without notice, it has been not only permitting, but encouraging, the building of small private homes.

It initiated this concession to stimulate the "new lands" program: to make people willing to move to these remote lands; and to save itself from having to put an inexpedient amount of its investment capital into vast emergency housing projects. So eager did people prove to be to build their own homes that the State—faced with widespread discontent about the perennial housing shortage—has extended the program to various other rural areas.

That this concession is temporary, however, is doubly underscored: by the constant "downgrading" of private property in speeches and doctrinal pronouncements; and by the flat statement in the Seven Year Plan that while "economic and cultural developments" are now chiefly financed by Socialist accumulations of capital, these accumulations will, as the Plan progresses, "become the only source" of a further rise in living standards. (20)

If, in brief, the urge for private property is not yet disappearing from the mind of the Soviet citizen, and is even being given a temporary right to lodge there, it is slated to disappear from the mind of that blueprint character, *Communist man*. In the next chapter, we shall consider some of the means by which its disappearance is being encouraged.

Meanwhile, we turn to yet another trait of the blueprint character. Communist man is a new kind of provincial: we might say, a provincial of the Iron Curtain. His curiosity about the world stays within approved limits. He does not spend time trying to catch fragments of jammed radio programs; nor does he welcome every chance to lay his hands on Western books and recordings. He finds Soviet culture sufficient to his needs.

Both the Seven Year Plan and the Central Committee's Resolution on Propaganda stress to the point of tedium that "the masses" must be urgently schooled in the spirit of "socialist internationalism." And running parallel to this theme is another: namely, that Party cadres must "wage a relentless struggle against individual manifestations of . . . cosmopolitanism which still occur in Soviet life." (21)

The "spirit of socialist internationalism" is invariably linked to "the spirit of collectivism." But "cosmopolitanism" is always catalogued as an individual vice. It smacks of a readiness to blur the dividing line between the "two worlds" in a manner that becomes all the more dangerous, the Party contends, when "peaceful coexistence" is the strategic order of the day.

Perhaps there is no better way to make plain the Party's determined provincialism—and anti-cosmopolitanism—than to quote a few lines of a poem and an official response to it. During the brief post-Stalin "thaw," a Soviet poet, Evgeni Evtushenko, expressed his hunger for foreign travel: a hunger, incidentally, which more than a few Soviet citizens have expressed to American tourists. He wrote:

> The frontiers oppress me . . .
> I want to wander

As much as I like
In London,
To talk, however brokenly,
With everybody . . .
I want to ride
On a bus
Through morning Paris . . . (22)

Evtushenko wanted only the sort of experience which thousands of free individuals enjoy every year, and which they take to be rightfully theirs if they want it badly enough to plan and save. But the individual Soviet citizen is not supposed even to want to travel abroad. His view of the world is to be a product of the propaganda apparatus.

A "correct" reviewer pointed out the error of the poet's attitude. "It would not be so bad," this reviewer wrote in *Literaturnaya,* on April 8, 1958, "If Evtushenko wanted only to wander through London and Paris; the trouble is that he resents living inside Soviet frontiers." *Communist man* would have no impulse to say, "The frontiers oppress me."

Finally, Communist man is a resolute, unqualified atheist. For many years, now—from well back in the Stalin era—the Communists have been playing a double game with respect to religion. They have proclaimed as much "friendship" and "tolerance" toward established religious institutions—inside the orbit, as well as outside—as might help them to exploit or neutralize these. At the same time, they have stressed the "irreconcilable" conflict between religion and the "science of Marxism-Leninism"; and between the Party and any religious spokesman with whom they are unable to establish an expedient form of "peaceful coexistence."

Khrushchev has stepped-up both these policies. In particular, however, his vast program of indoctrination is putting reinforced emphasis on the teaching of atheism—with children and young people as the main targets. Thus, we are reminded once more that Communist man must have no spiritual "standing place" that is, by its very nature, beyond the Party's authority.

Communist man must attach no such worth to the individual human being that he will live and, if need be, die to proclaim and defend this worth. If he is to give unqualified support to policies which derive from "class morality," he must not conceive of himself as obedient to moral principles which transcend the class struggle.

He must not have that peculiar independence which comes from the inner peace of being at home in the universe—and not merely within the Communist frame of reference. He must not project inner peace into an "apolitical" concept of what peace should really mean in the human situation. If, for reasons of Party discipline or "communist construction," he is made subject to the pressure of "collective disapproval," he must not be able, standing alone, to draw on a source of strength which keeps him from feeling alone.

Finally, he must not exhibit a compassion that is in no way tied up with political strategy. To minister to human needs simply because they exist serves no purpose that a Communist can respect. This, at least, would seem to be the import of Khrushchev's speech in Calcutta, on February 15, 1960, as reported by the Associated Press. Condemning as a "dole" an American shipment of wheat to India, he said that the Soviet Union "believes in aid only to build industries." Ignoring the fact that America and the other Western powers are engaged *both* in feeding the hungry *and* helping to build industries, he implied that the sending of food to those whose need is immediate and desperate is useless, because "once you eat, you are hungry again."

No one—and least of all, the Western powers—would question the importance of basic industries to India's future well-being. But why the rigid *either-or* pattern, since people are alive and hungry now? What was the standard that obligated Khrushchev to resent the American shipment of wheat? The fact that it was a strictly political standard was made plain by a further portion of his speech. Precisely because the building up of basic industries in the backward countries is so important, the Western powers were, at that time, urging that all resources available for aid be made more effective by being pooled and channeled through the United Nations. "Well, no thank you," said Khrushchev. "We will render our aid ourselves."

Here, then, are the "new moral traits" of that blueprint character, *Communist man*. He does not attach worth to individuality or claim individual rights. The "spirit of collectivism" is so developed in him that, for all purposes of work, recreation, learning, and thinking, the organized group is his preferred element. Not even as a specialist does he feel that his mind is his own, in the sense of its being free to seek truth along paths other than those mapped by the Party.

He has a "reasonable" interest in material goods, but no interest in private ownership, preferring the "really Communist way" of enjoying access to goods and services.

His thinking about the world is made in the image of "socialist internationalism," not "bourgeois" cosmopolitanism. Similarly, his thinking about the universe and human destiny is made in the image of Marxist-Leninist materialism, untainted by religion.

It is hard not to feel that the stereotyped "new man" whose portrait is drawn in the key documents of the Khrushchev era is too obvious a caricature of the complex human being to deserve attention. Yet he does deserve attention—on several counts.

He deserves it, first, because he reminds us that *only* a mass-produced caricature of the complex human being can really serve the needs of a system based on Marxism-Leninism, which is itself a caricature of science, and operated by a

Party which, by its very nature, and its every policy, caricatures "the dictatorship of the proletariat." This Communist man, in brief, tells us more about what is basically, incurably wrong with Communism than did even the cowed man of the Stalin era. For this "new man" is what the system counts on for its own survival in perpetuity—after the blood-letting is over; after the world is conquered.

He deserves attention, also, because all his traits are designed to insure his remaining, throughout his life, and in all phases of his life, a *dependent*. He is a caricature, in short, not only of the complex human being, but also of the adult human being. He is deliberately fixated at the pre-individual, pre-independent stage of development—and is conditioned to believe that papa, called Party, knows best. He does not have even the tough identity of the rebellious child. He is compliant, sober, diligent at the tasks set for him, conventional, and, above all, "collective."

He deserves attention, in the third place, as a warning to ourselves of what it means to have Communism, anywhere, extend its control over human beings; and as a warning, also, of our own need to strengthen those forces in our culture which encourage the growth of the individual into a mature responsibility and a mature compassion—thus keeping him, as a free person, "worthy to raise issues."

Finally, this Party-made caricature of man deserves our attention because of the contrast he presents to the type of human being whom we have most honored in our own tradition. By what Communist man is encouraged to become, and by what he is not permitted to become, we are forced to take stock of the elements in our heritage which would be liquidated and of the persons who would be converted into "unpersons" and dropped from history if the Communist Party ever had a chance to call the tune.

FIFTEEN

METHODS OF MIND-MAKING

NUMEROUS studies have been made of Communism's extreme measures of "brain-washing." We think, for example, of such different but complementary books as Joost A. M. Meerloo's psychiatric study, *The Rape of the Mind,* and Duane Thorin's *A Ride to Panmunjom*—a novel which is, in effect, a vehicle for what he learned about "brain-washing" while he was a prisoner of the Communists during the Korean War.

It has become increasingly important for the free world to understand this calculated process of taking away from a human being his individual judgment and, as it were, grafting into his mind the thoughts which he is to accept as his own. It has become equally important—as both Meerloo and Thorin indicate—for us to understand the type of mental and spiritual integrity that best fortifies the individual against this assault.

With respect to such integrity, we ourselves remember a long visit we had, in the Summer of 1959, in London, with a

Polish exile: a man who had been subjected, within a period of a few years, to the impact, first, of a Nazi concentration camp, and then of Soviet imprisonment and "brain-washing."

What impressed us most, as we talked with him, was what these ruthless assaults upon his mind and personality had *not* been able to take away from him. So we turned the conversation from the nature of the assault to the individual's resources for resisting it. This exile's thoughtful conclusion movingly confirmed what scientific researchers have said on the subject. What it came to was that the person who is best fortified is the one who most deeply knows, with his whole being, that he believes in the dignity of man and the profound worth of human life.

This age in which we live, he said, is one in which "history cuts across personal choice with appalling violence." The problem of all free men, therefore, is to "embody and enact the courage of the gentle."

The unusualness of this phrase—"the courage of the gentle"—invited exploring. What he meant, he told us, was that free men have to be "as brave as circumstances may require" —not to show off, but simply to support the dignity of life and to serve life rather than hurt it.

In the Soviet prison, in the wake of a "brain-washing" session that had tested his inner resources to the limit, he had discovered that "courage is born at the intersection of imposed necessity and love of life"—not love of one's own life alone, but love of what life mysteriously is, and of what it can become when it is "disciplined by freedom."

Neither concentrated "brain-washing," however, nor the individual's power to resist it is our main concern in this chapter. We have referred to them, rather, because of the light they throw on the Party's sustained effort to produce Communist man. In both its rationale and its methods, the

Party's attack upon the mind of the "bourgeois" prisoner whom it has at its mercy is strangely akin to its ongoing war against the mind of the Soviet citizen.

In both cases, the Party treats the mind as a container that can be emptied of "erroneous" ideas and refilled with "correct" ones. According to Marxism-Leninism, the content of the mind is determined by the socioeconomic environment: by the mode of production and the legal, political, and cultural "superstructure" which has been built upon this. All that need be done, then, to change "bourgeois" man into Communist man is to replace the old environment with a new one, and to prevent the "contamination" of this new one by alien influence. All that need be done to insure a person's developing "correctly" from the start is to control his environment from his childhood on.

In the typical "brain-washing" procedure, every effort is made to deprive the prisoner of his status as a *self-motivated* being and to make him purely reactive. He is left no room for initiative or even for an accurate anticipation of events. The timing of impact-sessions—of questioning, and of the repetitive implanting of ideas—is unpredictable. So is the degree of "friendliness" or "toughness" of his captors.

The only "success" open to him is that of satisfying his captors by his reaction to the stimuli they provide. The goal is to make him, by stages, into a psychological dependent who feels that he has given "right" answers and expressed "right" ideas when he has followed the lead of these captors.

Thus, "brain-washing" can best be understood as an effort to induce regression: to make the adult into a child again; and, ultimately, into a "good" child who has internalized and *made his own* the concepts of right and wrong which have repetitively been brought to bear upon him—in an environment from which all contrary influences have been excluded.

How different *in essence* is this process of remaking a

prisoner's mind from that of producing Communist man on a
mass scale? There is, of course, a difference in the intensity
of the process and in the range of experiences open to the
individual. But for prisoner and Soviet citizen alike, the only
approved type of "freedom" is that which the Soviet dictionary defines as *the recognition of necessity.*" To repeat
a statement quoted in an earlier chapter, "A person is free,
then, to the extent that he understands why the Party line
is right."

In the course of his psychological study of the Soviet
leaders' methods of manipulating minds—a study in which
he brought together the results of first-hand observation and
intensive research—Hadley Cantril collected statements
made by Soviet educators with respect to educational aims.
Some of these statements are much to the point here.

Thus: "The meaning of a collective for children or youth
and the part it should play from an educational point of view
consists of this: the collective removes the individualistic,
small property psychology and creates the psychology of a
collectivist . . ." The word *removes* is significant. One psychology is taken out of the mind. Another psychology is put
in. And, behold, a "collectivist" has been made.

Again, we read, from another educator: "The ultimate goal
of education is to reach such a level of consciousness, that
pupils will receive the demands of Soviet society as if they
were their own." (1)

The Soviet child, obviously, is the Soviet citizen in the
making. The environments and conditioning experiences of
both are, to the greatest possible degree, shaped by the
Party. In school, factory, study group, sports club, trade
union, collective farm, or whatever, the Party provides the
leadership.

Moreover, Cantril notes, "The implicit role of leadership

is interestingly revealed by the use of the word *rukovoditel* —a compound noun, uniting two roots: *ruka,* meaning "hand," and *vodit,* meaning "to lead." The word thus conveys the sense of "by-the-hand-leader." To be this type of leader—the type that takes the Soviet child or the Soviet citizen by the hand, symbolically at least, and guides him on the correct course—is the task of every person in a position of authority; and "thus the Party is the sum total of these leaders." (2)

What, then, are some of the discernible methods on which Khrushchev is relying for the making of Communist man? How is he insuring that the Soviet citizen—working, playing, learning—will be led by the hand in the right direction?

To an extent never approximated by his predecessors, Khrushchev has located Party members in strategic positions throughout the whole of Soviet society. To study his program for creating the "new man" is, then, rather like watching a play in which one character—the Party cadre—is never off stage. The roles of this cadre are as many as the things that must be done if "bourgeois remnants" are to be removed from the minds of the Soviet people; if "socialist diligence" is to be instilled in these minds; and if unfree men are to be induced to feel free.

In the conspiratorial days, before 1917, when the task of the Bolshevik Party was to lead "the masses" toward revolution, Lenin said that, in order to capitalize every discontent and antagonism, "we must have 'our own men' everywhere, among all social strata . . ." (3) After the *coup d'état,* the task of the Party became that of leading "the masses" toward a state of obedient compliance. Yet this post-revolutionary purpose did not render obsolete Lenin's pre-revolutionary edict.

Stalin, to the extent that he could contrive to do so, had his own men everywhere, "among all social strata." The omnipresence of the secret police was the core of Stalin's terrorism.

Khrushchev, also, has set himself the goal of having his own men everywhere. The omnipresence of the Party cadre is the core of Khrushchev's veiled coercion: of his "peaceful coexistence" with the Soviet people.

Khrushchev's expansionist program abroad and his domestic program of "communist construction" can both be better served and better advertised by controlled people *who feel free* than by resentful and terrorized masses. The embracing task, then, assigned to the Party cadres is that of making the Soviet Union safe for a pretense of democracy.

A key Resolution adopted by the Twenty-First Congress of the CPSU stated that, under present-day conditions, a new emphasis must be laid "on the all-around development of democracy, on drawing all citizens into taking part in the management of economic and cultural affairs . . ." (4)

How can this directive be implemented and yet leave the structure of power unchanged and unthreatened? Khrushchev's answer to this question is to be found in other statements in the same document and in the Seven Year Plan; and it is simplicity itself. There is no great risk in drawing all citizens into "the management of economic and cultural affairs" if a Party cadre is always present to provide "by-the-hand" leadership.

Not only is there no great risk, but the gains to be netted from such an "all-around development of democracy" are enormous. The process of citizen participation would mean that more and more people could be reached by Party propaganda; and that more and more of them might be brought to accept *as their own* the aims of the Party.

During the past few years, according to the Seven Year Plan, thousands of individual Party members have been put into key command posts throughout the Soviet Union. The Plan affirms that "thousands of such people have taken over the management of State and collective farms." The decentralization of industry, with the forming of wide-flung economic councils, has further "seeded" the remote reaches of the Soviet Union and the vast industrial compounds with Party members. Thus, "decentralization" has had the odd effect of bringing the monolithic structure of "democratic centralism" into contact with the life and mind of the Soviet citizen at more points than ever before.

Here, as in so many other instances, the words of Lenin fit the text of Soviet practice in spite of all the changes that have taken place since they were first spoken. April 1917, we recall, was the month when Lenin returned from exile in Switzerland and began working out his plan for the overthrow of the Provisional Government which had been set up on a broadly representative base after the fall of the Tsar. To this end, he undertook so to infiltrate society with his Bolsheviks that this minority group could shape and lead public opinion. "The question," he said, "is not one of numbers, but of giving correct expression to the ideas and policies of the truly revolutionary proletariat." (5)

Khrushchev has expanded the membership of the CPSU beyond its previous limits. It appears, now, to have reached a total of some eight million. The Young Communist League —the *Komsomol*—has been expanded even more. Khrushchev speaks of it as having a membership of eighteen million. Even on the improbable assumption, however, that all or nearly all of the persons in this latter group would eventually be admitted to the Party, the Communists would still be a decided minority in the Soviet Union.

But Khrushchev's strategy, like Lenin's, is that of so

deploying this minority that it can insure the majority's "giving correct expression to the ideas and policies" of the Party. "The question is not one of numbers . . ."

To understand the method by which the Communists are making the Soviet Union safe for a pretense of democracy we must, however, go beyond the planting of individual Party members in command posts in industry and agriculture. We must take account of the peculiar character of so-called "public organizations."

In specifying what was meant by "the all-around development of democracy," the Resolution from which we have quoted had this to say: "Many of the functions now performed by state agencies should gradually pass to public organizations . . ." What does this statement signify? What are these organizations?

The *soviets* are one type. They are always described as "mass organizations of the working people." This would seem to imply that they are bodies in which the membership as a whole determines policy. This would certainly appear to have been Marx's expectation when he first visualized the post-revolutionary order of things. Yet the soviets, in actual practice, have never been other than "fronts" for the Party. As far back as 1921, the striking Kronstadt sailors protested the Bolshevik Party's domination of the soviets—and were shot down for their pains. Today, the giving of more responsibility in public matters to these "fronts" is one of the much publicized steps toward "democracy." What it really does is to strengthen Khrushchev's chosen chain of command; and to do so, ostensibly, by the will of the people.

Soviet trade unions are also "fronts" for the Party; and the Young Communist League might be called its "prep school." Khrushchev himself has said that the "activities of the trade unions are directed by the Party"; and that the

Young Communist League "has always been the Party's true assistant in carrying out plans for communist construction." (6) He made this statement in his Theses of the Seven Year Plan. Yet at the same Congress where the Plan was adopted, the assigning of new tasks to the trade unions and the Young Communist League was said to make the Soviet Union more "democratic."

The true relationship of these organizations to the Party can best be confirmed, perhaps, by our recalling the fact, from the chapter on Berlin, that among the first acts of Sovietization in the East zone of Germany was the taking-over of the trade unions; and that this was swiftly followed by the forming of Communist Youth groups.

With a fine disregard for historic fact, M. A. Suslov, in his speech at the Twenty-First Congress of the CPSU, said that coercion "has never been a main method used by the socialist state in its activities"; and added that the "sphere of coercion is today becoming still narrower." To "document" this statement, he proclaimed that the "trade unions, the Young Communist League, the co-operative and other mass organizations" reflect "the profoundly democratic character of the socialist system . . ." (7)

In the Seven Year Plan, however, it is stated that the Communist Party, "the leading detachment and trusted vanguard of the people, gives leadership to all organizations of the working people." (8) The phrase for us to reckon with is "gives leadership"; for whether in the Soviet Union or in the free world, a "front" organization that is "led" by the Party is progressively dominated by it. Khrushchev, in his Theses, actually makes this fact plain when he quotes Lenin on the function of Party-led organizations: they are to "educate and enlighten the masses . . . directing all the masses' activities along the road of class conscious policy." (9) Further, today, in Khrushchev's own words, they "are called upon to inspire the people to fulfill concrete production tasks."

What does all this have to do with the making of Communist man? It has much to do with it. Since Communist man is to be satisfied, compliant, dependent, and diligent to perform tasks set by the Party, it would be hard to overestimate the importance of his being made to feel that he is enjoying "democracy" while he is actually being denied the basic experiences through which democratic habits are formed. Khrushchev's "democracy"—in which rigged organizations are used to make people feel that they are taking part in public affairs when they are simply being manipulated by Party propaganda on a mass scale—is exactly as "democratic" as rigged elections, and no more so.

The Soviet citizen is given no chance to engage in honest give-and-take; to probe into governmental policies; to operate as part of a "loyal opposition"; to practice the difficult art of being now in the minority and now in the majority; to join or form free voluntary associations; to vote, or to refrain from voting if the conduct and platforms of opposing candidates impel him to say, "A plague on both your houses"; or to go out on a limb in behalf of a lost cause.

Instead, he is introduced to "correct" policies; allowed to "discuss" these within specified bounds and under the guidance of Party cadres; and persuaded, then, that "democracy" consists in his giving these policies his "enthusiastic" support.

The Soviet citizen, thus politically pap-fed, is never required to experience what Edward P. Morgan has called "enfranchised frustration." (10) Such "enfranchised frustration" is all too familiar to democratic man. It is the feeling he has when he does not know what should be done, but is sure that something should be done, and that he should be doing his part of it. Neither, however, is the Soviet citizen ever privileged to feel an honest sense of accomplishment *in his role as citizen.* He does not know what it means for two or three, or twenty or a hundred, to be voluntarily "gathered together" to tackle some problem related to the common welfare. The genuinely free citizen, never knowing as much as he needs to know about any public problem, can easily make a fool of himself. But also, undertaking the "impossible" and bringing it to pass, he often turns out to be "a fool of God." The Soviet citizen is privileged only to be a fool of the Party.

It is doubtful whether any system has ever been as well devised as Khrushchev's pseudodemocracy to save the citizen from "growing pains"—and thereby to check his growth. Khrushchev needs a "new man" who thinks he is more free than he is and who, therefore, is not prone to demand more freedom. Khrushchev could not use, and would have to liquidate, men of the type who made our own American Revolution: ". . . able and courageous freemen, worthy to raise issues."

For Khrushchev, the "saturation" of Soviet society by Party cadres makes all things possible. At least, it does so within the Marxist-Leninist frame of reference, and for as long as the complex human being has not yet learned to laugh at this—having taken stock of its dimensions and discovered that it is much too small to contain the full nature of even one individual, let alone "the masses."

Not the least service which this "saturation" renders to the Party is that of providing innumerable channels through which the citizen body can be indoctrinated on a day-to-day basis. We have already quoted several times from that Resolution on the tasks of propaganda which the Central

Committee of the CPSU adopted in January 1960. In its 4,000-word entirety, this document amounts to a campaign plan for the Party's all-out attack on the mind of Soviet man.

The Resolution declares that conditions are now uniquely favorable for ideological work. Much experience "has been amassed." Also: "Cadres of propagandists have grown, their theoretical and methodological training has improved and the material basis for party propaganda has become much stronger." (11)

Yet all is not well. Propaganda has been too abstract; not geared to the special interests of different elements in society; not firm enough in opposing "reactionary ideology and cosmopolitanism"; not alert to make full use of "such propaganda tools as the press, radio, television, movies, clubs, libraries."

Moreover, many persons to whom the State has given a higher education—"economists, philosophers, historians, and scientific workers"—have a "dogmatic" concept of what their work should properly be. Many of their professional associations, as in the field of social science, "are still linked too loosely with the life of the party organizations and do not always help in ideological work in an active and creative manner." (12) Translated out of Communist jargon, this means that they tend to put professional standards above the interests of the Party.

Even the leaders of some Party organizations "do not wage an incessant struggle against alien ideology. . . . They sometimes take up passive and defensive positions regarding idealistic and revisionist ideologies which are hostile to Marxism-Leninism. . . . They adopt a conciliatory attitude toward the remnants of the past in the consciousness of the Soviet people." (13)

Among these "remnants of the past" are not only "apolitical attitudes" and "cosmopolitanism," but also "neglect of labor and public duty, theft of public property, bureaucracy, corruption, speculation, toadyism, drunkenness, hooliganism, and other phenomena which are alien to our system." (14)

In view of all this—and, we might add, in view of the Party-State's need to make its hold on the people *totalitarian* —the Central Committee "resolves" to place certain responsibilities upon Party cadres throughout the whole vast apparatus.

These cadres are instructed to take the offensive "against bourgeois ideology"; to "arouse in every Soviet person an ardent desire to strengthen the might of the Soviet Union and the whole socialist camp by his selfless labor"; to create "moral stimuli to labor" among the intelligentsia; to make young people "unshakably convinced of the final truimph of communism"; and to bring the value of atheism home to all the people—"particularly housewives."

How are Party cadres to insure that no corner of the Soviet Union or of the citizen's mind will remain unchanged? They will have to draw vast new numbers of persons into "collective" forms of political education: lectures, seminars, classes, study circles. Also, they will have to "call regular conferences and meetings of agitators, propagandists, and intelligentsia under the central committee of communist parties of the union republics." This edict is particularly interesting when we recall that these "union republics" are the "rim countries"—discussed in the chapter on colonialism— to which Lenin, by force of arms, denied the right of self-determination. The stress which current programs of indoctrination are putting upon these "republics" would suggest that a disturbing number of dissidents still remain within them.

Further, Party cadres must "intensify ideological and educational work among working people in their places of residence." And here we are reminded of the extent to which

Khrushchev's "peaceful coexistence" is a domestic policy as well as a foreign one. The cadres must practice a new friendliness with "the masses"—even "in the form of a visit" —in order "to elucidate the very important tenets of Marxism-Leninism." The relating of these tenets to "communist construction" and the Seven Year Plan must be made "a heart to heart business . . ."

More broadly still, the elements of indoctrination must be so injected into the atmosphere of daily life that Soviet man will be influenced by them constantly and everywhere. To this end, it will be necessary to increase "agitation and propaganda work" in clubs, libraries, museums, parks; to popularize the presentation of "socialist realism" in art and literature; to make programs directed at youth more "lively" and "picturesque"; to cast radio and television programs in a form to attract the masses; and to "raise the role played by propaganda sectors of editorial offices of newspapers . . ."

Certain aspects of Soviet education as "reformed" by Khrushchev are peculiarly relevant to this vast effort at mind-making. The Party must, according to the Seven Year Plan, "raise the role of the State and society in the upbringing of children. . . .

"For this purpose it is planned to build many new boarding schools, nurseries, and kindergartens. In 1965 boarding schools will have no fewer than 2,500,000 pupils. . . .

"In future it is planned to give all children the opportunity of attending boarding schools, which will enable society to cope successfully with Communist education of the younger generation . . ." (15)

In recent years, the free world has been more aware of Communism's attack on the institution of the family in Red China than in the Soviet Union. But this projected removal of all children—even very young children—from family circle to boarding school reminds us that the attack is not only orbit-wide but intrinsic to Communism. The family represents an authority other than that of the Party-State, and one that is fortified by the intimacy of its relationships. It represents, also, the *individuation* of children; the giving of attention to what is unique in each.

One of Khrushchev's strangest allies in separating children from the family circle is the acute housing shortage. In the case of all save the favored few, living space is still allocated in terms of so many square meters per person—with the result that two or more families commonly inhabit even a small apartment, and often a single room, with only a curtain to provide a semblance of privacy. Under these conditions, the parents welcome a chance, more often than not, to get the children out of the home—into boarding school, but also, into camps and youth groups. The housing shortage contributes so much, in fact, to the Party's taking over of children and young people that the hierarchy—in spite of all its promises to speed up the building program—may well elect to postpone as long as possible the return of domestic privacy.

A second aspect of Khrushchevism in education—as set forth in the "reforms" adopted by the Supreme Soviet in December 1958—has to do with "the strengthening of ties between school and life." As explained in *Pravda* on December 25, 1958, the new law provides that the compulsory elementary school—from which pupils normally graduate around the age of fourteen—will be designed to be *terminal*. The vast majority of young people who complete this "first stage schooling" will then be assigned to "socially useful" work; and "all education thereafter is to be carried out in conjunction with productive labor in the national economy." Such further education will be either a direct apprenticeship or a part-time addendum to a full day's work.

Unusually gifted children will be treated as exceptions. They will be permitted to secure a full-time secondary education; and from among their number, the few who excel in mathematics and the natural sciences will be allowed to go on to higher education.

Higher education itself, however, is to be reorganized. Except for the few students who come directly from schools for the gifted, education will be on a part-time basis for the first two years. Only those who, during these two years, prove "deserving" will be permitted to continue their higher education on a full-time basis.

The word *deserving*, moreover, is given a peculiar two-pronged meaning. In the selecting, or weeding-out, of students, as much weight is to be given to political orthodoxy as to academic qualifications. Quite apart from intellectual capacity, in brief, or the urge to learn, higher education is to become a reward for toeing the ideological line and for being a political "activist."

This educational "reform" will increase the labor force; will advertise to all who are studiously inclined the clear advantage to be gained from an uncritical acceptance of Marxism-Leninism and of showing an interest in "collective" enterprises; and will protect the system against the growth of a nonpolitical, non-Party, liberally educated intelligentsia.

This final point ties in with a speech at the Twenty-First Congress in which Ekaterina Furtseva described the type of education which the Party will henceforth designate as appropriate for persons of "artistic bent." (16) It is not "normal," the speaker declared, for a writer, artist, or musician "to get a full-scale training and then become a 'free artist.'" He should not, then, be among those who are given a full-time higher education. He should be added to the labor force after his "first stage schooling" is completed; for it is "an indisputable fact that everyone who embarks on artistic creation must have experience of life." Part-time education, added to daily work, should provide the correct training for those who are to portray "socialist realism." Therefore, an "extensive system of correspondence education" should be set up for "training art workers."

Khrushchev's Party-State, in brief, is going even further than Stalin's Party-State in eliminating the risk that Soviet man will be exposed to the influence of either the liberally educated thinker or the "free artist": two types, incidentally, which the Party has singled out as prime targets in every non-Communist country.

The vast project of "standardizing" the Soviet citizen and insuring his chronic dependence is further supported by what we can only call pervasive meddling: a constant intrusion by Party and State upon private lives at points where independent interests and habit-systems might otherwise be formed.

A Soviet child, for example, manages to earn some money of his own. He wants a bicycle; so he decides to put his money in the bank and add to it by further earnings until he has enough to buy one. But the meddling Party-State says, in effect, "No, no." It is all right for him to have the bicycle if his parents can get it for him. But it is not good for a child to save his money. The act bespeaks a "bourgeois" taste for private property and the making of long-range individual plans. According to *Komsomolskaya Pravda*, the child who begins in his school days to put money in the bank to satisfy a personal wish will become "an acquisitive, stingy egotist." (17) His habits will become those of a "greedy" individualist; not those of a "collectivist."

Party meddling operates equally on the adult level. Throughout the centuries, for example, one basic way in which man has made his soul his own—in freedom, but also in servitude—has been by a skilled relationship to his job and to the working materials associated with it. Robert Frost has expressed one angle of this self-respecting relationship in "The Code":

> The hand that knows his business won't be told
> To do work better or faster—those two things. (18)

But where Communism prevails, skill and love of the job are no defense against intrusion. Neither do they constitute a license to exercise ingenuity: to try out on one's own a new way of doing things.

A Polish poet, Wiktor Woroszylski, availed himself of the opportunity provided by the post-Stalin "thaw," in 1956, to ask certain questions:

> Must I, a shoemaker,
> Ask the Central Committee
> How to make shoes?
> Must I, a gardener,
> ask how to tend apple and cherry trees?
> Must I, a musician,
> explain the dancing notes in my head? (19)

The Party's answer, as expressed in its policies, is "Yes, you must." Thus, Khrushchev, in the Seven Year Plan, happened to be talking about roofs instead of about shoes or apple trees or the notes of music. But he made clear that it is the task of the Party, not of the craftsman, to decide upon the correct —and standardized—way of doing a job. He was describing certain new methods of roof-building which "should be introduced more widely." How should the introduction of these methods throughout the Soviet Union be guaranteed? "Perhaps it will be necessary to adopt a special decision in which the dates for carrying out this measure are to be stipulated . . ." (20)

Examples could be multiplied, but would only underscore the same point: Communism has instituted on a colossal scale the *cult of interference*. If the citizen is a "good child," he need not suffer coercion in any obtrusive form. If he works hard, and urges others to work hard, he can enjoy more and more material benefits. But he will still have no defense against the intrusion of the Big Parent—the Party-State— which claims the right to ask him what he is thinking, and why he oddly wants to be alone, now and then, instead of always in the "collective"; and that takes his work out of his hands, no matter how skilled these hands are, saying to him, "No, no. Don't do it *that* way. Do it *this* way."

We are accustomed to think of Communist propaganda as directed against the free world. Thus, our minds have to do a sort of "double take" to encompass the meaning of the Party's calculated assault upon the consciousness of the Soviet people.

That this is to be a full-scale assault, and no sideline affair, is shown by the fact that the Central Committee of the CPSU has ordained that Party propagandists are to enjoy a new "authority." They are not to be overloaded with other duties. Propaganda work is to rate as "a basic and most important party mission." (21)

Here, again, we can almost see Lenin looking over Khrushchev's shoulder. Lenin stated that his Bolsheviks, with the Tsarist regime as their target, must "devote to the revolution not only their spare evenings, but the whole of their lives." (22) In like manner, Khrushchev's agitators and propagandists, with the Soviet citizen as target, are to become full-time professionals.

What is most startling in the Central Committee's Resolution on Propaganda is the battery of specified methods. These methods—to be used, now, in a country where the Party-State has held dictatorial power for more than four decades—are in *essence* those which Lenin laid down for use, first, against Tsarism; and then against all non-Communist

countries. Our minds can scarcely help asking: What goes
on here? What kind of system, after forty years in power,
must base its "peaceful coexistence" with the people it rules
on methods devised for the waging of revolution against the
"enemy camp"?

Lenin's chief target groups—workers, young people, intellectuals, the armed services—are still Khrushchev's targets.
To reach these, and other groups as well, Lenin instructed
his revolutionaries to study the strengths and weaknesses of
each, and "even the catchwords." The Central Committee's
Resolution, adopted in 1960, points out to Party cadres the
need "for taking account in every way of the peculiarities
of profession, age, education, nationality, and other factors
inherent in different strata of the population." (23)

Lenin's propaganda aim was to "utilize every grain of even
rudimentary discontent." (24) Khrushchev's propaganda aim
on the home front—in contrast to his propaganda aim on
the world front—is to induce compliance and content. But
whether employed by hard-core revolutionaries, intent on
overthrowing Tsardom, or by Party cadres intent on upholding the totalitarian power of the Soviet system, Leninist-
Khrushchevist "methodology" has as its aim the *manipulating of minds* by a self-appointed elite.

Above all, this methodology points up the fact that Khrushchev's policy of "peaceful coexistence"—whether applied
in the Soviet Union, the satellites, or the free world—is a
policy of veiled warfare. There is simply no way in which
the Communist Party can make more than a strategic peace
with any element outside itself. It is still a Leninist Party;
and Lenin both designed and commanded it to take power
alone.

In Chapter I, we spoke of the dividing line that runs across
the great land mass of Europe and Asia, setting the Communist orbit apart from all that lies outside it. Here, we

must weigh the significance for the human future of a different dividing line: a line that runs between the Communist Party and its "fronts," on the one hand, and the rest of the human race on the other. This line is not drawn on any map. It cuts through an organization in America or Japan or Italy or India or Mexico that has been infiltrated by Communists. But also it cuts through a trade-union or study circle within the Soviet Union itself—and through any other group in which "the working masses" are manipulated and "led" by the Party.

In his *Foreword* to *The Future Is Ours, Comrade,* Joseph Novak—who does not write under his real name, being still within the Communist orbit—tells of his journey to the Soviet Union as a private but officially approved guest from his satellite homeland.

The man who shared his seat on the train was a Soviet official on his way home from a diplomatic post in East Europe. He not only called Novak a very lucky young man to have a chance to visit in the USSR but suggested how he might best get a real picture of that country.

Urging the young traveler not to look at externals only, he told him that he must, above all, try to understand "the greatest pride of Russia, the main Soviet contribution to the march of mankind." This contribution, he said, "is the Soviet man, the citizen of the first Soviet country of the world.

"Remember, young man, fascinating scenery, heterogeneous cultures, and monumental architecture may be found all over the world. But the generation of *new people,* raised by us, can be found only in the USSR, nowhere else.

". . . Try to find, in the daily life of the Soviet people, the mechanism shaping the New Man . . ." (25)

This "New Man" and the mechanism by which he is being shaped have been our concern in this chapter—as in the chapter immediately preceding it. The Soviet official on the train told Novak that "the future of the world" belongs to this "New Man." It would take a Communist to rate this prospect as a happy one.

SIXTEEN

THE UNITED NATIONS AS TARGET

O N OCTOBER 20, 1960, the *Manchester Guardian Weekly* summed up Khrushchev's performance in the General Assembly of the United Nations: "That he aimed at striking terror into the hearts of all who do not agree with him became plainer every day." His design was made doubly plain in his threat that "he would annihilate Britain on the first day of any war" and that "he would walk out of the UN if it refused to be remoulded by him."

On the same theme, the usually restrained *Times* of India said in disgust that "both the United Nations and international diplomacy have been compelled to reduce themselves to the level prescribed by Mr. Khrushchev—a level in which political billingsgate sets the tone."

And this paper went on to say, "The entire purpose of the Soviet leader's performance in the United Nations appears to have been to . . . give notice of the Soviet Union's determination not to be inhibited by the conventions and principles of normal diplomacy but to seek solutions on the basis of unadulterated power politics."

As early as September 24, reporting on Khrushchev's first speech in the General Assembly sessions, Chalmers Roberts wrote in the *Washington Post* that the speech marked the opening of a new chapter in the Soviet Union's determination to use its group power to dominate the world. His two-and-a-half-hour speech, said Roberts, "reflected his confidence that the Soviet power is now so great, in comparison with that of the United States, that the Communist world today can challenge the United Nations . . ."

And Roscoe Drummond, in the *New York Herald Tribune* of September 26, dovetailed Khrushchev's attack upon the United Nations and the failure of his attempted *coup* in the Congo. "The Soviet Union," wrote Drummond, "is an ally of the United Nations only when the United Nations can be used to further Soviet purposes. The United Nations must be treated as an enemy whenever the U.N., however overwhelmingly it may be responding to the vote of the whole non-Communist world, stands in the path of the Kremlin."

These comments from the free-world press are sample expressions of a conviction that was being forced, day by day, upon the delegates in the Assembly sessions and upon myriad anxious minds around the globe: Khrushchev's fingers, now, are digging deep into the United Nations, probing to tear it apart.

In a sense, both Khrushchev's performance in the General Assembly and these reactions to it might be said to round out what had been started, some four months earlier, at Khrushchev's press conference in Paris.

At that press conference, we recall, newsmen who had come from many nations to cover the Summit meetings which did not take place listened with incredulity and revulsion while the Soviet dictator, as a "preview" of what he would do to those who opposed him, demonstrated how he had, in his boyhood, beat out the brains of a cat against a wall.

As we noted in Chapter III, Theodore Draper—among others—undertook to extract the core of meaning from Khrushchev's conduct: not only in Paris, but during the subsequent weeks of threat. He concluded that this abrupt change of manner on the part of the world's self-appointed spokesman for "peace" signaled a new Soviet appraisal of how further Communist expansion could best be achieved: "In this case, the style is not only the man but also the policy."

By the time Khrushchev left New York for Moscow, in mid-October, his use of the magnified tantrum as a weapon had become an expected routine. Obviously, all that it took to make him go into his act was for someone to disagree with him on a sensitive point; or, more particularly, for someone to point out the discrepancy between Communism's word and practice.

Khrushchev might scowl or he might grin as he and his puppets from East Europe drowned out an opposition speaker with shouts and desk-thumpings. But either way, the purport of the action was clear: the General Assembly was to be *his* forum platform and not that of anyone who questioned the rightness of Communism's drive toward world empire.

After Khrushchev's departure, Draper, as witness and interpreter of his tactics, again took up the task of analysis: this time, of the relationship between Khrushchev's assault on the United Nations and his new "grand strategy." Draper's analysis—entitled *Ordeal of the UN: Khrushchev, Hammarskjold and the Congo*—was issued, in pamphlet form, as a special supplement to the *New Leader* of November 7, 1960. (1) It should be read by every person who wants to be armed to the brain, we might say, for the struggle that lies ahead: a struggle to preserve the integrity, and even the entity, of the United Nations.

"Soviet policy in Cuba, the Congo and the UN are all pieces of the same puzzle," writes Draper. "They have their common basis in the fact that the most dynamic revolutionary force in the world since the last war has been the national-revolutionary movements rather than the Communist movement. Wherever they have been in direct competition, the Communists have come off second best." (2)

Thus, it is a matter of record that after India achieved its independence, the Communists tried to keep the Congress Party from being able to form a stable government. At that time, Nehru was, in Communist verbiage, a "lackey of capitalism." Only when he had conclusively proved that he could outbid the Communists for popular support did the Soviet Union shift its policy. It began, in short, to cultivate "friendship" with Nehru only when it had to find an alternative to its first hope of taking charge of the Indian nationalist revolution.

If we hold this part of the record in mind, we are that much more able to put into context both Khrushchev's policy with respect to Cuba, the Congo, Guinea, Ghana, and other nationalist-revolutionary countries and his virulent attack upon Hammarskjold and the United Nations.

In an open bid for popular support in the underdeveloped countries, Draper reminds us, "the Communists have rarely been able to compete with the nationalists for power." Thus, in Cuba, "the official Communists scorned and opposed Fidel Castro until victory was almost in his grasp." Then—in accord with the Leninist axiom that what cannot be destroyed must be controlled—they claimed the Cuban nationalist-revolutionary movement as *their* "cause." Its indigenous anti-

Americanism was stimulated into rampant growth and made part of the Soviet Union's worldwide anti-American drive. Today, on the word of competent observers, Castro is Cuban leader in name only. He has become one more puppet of Communism.

Long before Khrushchev, Draper points out, "the world Communist movement faced the problem of competing or collaborating with national-revolutionary movements and, from time to time, it did one or the other.

"Khrushchev's grand strategy has swung the pendulum far over to the side of collaboration. It represents a supreme effort to harness the dynamic of the national-revolutionary movements to the dynamic of Soviet expansionism. It recognizes that a Castro, a Sékoú Toure, a Kwame Nkrumah is vastly more popular with his own people than the Cuban, Guinean and Ghanaian Communists are." (3)

One fact which the Communists have on their side in this effort to expand the "world camp of socialism" by seizing control of revolutions which others have made is that most national-revolutionary movements in underdeveloped countries "are characteristically far more effective and self-sufficient before taking power than afterward." During the struggle for independence, these movements "are held together by a common enemy rather than by a social and political program." After independence is gained, however, a *program* is what they must provide; and this program must not only work on a day-to-day basis but must, in some measure, satisfy popular expectations. At this point, "the Communists stand ready to fill the post-revolutionary vacuum with ready-made slogans and prefabricated formulas as well as the allure of Soviet aid and trade." (4)

The Communists' ability, however, to take charge of the nationalist revolution depends upon certain other factors; and not the least of these, today, is their power to keep at fever pitch the world's fear of war. Here, the Soviet Union's scientific and technological advance is their best ally. It affords them the hope that by well-timed "rocket-rattling" they can, at one critical juncture and then another, divide world opinion and paralyze the world's will to call them to account for any *coup* which they may be able to effect in an underdeveloped country.

It is in the light of this Communist need to keep the fear of war in the forefront of people's minds that we must interpret one of the most curious phenomena of the May–October interval of 1960: the fact that while Khrushchev continued to claim the role of "peace-maker," he was the only head of state—except Castro—who threatened the world with war; and he did so repeatedly.

Again, the success of Khrushchev's strategy depends upon his being able to keep the issue of Western colonialism alive when history has made it dated; and upon his being able to prevent the underdeveloped countries from becoming concerned about the issue of Soviet colonialism—which is by no means dated.

Further, it depends upon his being able, in the underdeveloped countries, to induce *neutralism;* not *neutrality.* The two are very different. Switzerland, for example, has a long and honorable record of neutrality; and in its role as neutral, it has served the world well. Postwar Austria, having had neutrality imposed upon it by international treaty, is building a similar record. There is evidence that Ireland aspires to join this company, as India has already joined it. But no one of these nations is neutralist.

That is to say, no one of them has relinquished the right to form and express moral judgments in the area of world affairs and to exert whatever influence it can. They are all neutral in the accepted sense of not being tied in with any other nation or any power bloc by political or military alliance.

In contrast, neutralism is a Communist invention for maneuvering a nation into moral limbo and keeping it there till it can be taken over. To be neutralist, a country must indeed be free of political and military ties that would automatically bring other nations to its support in time of crisis. But also it must be "anti-imperialist" enough that the fear and hostility which it directs against the West will more than offset whatever suspicions it may entertain with respect to Communist motives. Thus, when it needs help, it can be drawn into the orbit of Khrushchev's economic diplomacy.

This is closely related to a final, determinative factor upon which the success of Khrushchev's strategy depends. He must be able, in one area and then in another, as we have noted in earlier chapters, to create an "authority vacuum" into which the Communists can move.

Against this background of Soviet strategy we can locate, now, Khrushchev's attack upon Hammarskjold and the United Nations. He regards the United Nations as an enemy for the simple reason that, in spite of his effort to brand it as a "tool of American imperialism," it is not thus regarded by most of the world's newly independent peoples. They see it as the friend of small nations: a role which Khrushchev wants to pre-empt for the Soviet Union.

In effect, we might say, the UN gives *size* to small nations. In its General Assembly, their voices and votes count. Through its agencies, they enter into civilization's effort to solve the basic problems of man's life on earth: problems of food, health, education, and the rest. Not least, it is a body to which small nations can turn for help in time of need without having their independence put in jeopardy.

The United Nations neither owns territory nor carries on trade. Hence, it cannot aspire to *add* to its territory or its economic sphere of influence. In short—and in spite of Khrushchev's shrill and insistent propaganda—no imperialist motives can be concealed in the help which the UN gives.

All this adds up to a fact which Khrushchev finds intolerable. As now constituted, the United Nations can keep the new underdeveloped countries from having to subordinate themselves to either great-power bloc in order to survive; and it can prevent the creation within them of an "authority vacuum." Hammarskjold, in word and act, has become the embodiment and defender of that very concept of the United Nations which makes it a barrier to Soviet expansionism.

The Congo, by reason of the virulent hostilities which exploded within it after liberation, became the testing ground where the policy of the United Nations collided, head-on, with Communist strategy. The latter suffered defeat—with the world watching. This made it "obvious" to Khrushchev that Hammarskjold must go; and, further, that the United Nations must be so altered in structure that no one could take his place and enact a similar role.

With respect to the nationalist-revolutionary movements, we have noted, the Communists are determined *to control what they cannot destroy*. With respect to the United Nations, now, they are determined *to destroy what they cannot control*. Thus, one grand strategy has been compounded by Khrushchev out of two supplementary parts.

The Congo became independent on June 30, 1960. A week later, Congolese troops revolted against their Belgian officers —who were in command by treaty agreement, but who bore the onus of Belgium's past colonial policy in the country.

Having revolted, the troops went on the rampage, committing various acts of violence against the white population. Soon, the country was swept by a panic which both exaggerated the extent of the initial violence and induced further violence. Abruptly, then, tribal conflict was added to racial conflict. On July 12, President Kasavubu and Premier Lumumba of the Central Government of the Congo called on the United Nations for aid.

Also, however, they called on a number of separate nations, including both the United States and the Soviet Union. All of these except the Soviet Union replied that their aid would be channeled through the United Nations. But the Soviet Union chose to follow a double course: to support, in the Security Council, the resolution that authorized the sending of UN troops to the Congo; but also to rush its own tanks and troops to the scene—to establish "squatter's rights," as it were, in the "authority vacuum" before the UN forces could arrive.

What frustrated the Soviet Union's projected *fait accompli* was the swift efficiency with which Hammarskjold organized and delivered the UN forces. It was on July 13 that the sending of these forces was authorized in the Security Council. Within five days—on July 18—Hammarskjold was able to report that 3,500 UN troops had arrived in Leopoldville. Their unexpectedly prompt arrival set the stage for the Hammarskjold-Khrushchev struggle. For it filled the "authority vacuum" which the Soviet Union was prepared to pre-empt.

The presence of Soviet tanks and troops was simply announced as a fact for the UN to accept. But Hammarskjold refused to accept it. In the showdown that swiftly followed, Hammarskjold won: the Congolese government asked the Soviet forces to withdraw, and they had no choice other than to do so.

During this rush of developments, Khrushchev was on board ship, bound for the General Assembly of the United Nations. His subsequent behavior suggests that his propaganda war against Hammarskjold and the UN was declared when the news reached him of the forced withdrawal of Soviet troops and agents. The "intolerable" had happened. A drive for Communist expansion which had all the makings of success had been stopped in its tracks. The man and the organization responsible for this "outrage" must go.

Khrushchev's first approach to the problem of rendering the United Nations impotent was calculatedly "reasonable." He proposed replacing the one-man post of Secretary General with a triumvirate.

There are no longer, he said, just two blocs of nations in the world, but three: imperialist, socialist, and neutral. No one man can express the will of all three. Thus, the type of decision which Hammarskjold has hitherto been empowered to make on his own should be made by representatives of these three blocs; and to reduce the danger of an unjust decision's being carried into action, each of the three should have veto power.

Those who felt least impulse to applaud this "reasonable" effort to replace "one-man rule" by "true world representation" were those who best knew the Soviet Union's fifteen-year record of exploiting its veto power in the Security Council. At the time when Khrushchev proposed the "reformation" of the Secretary General's office, the Soviet Union had exercised its right of veto in the Security Council *ninety-two times*—and had thereby nullified on that many occasions the majority decision. Its supporting satellites had run the total of Communist vetoes well over the hundred mark.

To put this record in perspective, we can note that during the same fifteen-year span, since the UN's founding, all non-Communist countries put together had exercised their veto right only seven times: China, once; France, four times; United Kingdom, twice; and the United States, not at all.

Throughout the whole history of the UN, in short, the Soviet Union has used the veto as a weapon in the struggle between the "two camps"; and has exhibited, all along the line, a Communist contempt for majority decisions. What Khrushchev proposed in 1960 was that the "two-camp" struggle be extended to the level of UN operations now occupied by the Secretary General's office.

In practical terms, what would his "triumvirate" mean? It would mean—to judge by the record of the Security Council —that when the neutral representative and the Communist representative voted in agreement, the representative of the "imperialist" bloc would, except in the most rare and critical instances, refrain from using his veto—because of his ingrained respect for majority decisions; but that the Communist representative, with his thinking geared to the "two-camp" struggle, would not hesitate to nullify any majority vote not favorable to "the camp of socialism."

Further, it would mean that no swift and decisive action could be taken even when *only* such action would insure the success of UN policies. Let us suppose, for example, that the triumvirate extolled by Khrushchev had occupied the Secretary General's post in July 1960. In this hypothetical case, as in the actual case, the Security Council has authorized the sending of a UN force to the Congo. But—again as in the actual case—the Soviet Union wants to pre-empt the "authority vacuum" in the Congo before the arrival of the UN troops. Under these circumstances, what chance would there have been that a three-bloc triumvirate, in which each member held veto power, would have reached a prompt executive decision—and have delivered 3,500 UN troops to Leopold-ville within five days?

Finally, we must note, the adoption of Khrushchev's proposal would have meant that flexibility of alignment would vanish from the United Nations, to be replaced by a predictable rigidity. The "bloc" pattern which dominates all Communist thinking would have replaced the pattern of nations voting in accord with their own convictions on one issue and then another.

Khrushchev's effort to control or destroy the United Nations by changing the character of the Secretary General's office was overwhelmingly voted down—as was his effort to oust Hammarskjold from that office.

Casting aside, therefore, the guise of "reasonableness," he took up the weapon of open threat. If the organization was not reshaped to fit his purposes, the member nations of the Soviet bloc would walk out—and form their own "United Nations." He would, in brief, carry the "two-camp" theory to its ultimate logic: he would bring to pass a state of affairs in which no international body bridged the gap between the two camps. Thus, he would make difficult almost to the point of impossibility the peaceful exploration and solution of any world problem; and he would make any "authority vacuum" anywhere on earth a prize for which the great-power blocs would have to compete. No newly independent nation could escape the fate of being dragged into the "two-camp" struggle prescribed by Marxism-Leninism.

It is at this point that we can best turn from Khrushchev's view of the United Nations to Hammarskjold's. For that which, above all else, divided these two men in the General Assembly sessions of 1960 was the diametrically opposed interest they had in the future of the small, newly independent nations. For Khrushchev, these nations were "prizes" to be struggled for and added to the "world camp of socialism." For Hammarskjold, they were nations that must have their independence so underwritten by the strength of the United Nations that no great-power bloc could infringe or exploit this independence.

It was Hammarskjold's stand on this point—a stand dramatized by the showdown in the Congo—which made Khrushchev his implacable enemy. For Khrushchev's grand strategy demands for its success that each small nation, in its throes of post-liberation unrest, must stand vulnerable and alone; and, further, that even the greatest of non-Communist nations must be kept on the sidelines by its fear of war while the Soviet Union moves in to kill by "friendship." The whole strategy falls apart if the new small nations, singly and together, know that they can rely on the United Nations—not only to fill a dangerous "authority vacuum" in a time of crisis, but also to help them grow into a fruitful independence and a fruitful mutuality.

Out of the stresses and strains of the Congo crisis, there emerged one of the remarkable documents of our time. Entitled "The Positive Role of the United Nations in a Split World," it is Hammarskjold's *Introduction* to the Annual Report, June 1959–June 1960, which he presented to the General Assembly in his capacity as Secretary General. (5)

What Hammarskjold had to say in this document marks a departure, certainly, from the original 1945 concept of the United Nations. But this departure is designed to take account of developments in the world that were not anticipated in 1945, and to give the United Nations a role appropriate to these developments. His thesis may well become the rallying conviction of the world's free peoples.

The United Nations, we must remind ourselves, was brought into being as a carrying forward of the wartime alliance into the postwar period. Whatever intentions Stalin may have been holding in reserve, the Western powers looked forward to continued East-West collaboration. The structure of the UN was so set up as to express both the faith that such collaboration would continue and the expectation that while the big powers might pull against one another on various specific issues, they would, on the whole, be a unitive force for peace. The institution of the veto in the Security Council reflects the assumption that the big powers would exert the dominant influence: it was designed, we might say, to prevent the basic interests of any one of these powers from being put in jeopardy.

Three changes have obviously taken place since the United Nations was thus conceived and brought into being. First, the wartime alliance has yielded place to cold war. Second, the major power blocs involved in this cold war have reached a point of military stalemate at a level of high potential destructiveness. Third, independent nations have greatly increased in number, with the vast majority of the new nations located in the world's underdeveloped areas. In view of these changes, what role can the United Nations properly and usefully claim?

As we have noted, Khrushchev is determined to infect the whole organization with the tensions of the "two-camp" struggle; and either to make it serve the "world camp of socialism" or else render it impotent. In like vein, he is determined to carry the struggle into the underdeveloped countries.

Hammarskjold, in contrast, with special reference to the new African nations, takes the stand that the United Nations must help these newly independent nations "to choose their own way without undue influence being exercised and without attempts to abuse the situation. . . . As a universal organization neutral in the big-power struggles over ideology and influence in the world, subordinated to the common will of the member governments and free from any aspirations of its own to power and influence over any group or nation, the United Nations can render service which can be received without suspicion and which can be absorbed without influencing the free choice of the peoples." (6)

The key phrase, here, is "neutral in the big-power struggles." This concept of the United Nations as a neutral guarantor of the neutrality of nations that are seeking to develop without being intruded upon by the "two-camp" struggle is Hammarskjold's unique contribution.

"Fundamental though the differences splitting our world are," he writes, "the areas which are not committed in the major conflicts are considerable. Whether the countries concerned call themselves non-committed, neutral, neutralist or something else, they have all found it not to be in harmony with their role and interests in world politics to tie their policies, in a general sense, to any one of the blocs . . . in the major conflict. . . .

"This clearly defines the main field of useful activity of the United Nations in its efforts to prevent conflicts or to solve conflicts. Those efforts must aim at keeping newly arising conflicts outside the sphere of bloc differences." (7)

In the sphere of "preventive diplomacy," Hammarskjold states, the United Nations must aim to prevent "the creation of a power vacuum between the main blocs"; but if such a vacuum appears—as it did in the Congo—the aim must be so to fill this vacuum that its existence "will not provoke action from any of the major parties." For if any nation associated with either major power bloc were to move in to fill the vacuum—whether it did so to exploit the situation or simply to prevent the opposing bloc from getting in first— the result could be catastrophic for the whole world. Far more than the independence of the invaded nation would be at stake. The risk would be that this nation would become a battlefield where the big powers would engage in a conflict that would spark a world war.

Many persons, Hammarskjold notes, are ready to dismiss the United Nations as useless because it cannot resolve the East-West conflict. To take this attitude, however, is to ignore the many tasks which it can perform "as an instrument for the world community."

These tasks are almost as various as the human enterprise itself. In their separateness, most of them are modest. In their aggregate, however, they become tremendously important. They may well mean, to the underdeveloped nations which occupy a good part of the globe, the difference between having a chance to achieve a viable independence and being destroyed at a point of conflict between the big powers. And they may well mean to the world as a whole the fending-off of a catastrophic, all-embracing war.

By standard Communist label, the Western powers are "warmongers." Also, they are constantly animated by "imperialist" motives. At the very meeting of the Security Council, on July 13, 1960, at which the sending of UN troops to the Congo was authorized, the Soviet representative, Arkady Sobolev, accused the Western powers of "conspiring" against Congolese independence; and soon thereafter, in the General Assembly, Khrushchev tried to brand the whole United Nations as a "tool of American imperialism."

In view of these charges, it is significant that every Western nation supported Hammarskjold in his determined stand for a *neutral* United Nations that could prevent the big-power conflict from invading the small, newly independent countries. The free world—committed and neutral—showed itself to be overwhelmingly in favor of the right of these new nations to have their independence secured and their growth encouraged by the international body. It was the Soviet Union that sought to exploit the crisis in the Congo for the benefit of the world Communist movement. It was Khrushchev who responded to the blocking of this effort by declaring all-out war on Hammarskjold and the United Nations.

This war did not end when Khrushchev left New York. It continued to develop through phase after phase. In late October, for example, it took the form of a Soviet demand, voiced by delegate Alexei Roschin, and repeated by Hungarian delegate Tibor Keszthelyi, that the worldwide information service of the United Nations stop its broadcasts in the Russian, Hungarian, and Chinese languages. This amounted to an assertion that the right of the international body to beam its proceedings to the peoples of member nations behind the Iron Curtain depends upon the current policy of the Communist dictator. Indirectly, it amounted to an assertion that Khrushchev prefers to deliver to these peoples his own strategically amended version of the proceedings. By late November, Khrushchev was demanding that UNESCO, as well as the United Nations as a whole, adopt the "Triumvirate" pattern of executive leadership.

We must assume that the struggle will go on. Each of us, therefore, must decide both what the role is that he wants the United Nations to perform in this "split world" and what he can do to support it in this role.

SEVENTEEN

TOO LATE FOR CREDULITY

KHRUSHCHEV is playing for keeps. He has left no room for doubt on this score. Moreover, his current tactics serve notice that his drive for power will be urgently stepped up in the period ahead. These tactics—of which his attempted grab in the Congo and his assault on the United Nations are samples—have about them a now-or-never quality. By their very nature, it would seem, they must yield him either swift gains or diminishing returns.

If tactics of this sort leave the free world divided against itself, and transfixed with fear of what he may do next, they may net him, at some point in the near future, some gain that will let him forge ahead to another gain, and another.

But if the free world, instead of being divided and transfixed, is moved by these tactics to make a clear appraisal of itself and of what a Communist world victory would mean, the balance of power may just as decisively shift against Khrushchev.

It seems imperative, then, for us to take stock, in this final

chapter, of some of the types of help that he needs from us—
but that we are under no obligation to deliver. Our best clue
to what he wants from us is to be found in the propaganda he
directs at our minds.

First, quite obviously, he wants us to be self-confused
about the meaning of such terms as *freedom* and the *free
world:* confused and abashed and guilty in our use of them,
because we are always reminding ourselves that no one is
absolutely free and that the free world is pockmarked with
despotisms.

It is of the utmost importance to Khrushchev's grand strategy that we be kept too hesitant, self-conscious, and embarrassed in our use of these terms to speak with pride of what
freedom has actually meant to mankind and what it can mean
in the future. If, in our embarrassment, we are moved even a
step further and made to feel proud of our capacity for self-
condemnation, and proud of our inability to see any intrinsic
difference between the Communist system and our own, so
much the better for his strategy. It is of the utmost importance, then, that we use the terms *freedom* and *free world*
without embarrassment—and with legitimate pride.

Even though we recognize that no one is absolutely free,
the fact remains that the human race has long been able to
make a practical distinction between a state of freedom and
a state of coerced submission. Likewise, the term *free world*
has a commonsense utility on two different levels of meaning.
On one level, it can be used to designate the whole non-
Communist orbit. On another level, it can be used to designate that complex of nations in which, roughly speaking, government is not only *for* the people but *by* the people, and in
which certain basic civil liberties have a recognized status.

The term can be applied to the whole non-Communist
orbit, not because all parts of this are equally free, or because

any part of it or any person in it is absolutely free, but because it is that portion of the world within which the Communist Party cannot call the tune.

Against this orbit, Khrushchev can level threat and propaganda. But—so far, at least—it is Communism's target, not Communism's domain. It is free, then, in the sense that it is still the home of diversity, not of "monolithic unity"; and in the further sense that the nations which comprise it enter into larger international unities by voluntary action. They are not subject to "socialist solidarity." Finally, and not least, this orbit is that three-fourths portion of the earth's surface in which the future is still regarded as open, not as pre-designed by a dogma in which history is fate.

Again, the term *free world* can be applied—without apology—to the complex of nations characterized by responsible government and civil liberties, not because these have achieved perfect freedom, but because they have elected to build, by an evolutionary process, customs and institutions to express the belief that individual man has intrinsic worth and inviolable rights; and that he is capable of learning to exercise self-government.

Most of the nations in this category lie in the West. They are heirs to the Hebraic-Christian religion, the Greek respect for rationality, the Magna Carta tradition, and a long on-the-job experience of self-government.

These Western nations, however, do not comprise some sort of exclusive club. The world's democratic community is one into which "whosoever will may come"; and if we really believe in democracy, our hope must be—as it traditionally has been—that more and more of the earth's nations will come.

No matter what Khrushchev may say to the contrary, our hope on this score is not "imperialistic." Neither is it "chauvinistic," no matter how many times we may self-accusingly hit ourselves over the head with the charge that it is. Further, it is not merely a strategic hope that "our side" will become progressively stronger than "their side." And finally, it does not contain within itself a demand that all nations, or any nation, in order to join the world's democratic community, forsake the unique and indigenous and become like us. Even such kindred nations as England and America have evolved markedly different democratic forms.

India has made its choice and must be counted as a viable democracy. So must Israel and Burma. Pakistan is not yet a democracy; but the direction which it intends to take, at a pace geared to the practicalities of change, seems indicated by the fact that its villages are being deliberately turned into laboratories of "basic democracy." And other nations are coming along.

There is, in short, no perfect and absolute freedom on earth, nor is there any perfect formula for bringing it to pass. But there is an orbit that is still free of Communism's "monolithic unity" and "socialist solidarity": an orbit where creative diversity still resides and where the future is still open. And there is a growing community of nations committed to the belief that man both deserves freedom and is capable of enacting a progressive measure of it within a frame of law that is not "class" law and according to codes that are not those of "class" morality.

A second thing which Khrushchev wants from us is a naive credulity with respect to his aims when he calls for negotiations. We have discussed in an earlier chapter the Communist meaning of the verb *to negotiate*. But we return to the subject, here, because Khrushchev appears certain that he can, by manipulating world public opinion, force a Summit or other conference into being whenever he wants one; that he can net propaganda gains from it, at the very least; that sooner or later, he can contrive some more tangible gain in the way of a one-sided concession from the West; and that he can always disrupt a conference by a tantrum or a walkout if it begins to go against him.

It cannot be said too often, therefore, that Communist diplomacy is a projection of Communist ideology into the field of international relations. "Churchill once remarked," writes G. F. Hudson, "that the rulers of Russia 'do not want war, but they want the fruits of war.'" (1) That statement contains the essence of Communist diplomacy. Khrushchev's aim, when he calls for negotiations, is "to get something for nothing, to gain without paying a price the kind of advantage which is normally to be obtained only at the point of a gun." (2)

Non Communist nations—be they democratic or otherwise, highly developed or underdeveloped think of the council table as a *substitute* for the battlefield. When they come to it, they bring with them the assumption that all nations there represented *have a right to continue existing.* Their conflicts may be deep and bitter. Yet each party to the negotiating process expects to give as well as to take; for no one of them thinks of this process as a means of eliminating the others from the world scene. One triumphant example of what can be accomplished by the type of negotiation that takes permanent coexistence for granted was the agreement reached by India and Pakistan, in 1960, with respect to the long-disputed waters of the Indus River.

Communist nations think of the council table as an *extension* of the battlefield. As Hudson points out, they cannot think of it otherwise; for in their ideology "all non-Communist governments are only interim authorities; they are representatives of the class enemy, historically doomed to destruction sooner or later."

From this it follows that these non-Communist govern-- ments "cannot in any circumstances be right in a dispute with a Communist state and they cannot have points of view for which a true believer should have any sympathy. Communist diplomacy, to accord with the processes of history, should always be on the offensive against them; the task of the Communist statesman is to make them yield to his demands, and if he cannot do that, to manifest a proper hostility toward them." (3)

When, in short, Khrushchev demands a conference—on Berlin, or disarmament, or whatever—he comes to the council table doubly obligated. His primary Communist obligation is to gain a one-sided advantage. Failing in this, his secondary Communist obligation is to disrupt the conference and, by propaganda, to put upon the "class enemy" the blame for nothing having been accomplished.

"In the Western view," Hudson continues, "peaceful coexistence should mean a diplomacy of normal negotiations on a give and take basis. But an examination of the record of the last two years shows that this is just what Khrushchev has never been prepared to contemplate. At no point has he had anything to offer in return for acceptance of his demands about Berlin and Germany except reduction of the danger of war—a danger which Soviet policy has created . . ." (4)

Khrushchev's diplomacy is never more than a pretense of diplomacy. It is a blend of offensive maneuvering, to catch the free world off guard, and of outright blackmail when the maneuvering does not get results. There is no reason to think that it will be safe, at any time in the foreseeable future, for either non-Communist governments or the people upon whom they must rely for support to entertain the naive hope that any true resolution of international problems can result from any negotiations to which the Communists are a party.

In the third place, Khrushchev wants us to become enchanted with the idea that disarmament is equivalent to peace. It is not. "Blaming armaments for war is like blaming fever for a disease," writes E. B. White. "Total disarmament would not leave anyone free of the threat of war; it would simply leave everyone temporarily without the help of arms in the event of war." (5)

The solving of the war problem lies not in the giving up of weapons but "in the creation of the machinery for the solution of problems that give rise to the use of weapons." What is the main obstacle in the world today to the creation of such machinery? It is Communism's dogma translated into Soviet policy. Khrushchev asks us to credit his claim that all Communist nations are "peace-loving." But he also insists that all non-Communist nations must learn to accept the fact that they are headed for oblivion, and that Communism's historic role is to help them reach that state. How much support this view can give to "the creation of the machinery for the solution of problems that give rise to the use of weapons" was shown by Khrushchev's drive either to control or destroy the United Nations.

Khrushchev knows, however, that a vast number of people throughout the world do believe that disarmament would be equivalent to peace; and he hopes that if he calls for total disarmament loudly and persistently enough, he will become for these people the apostle of peace. This hope of his rests on the expectation, it would seem, that the world's naivete is unlimited and incurable.

"In a letter to Dag Hammarskjold," E. B. White reminds us, "Khrushchev said: 'General and complete disarmament cannot result in advantage to any side.' This is nonsense. The side that enjoys numerical superiority stands to gain by disarmament, the side that does not have any intention of remaining unarmed for more than a few minutes stands to gain, and the side that uses the lie as an instrument of public policy stands to gain. If disarmament carried no chance of advantage, Mr. Khrushchev would not be wasting his breath on it. He likes it because of its propaganda value and because it gives him a chance to oust us from our advanced military bases—which is the Soviet's precondition of an arms agreement." (6)

That final sentence deserves to be memorized by every person in the non-Communist world who is still trusting enough to become a victim of naive hope whenever he hears the phrase *total disarmament*. Khrushchev's *precondition* of an arms agreement—a precondition which he never modifies and from which he never departs—is one that would, from the moment it was fulfilled, leave the free world helpless to defend itself.

In an earlier chapter, we made note of the Soviet Union's sustained effort, with respect to both disarmament and the control of nuclear weapons, to secure agreements with loopholes in them: loopholes that would enable the Communists to convert ostensibly fair agreements into advantageous ones.

One phase of this effort, from at least 1957 to the present, has been Khrushchev's "benign" insistence that nations must first learn to trust each other enough to reach an agreement and put it into operation and *then*, in a spirit of mutual trust, work out its detailed implementation. In an interview with William Randolph Hearst, Jr., for example, in 1957, he discussed the problem of the control of nuclear weapons. "The way you put the question," he said, "is, first inspection, then the establishment of confidence. But we believe that first confidence between countries should be achieved and then inspection established."

Khrushchev was still on this theme in 1960. He was perfectly willing, he said—speaking, this time, of total disarmament—to accept any kind of controls the West wanted to specify, but on condition that an agreement was, first, in a state of "mutual confidence," reached and put into operation.

To appreciate the irony—but also the grim danger—of this insistent approach, we have only to remember that the Soviet Union holds, by a wide margin, the world's record for broken treaties; and that its ideology justifies its breaking them. Treaties made across "class" lines, Lenin specified, are instruments of war; and they are not designed to be kept a minute longer than expediency dictates. On what, then, is "mutual confidence" to be based? If the free world were to accept Khrushchev's formula of disarming first, and then working out the machinery of controls, what would happen *during the interval between these two operations?*

There are two Communist reasons why Khrushchev cannot actually want total disarmament—no matter how much he talks about it. His attempt to stage a *coup* in the Congo illustrates one reason: namely that his grand strategy with respect to the underdeveloped countries demands his being able to exploit, swiftly and conclusively, by force of arms, any "authority vacuum" that shows up in these countries. He is not, at the very time when he is trying to eliminate the United Nations as a competitive "vacuum filler," likely to be trying also, in good faith, to eliminate the Soviet Union's armed capacity to move in when the time is ripe.

The second determinative reason why he cannot actually want the total disarmament which he demands is that a disarmed Soviet Union would promptly lose its satellite empire. No puppet regime in East Europe could long survive without the presence of the Red Army. According to the best figures available, between 50,000 and 80,000 Soviet troops are today stationed in Hungary alone—to ward off the danger of "counterrevolution."

But we can let E. B. White have the final word on the subject: "Disarmament in this day would increase, not diminish, the danger of war. Today's weapons are too destructive to use, so they stand poised and quiet; this is our strange climate, when arms are safer than no arms. If modern weapons make war unlikely, had we not better keep them until we have found the political means of making war unnecessary?" (7)

In the fourth place, Khrushchev wants the world—and particularly the underdeveloped countries—to believe that the Soviet Union has been able to achieve by Communist methods a spectacular economic development that would have been utterly impossible by any other methods.

He knows, as we all tragically do, that our world today is a hungry world, a world desperately in need of economic progress. And he appears to be betting, therefore, that there are countless people who, if they can once be persuaded of the truth of his claim, will tacitly agree not to look too closely at the *human* cost of Communist methods; and not to look too wistfully at the political liberties they must renounce in order to embrace these methods.

What are the facts? In an earlier chapter, we appraised the heavy and unacknowledged debt which the Soviet economy owes to the millions of persons who, in slave labor camps, were literally worked to death to "prove" the efficiency of Communism; and the other heavy and acknowledged debt which it owes to East Germany and the East European satellites for the wealth of materials and industrial installations of which it plundered them.

But since this is a period when Khrushchev is seeking advantageous trade relations, let us look, also, at what the Soviet economy owes to the despised capitalism of the United States. In 1944, Stalin told Eric Johnston that "About two thirds of all the large industrial enterprises in the USSR had been built with U.S. material aid or technical assistance." (8)

And again: "In 1931 Russia apparently bought sixty-five per cent of the exports of the United States machine-tool industry . . . the General Electric Company played a major role in rebuilding the famous Dnieper Dam in the immediate post-war years." (9)

Quite apart, however, from these considerations, how does the Soviet Union's claim of spectacular success actually stand up? The only comparison which appears to interest Khrushchev is that between the Soviet economy and that of the United States—which is to be overtaken and outstripped. But it is interesting to make a quite different comparison: between the Soviet economy and that of a country which constantly infuriates the Soviet dictator—as it infuriated Stalin —by being Communist *in its own peculiar and experimental way:* namely, Yugoslavia.

Yugoslavia has had, over the past five years, a rate of economic growth "surpassing that of every country in the world except China." (10) Unlike Red China, however, and unlike the Soviet Union, it has focused on the production of consumer goods. Such production is still very far from being adequate. But Yugoslavia has not sacrificed its own people to the demands of "proletarian internationalism." Furthermore, it has achieved its own form of experimental diversity. Within a frame of almost total public ownership, it has effected a very considerable release of the people's initiative by allowing, between state-owned productive units, a remarkable measure of free competition; and it has granted to the workers in these productive units both enough tangible benefits from successful enterprise and enough policy-making power to insure such competition's being more than an empty pretense.

Yugoslavia is working, now, to build not only better relationships with the West but also economic ties with such Asian countries as India and Pakistan. Like all underdeveloped countries, these need, in their planning, to think of both basic industries and consumer industries. It would be an odd turn of history if Yugoslavia should prove uniquely able to convince them that the coercive, "monolithic" pattern of the Soviet economy is not essential to swift progress.

And finally, a comparison with free-world methods and results is in order. The best commentary on collectivization is provided by a comparison between the present state of Hungarian agriculture, which is still sluggish and woefully inadequate, and that of Austria. "Since 1945, Austria has had a 35–50 per cent increase in grain production and has now become self-sufficient in grain for the first time since the first world war—*with only one-third as much arable land as Hungary.*" (The italics are ours.) "Austria's progress is due to mechanization, which is spearheaded by some 120,000 tractors, while Hungary's total number of tractors is only about 30,000." (11)

When we add to these facts the discrepancy in the developments of West Germany and the Soviet zone of Germany, we can only conclude that Khrushchev's claim that the Soviet Union and only the Soviet Union can point the way toward economic progress simply does not stand up.

In the fifth place, Khrushchev wants us to have an inexhaustible capacity to feel reassured whenever he or any other Communist speaks reassuring words.

What such words amount to can be suggested by one illustration. Some seven months after Khrushchev gave his "de-Stalinization" speech, at the Twentieth Congress of the CPSU, in late February 1956, Antal Apro, a long-time henchman of Rakosi, the "Stalin of Hungary," laid down the new Party line to a Hungarian audience that had been on the receiving end of the most ruthless brand of terrorism.

In the new "correct" manner, Apro deplored the Stalinist

excesses by which the Hungarian regime had been marked in the past and stated that there must never again occur "such acts of terror as those which caused the death of our dear comrades."

Then he struck his note of reassurance: "Many will ask, 'What is the guarantee that similar infringements of the law will not be repeated?' . . . The guarantee is the Party. We are the guarantee, because we are determined and we can learn from the mistakes of the past." (12)

A month later, Soviet tanks rolled into Budapest—and those who welcomed their coming were precisely men of the Apro type. So were those who, like Kadar, were deemed most fit to fill the top Party posts after the "counterrevolution" had been crushed. If both the Communist ideology and the Communist record tell anything at all, it is that a "guarantee" given by the Party is at the farthest remove from a guarantee in which men can safely lodge their trust.

Khrushchev has one fear that outranks all others: the fear that the free nations will unite—in policy and determination —and stay united.

If this is his paramount fear, then the course the free nations must take becomes obvious. "If it is so very important to Russia that the West be a house divided against itself," E. B. White points out, "then it should be equally important to the free nations that they stand together, not simply as old friends who have a common interest but as a going political concern." (13)

This urgent need of the free world to achieve workable unity is, White observes, seldom referred to in exact terms. "England and America remind me of a fabulous two-headed sheep I encountered in a book by Laurie Lee: 'It could sing harmoniously in a double voice and cross-question itself for hours.'"

It is simply too late for the free world to go on indulging in the naivete of separateness. It is too late for us to hope that if we just go on thinking *primarily* of our separate national welfare, and making only a token gesture—and a reluctant one at that—to the demands of our common welfare, we will be able to handle, in the period that lies ahead, the Communist challenge as designed by Khrushchev.

In an article called "New World Culture," in the *Manchester Guardian Weekly* of October 20, 1960, David Marquand says that American culture, originally built on "the values of English dissent" has the mark of the "Non-conformist conscience." It is "a weapon of social revolution."

Surprisingly, his verbs are in the present tense; not the past. We so rarely hear our current American culture described in these terms, and so habitually hear it described as materialistic and conformist, that we are brought up short: what is he talking about?

The fact is that what has caught his attention is something which most of us have not noticed. "In Europe politics has generally been a battle between rival philosophies. In America it is a struggle between rival adherents of the same philosophy. Hence the failure of American Marxism. A society based on Jefferson has no need of Marx: all it needs is to bring Jefferson up to date. Hence, too, the intellectual bankruptcy of the American Right."

Extremism at both ends of the scale can make far more than its share of noise; and it can do no end of harm if it is allowed to have its divisive way. It can pull and haul at the non-extremist majority until it sets against each other persons and groups that should, with a recognition of common purpose, be resolving their differences "in open debate." Also, whether Communist or Rightist, it can distract our attention from our unfinished democratic homework and from those international responsibilities that have accrued to us as by-products of the fact that our system has functioned extraordinarily well.

Further, Marquand reminds us, the non-extremists who comprise the overwhelming American majority can easily lose sight of what their Jeffersonian enterprise is all about—and thereby forsake the values of a unique culture in which the indigenous struggle is not between rival philosophies but "between rival adherents of the same philosophy."

In spite of its extremist minorities, and in the midst of all the differences that threaten to splinter the majority, the America which Marquand portrays should be able to work out unitive policies for the period ahead. It should be able to infuse these with Jeffersonian vigor—not with a vague hope that if issues are avoided long enough, someone will somehow pull out of the international hat a rabbit called "peace."

A nation, moreover, which "has no need of Marx" because it is "based on Jefferson" should be able to make Marx look supremely unnecessary on the world front. For Jefferson has infinitely more than Marx could ever have to offer to those peoples and countries that want to keep their hard-won independence, and to move toward responsible government and responsible participation in the world community, while they are learning how to bring a workable economy into being and make it function.

Too many of us have come to a point where we think of Jeffersonian democracy with nostalgia rather than with purpose. Because he lived in a rural economy—as most of the world's people still do—we have let ourselves doubt that his faith and commitment can be ours.

Further, just as we have been embarrassed to speak about freedom because we have achieved no perfect freedom, and about democracy because we do not want to seem to be foisting our political forms upon other nations, so we have hesitated to say that when Jefferson spoke, he was speaking about *man.*

Every civilized nation has produced its quota of men who have both embodied its unique greatness and been too great to remain exclusively its own. Within a particular environment, in terms that express this particularity, these men have wrestled with the ancient, perennial problems of our human estate; and they have become, in the end, the property of the world. No man anywhere is diminished by learning from them; for each individual recognizes that what they have had to say has been about him.

We do not feel that Greece is thrusting some alien influence upon us when we adopt as mentor that Socrates who found an unexamined life not worth living. It was not an act of chauvinistic arrogance for Nazareth to give Jesus to the world.

It is no secret that Lincoln has long since ceased to belong to America alone. The world has claimed him because what he became on the American frontier was relevant to what countless human beings hunger to become. He lived for a specific span of years in a specific place; he belongs everywhere.

Today, it may be that our prime task is to tell the peoples of the world what Jefferson knew about them. He knew that they were never designed to take on any such stunted lineaments as those of Communist man. He knew that something was lodged in each of them that was of inestimable worth. He knew that they could come very far short of being adequately skilled in self-government and yet justify *by their potentialities* the hypothesis that governments must "derive their just powers from the consent of the governed."

Above all, he knew that they were *created;* not *manufactured.* And he knew that the more they respected themselves and one another as created beings, the more able they could become, by study and experience, to create a society free enough to be called free and imperfect enough to keep them on the job. A world learning to base itself on Jefferson would have no need of Marx.

NOTES TO THE TEXT

Chapter One—THE GEOGRAPHY OF COMMUNISM

(1) J. V. Stalin, "Two Camps," *Izvestia*, No. 41, February 22, 1919. Also, *Works*, Vol. 4, p. 243. Moscow, Foreign Languages Publishing House, 1953.

(2) "Andrei Zhdanov: 'On the International Situation,'" *Political Affairs*, December 1947.

(3) "Resolution of the 21st Congress of the Communist Party of the Soviet Union on Nikita Khrushchev's Report on the Target Figures for the Economic Development of the USSR from 1959 to 1965," *Soviet News*, No. 4004, p. 145, February 10, 1959. Published by the Press Department of the Soviet Embassy, London.

(4) Quoted by General John E. Hull (Ret.) in "Trade With Soviet Russia," *Soviet Economic Challenge: Proceedings of the Fifth National Military-Industrial Conference*, p. 19. The Institute for American Strategy, 140 South Dearborn Street, Chicago 3, Illinois. 1959.

(5) "Long Live the First of May!" *Communist International*, No. 1, p. 28, May 1, 1919.

(6) V. I. Lenin, *Works*, Vol. XXIV, p. 381. Moscow.

(7) Resolution of 21st Congress, p. 60.

(8) V. I. Lenin, *Selected Works*, Vol. II, p. 105. New York, International Publishers, 1943.

(9) "Comment," *Manchester Guardian Weekly*, June 16, 1960, p. 9.

(10) S. F. Singer, "Russian Reactions to the U-2 Incident," letter on Editorial page, Washington *Post* and *Times Herald*, September 15, 1960.

Chapter Two—THE MEANING OF "PEACEFUL COEXISTENCE"

(1) "Resolution of the CPSU Central Committee on the tasks of party propaganda in contemporary conditions," *Pravda* and *Red Star*, Moscow, Jan 10, 1960; *USSR National Affairs*, Jan. 11, 1960, p. 2.

(2) "7-Year Plan Target Figures: Report to the Special 21st Congress of the Communist Party of the Soviet Union and reply to discussion by N. S.

Khrushchev," Soviet Booklet No. 47, p. 107. Soviet Booklets, 3 Rosary Gardens, London, S.W. 7.

(3) Ibid., p. 65.

(4) Ibid., p. 57.

(5) Ibid., p. 66.

(6) Ibid., p. 101.

(7) Ibid., p. 11.

(8) Ibid., p. 85.

(9) Soviet News, Feb. 2, 1959, pp. 101–102. Published by the Press Department of the Soviet Embassy, London.

(10) J. Edgar Hoover, "Statement to the Subcommittee to Investigate the Administration of the Internal Security Act and other Internal Security Laws of the Committee of the Judiciary, United States Senate, Eighty-sixth Congress, First Session, concerning the 17th National Convention, Communist Party, U.S.A., December 10–13, 1959," p. 5. United States Government Printing Office, Washington, D.C., 1960.

(11) Nikita S. Khrushchev, "On Peaceful Coexistence," Foreign Affairs, October 1959, p. 14.

Chapter Three—IN THE WAKE OF AN ILLUSION

(1) For a summary of Soviet espionage in the United States, see Exposé of Soviet Espionage, May 1960, prepared by the Federal Bureau of Investigation, United States Department of Justice, J. Edgar Hoover, Director. Printed for the use of the Committee on the Judiciary, United States Printing Office, Washington, D.C., 1960.

(2) Edwin Arlington Robinson, "The Burning Book," Collected Poems, p. 48. New York, Macmillan, 1937.

(3) "Mr. K. Turns Down the Heat," Berlin Correspondent of the Manchester Guardian Weekly, May 26, 1960, p. 3.

(4) Foreword, The Soviet Economic Challenge, p. 3. Proceedings of the Fifth Annual National Military-Industrial Conference, the Institute of American Strategy, 140 South Dearborn Street, Chicago, Illinois.

(5) Max Frankel, "Russians Calm Amid Tough Talk," New York Times, September 12, 1960.

(6) Theodore Draper, "Khrushchev's Doctrine," The New Leader, August 1–8, 1960, p. 3.

(7) "Mr. Khrushchev's Offensive . . . Pie in the Sky and Chaos on Earth," New York Herald Tribune, September 24, 1960.

Chapter Four—DICTATOR OF THE IDEOLOGY

(1) Leonard Schapiro, *The Communist Party of the Soviet Union*, p. 558. New York, Random House, 1959.

(2) Neal Wood, *Communism and the British Intellectuals*, p. 112. New York, Columbia University Press, 1959.

(3) Edwin Arlington Robinson, *Roman Bartholow*, in *Collected Poems*, p. 757. New York, Macmillan, 1937.

(4) N. S. Khrushchev, *7-Year Plan Target Figures, Report to the 21st Congress of the Communist Party of the Soviet Union;* Soviet Booklet #47, p. 91. Soviet Booklets, 3 Rosary Gardens, London, S.W. 7.

(5) Leopold Labedz, "Ideology: The Fourth Stage," *Problems of Communism*, #6, Vol. VIII, November–December 1959, p. 2. United States Government Printing Office, Washington, D.C.

(6) J. V. Stalin, *Works*, Vol. XII, pp. 380–381. Moscow, Foreign Languages Publishing House, 1955.

(7) Tamas Aczel and Tibor Meray, *The Revolt of the Mind*, pp. 386–387. New York, Praeger, 1959.

(8) Ibid., p. 391.

Chapter Five—THE SUCCESS KHRUSHCHEV NEEDS

(1) For a study of the manner in which the Chinese Communists, in their struggle toward power, made someone in each community a "class enemy" to be hated, see R. J. De Jaegher and Irene Corbally Kuhn, *The Enemy Within: An Eyewitness Account of the Communist Conquest of China.* Allahabad 2, U.P., India, St. Paul Publications, 28-B Chatham Lines, 1957.

(2) Hugh Seton-Watson, *Neither War Nor Peace*, New York, Praeger, 1960, pp. 438–439.

(3) Ibid., p 451.

(4) Leonard Schapiro, *The Communist Party of the Soviet Union*, New York, Random House, 1959, pp. 547–550.

(5) Merle Fainsod, "The Party in the Post-Stalin Era," *Problems of Communism*, #1, Vol. VII, January–February 1958, p. 8.

(6) Harold J. Berman, "Soviet Law Reform—Dateline Moscow 1957," *Yale Law Journal*, Vol. 66, No. 8, July 1957, p. 1215.

(7) Washington *Post* and *Times Herald*, April 17, 1960.

(8) Leopold Labedz, "The Growing Sino-Soviet Dispute," *The New Leader*, September 12, 1960, p. 5.

Chapter Six—THE BODY AND SPIRIT OF A PLAN

(1) "Target Figures for the Development of the National Economy of the U.S.S.R. from 1959 to 1965: *Theses* of N. S. Khrushchev's Report to the Twenty-First Congress of the Communist Party of the Soviet Union," *Soviet Booklet* #43, p. 77. Soviet Booklets, 3 Rosary Gardens, London, S.W. 7, December 1958.

(2) Ibid., p. 20.

(3) Ibid., p. 75.

(4) Ibid., p. 13.

(5) Ibid., p. 61.

(6) "7-Year Plan Target Figures," *Soviet Booklet* #47, p. 20. Soviet Booklets, February 1959.

(7) Ibid., p. 66.

(8) *Second Five Year Plan*, 1956, pp. 3, xiii. Government of India Planning Commission.

(9) *Third Five Year Plan, A Draft Outline*, p. 3. Government of India Planning Commission.

(10) *Outline of the Second Five Year Plan (1960–1965)*, p. iii. Government of Pakistan Planning Commission. Government of Pakistan Press, Karachi, 1960.

(11) *Theses*, pp. 72, 18.

(12) Ibid., p. 77.

(13) "7-Year Plan," p. 69.

(14) Ibid., p. 39.

(15) Ibid., p. 73.

(16) Ibid., p. 67.

(17) *Outline of the Second Five Year Plan*, Pakistan, p. iv.

(18) *Theses*, p. 6.

(19) *Outline of the Second Five Year Plan*, Pakistan, p. 1.

(20) *Second Five Year Plan*, India, p. 5.

(21) Ibid., p. 6.

(22) V. I. Lenin, *Left-Wing Communism, An Infantile Disorder*, in *Selected Works*, Vol. X, p. 60. New York, International Publishers, 1943.

(23) J. V. Stalin, *Works*, Vol. 13, p. 176. Moscow, Foreign Languages Publishing House, 1955.

(24) "7-Year Plan," p. 77.

(25) Ibid., p. 77.

Chapter Seven—HISTORY AS A WEAPON

(1) Leonard Schapiro, *The Communist Party of the Soviet Union*, p. 472. New York, Random House, 1959.

(2) Bertram D. Wolfe, "The Gospel According to Khrushchev," *Foreign Affairs*, Vol. 38, No. 4, July 1960, p. 579.

(3) Ibid., p. 579.

(4) Ibid., p. 578, text and footnote.

(5) Ibid., pp. 579–580.

(6) "Speech of Nikita Khrushchev Before a Closed Session of the XXth Congress of the Communist Party of the Soviet Union on February 25, 1956," pp. 132–137. Printed for the Use of the Committee on the Judiciary, by the Subcommittee to Investigate the Administration of the Internal Security Act and Other Internal Security Laws of the Committee of the Judiciary, United States Senate. U. S. Government Printing Office, Washington, D.C., 1957.

(7) Leopold Labedz, "Khrushchev's New Party History," *The New Leader*, October 12, 1959, p. 20.

(8) Ibid., p. 20.

(9) Khrushchev, p. 41.

(10) Labedz, p. 18.

(11) Khrushchev, p. 31.

(12) *Istoriya Kommunisticheskoi partii Sovetskogo Soyuza* (*History of the Soviet Communist Party*), p. 645. Moscow, 1959.

(13) *History*, p. 603.

(14) Edwin Arlington Robinson, "Toussaint L'Ouverture," *Collected Poems*, p. 1185. New York, Macmillan, 1937.

(15) V. I. Lenin, *Selected Works*, Vol. VI, p. 46. New York, International Publishers, 1943.

(16) *History*, p. 209.

(17) Ibid., p. 227.

(18) Ibid., p. 567.

(19) Ibid., p. 567.

(20) Ibid., p. 161.

(21) Ibid., pp. 159–160.

Chapter Eight—COMMUNISM'S PRINTING PRESS

(1) Joseph Stalin, *Foundations of Leninism*, pp. 87–88. New York, International Publishers, 1934.

(2) A. Denisov, "International Cultural Bonds of the Soviet People," *International Affairs*, Moscow, July 15, 1955, p. 36.

(3) Ibid., p. 37.

(4) V. I. Lenin, *Selected Works*, Vol. II, p. 19. New York, International Publishers, 1943.

(5) Ibid., p. 18.

(6) Ibid., pp. 20–22.

(7) Ibid., p. 169.

(8) Ibid., p. 178.

(9) Ibid., pp. 179–180.

(10) Ibid., p. 180.

(11) Ibid., pp. 166–167.

(12) George S. Counts, *The Challenge of Soviet Education*, p. 180. New York, McGraw-Hill, 1957.

(13) Ibid., p. 196.

(14) Ibid., p. 196.

(15) *International Affairs* can be secured in the United States from three sources: Imported Publications and Products, 4 West 16th Street, New York City; Four Continent Book Corporation, 822 Broadway, New York City; or the Bookstore of Victor Kamkin, Inc., 2906 14th Street, N.W., Washington, D.C.

(16) For a report on the manner in which a long line of Soviet visitors to the United States have given their impressions in the Soviet press, after their return home, see *The United States Through Soviet Eyes*, prepared by the staff of the Subcommittee to Investigate the Administration of the Internal Security Act and Other Internal Security Laws of the Committee of the Judiciary, United States Senate, Eighty-Sixth Congress, Second Session. Printed for the use of the Committee on the Judiciary, United States Government Printing Office, Washington, D.C., 1960.

Chapter Nine—SPEAKING IN TONGUES

(1) *Khrushchev in America*, p. 70. New York, Crosscurrents Press, 1960. Translated from the book published in the USSR, in 1959, entitled *Live in Peace and Friendship* (Full texts of the speeches made by N. S. Khrushchev on his tour of the United States, September 15–27, 1959).

(2) To avoid repeating at length what we have written elsewhere on the

subject of how Communists negotiate, and the meanings which they attach to negotiation, we would refer our readers to Chapter XVII, "Negotiating With Our Eyes Open," in our book *What We Must Know About Communism*. New York, Norton, 1958.

(3) V. I. Lenin, *Selected Works*, Vol. IV, p. 201. New York, International Publishers, 1943.

(4) *Khrushchev in America*, p. 74.

(5) V. I. Lenin, *Selected Works*, Vol. II, p. 322.

(6) J. Stalin, *Works*, Vol. IV, p. 161. Moscow, Foreign Languages Publishing House, 1953.

(7) W. de Kohout-Dolnobransky, *The People's Right to Self-Determination*, p. 8. From the Archives of International Bolshevism, International Committee for Information and Social Activity (CIAS), Luxembourg, 1960.

(8) N. S. Khrushchev, *For Victory in Peaceful Competition With Capitalism*, p. 121. New York, Dutton, 1960.

(9) Stefan C. Stolte, "The Seventh Hungarian Party Congress," *Bulletin* of the Institute for the Study of the USSR, Vol. VII, No. 2, February 1960, p. 42. Mannhardtstrasse 6, Munich, Germany.

(10) David J. Dallin, *The Changing World of Soviet Russia*, p. 204. New Haven, Yale University Press, 1956.

(11) N. S. Khrushchev, *For Victory in Peaceful Competition with Capitalism*, pp. 282, 283, 287.

(12) Khrushchev, ibid., p. 278.

(13) *Theses and Statutes of the II Congress of the Communist International, 1920*. Issued by the Central Executive Committee of the Communist Party of America, New York, 1921.

(14) Elliot R. Goodman, *The Soviet Design for a World State*, p. 7. New York, Columbia University Press, 1960.

(15) S. P. Melgunov, *"Krasnyi Terror" v. Rossii*, 1918–1923. Berlin, Second Edition, p. 72, 1924.

(16) "History Revisited," *East Europe*, Vol. 9, No. 5, May 1960, p. 35.

Chapter Ten—BERLIN: A CASE STUDY

(1) For a much fuller list of dates, we refer the reader to *Berlin: a Compilation of Analytical Materials*. Institute for the Study of the USSR, Mannhardtstrasse 6, Munich, Germany, 1959.

Three other useful sources of facts and insights not specifically quoted in this chapter, but to which we acknowledge our debt, are as follows: Helmut Arntz, *Germany in a Nutshell*, published by the Press and Information Office of the Federal German Republic, Bonn, Germany, 1958; *Germany Behind the Iron Curtain: The Soviet Occupation Zone*, Edited by Karl Hermann Böhmer, published by Tellus-Verlag, Essen, Germany; and *The*

Soviet Note on Berlin: an Analysis. Department of State Publication 6757. European and British Commonwealth Series 52. Released January 1959. U. S. Government Printing Office, Washington 25, D.C. Price 25¢.

(2) V. I. Lenin, *Selected Works,* Vol. VI, p. 477. New York, International Publishers, 1943.

(3) *Confuse and Control: Soviet Techniques in Germany,* pp. 2, 15. Department of State Publication 4107. European and British Commonwealth Series 17. Released April 1951. U. S. Government Printing Office, Washington 25, D.C. Price 30¢.

(4) Flora Lewis, Special to the *Washington Post:* "Allies Move to Hit Back at Reds for Restrictions Put on Berlin," September 9, 1960.

(5) Flora Lewis, Special to the *Washington Post:* "Reds Back East Germany on Berlin Travel Curbs," September 14, 1960.

(6) *Berlin,* p. 8. Prepared by the United States Mission, Berlin, April 1959.

(7) Ibid.

Chapter Eleven—EXCHANGE PROGRAMS: WHOSE WEAPON?

(1) B. Litvinov, "The Soviet View of East-West Cultural Exchange," *Bulletin,* Vol. VII, No. 2, February 1960, p. 49. Institute for the Study of the USSR, Mannhardtstrasse 6, Munich, Germany.

(2) Ibid., p. 50.

(3) *Treaties and Other International Acts Series 3957.* Superintendent of Documents, U. S. Government Printing Office, Washington 25, D.C. Price 15 cents.

(4) *Arts,* Paris, November 4–10, 1959.

(5) *Sovetskaya Byelorussiya,* February 18, 1960.

(6) *Pravda,* October 11, 1959.

(7) *Arts,* Paris, November 4–10, 1959.

(8) *Saturday Review,* July 25, 1959. This issue contains a full article on Norman Cousins' speech in Moscow, and another on the discussion period which followed it.

(9) N. S. Khrushchev, "On Peaceful Coexistence," *Foreign Affairs,* October 1959, p. 14.

(10) Ibid., p. 3.

(11) John Herling, "U. S. Labor vs. Khrushchev," *The New Leader,* October 5, 1959, p. 18.

(12) "Remarks by Ambassador William S. B. Lacy at the Foreign Affairs Forum of the League of Republican Women of the District of Columbia," Feb. 6, 1959, p. 8. Mimeographed. U. S. Department of State.

(13) *Soviet News*, Feb. 2, 1959, p. 107. Published by the Press Department of the Soviet Embassy, London.

(14) Lacy, "Remarks," p. 5.

(15) *Trybuna Ludu*, Warsaw, December 15, 1957.

Chapter Twelve—COLONIALISM: SOVIET STYLE

(1) Alex Inkeles, "Nationalities in the USSR"; *Problems of Communism*, Vol. IX, No. 3, May–June 1960, p. 27.

(2) Ibid., p. 28.

(3) Ibid., p. 28.

(4) Leonard Schapiro, *The Communist Party of the Soviet Union*, p. 221. New York: Random House, 1959.

(5) Ibid., p. 221.

(6) Ibid., p. 222.

(7) *Tass*, March 26, 1957.

(8) *Soviet World Outlook: A Handbook of Communist Statements*, p. 17. Department of State Publication 6836. European and British Commonwealth Series 56. Released July 1959. U. S. Government Printing Office, Washington 25, D.C. Price $1.25.

(9) *Der Aktuelle Osten, Kommentare und Nachrichten aus Politik, Wirtschaftund Technik der UdSSR und der Satellitenländer*, p. 7. July 20, 1960. Published by the Volksbund fur Frieden und Freiheit, Member of the International Committee for Information and Social Activity (CIAS), 17 Bertha von Suttner-Platz, Bonn, Federal Republic of Germany.

(10) Ibid., p. 7.

(11) Ibid., p. 8.

(12) Ibid., p. 8.

(13) "Integrating the Satellites: The Rule of COMECON," *East Europe*, Vol. 18, November 1959, p. 3.

(14) *East Europe*, p. 11.

Chapter Thirteen—THE PARTY'S WAR AGAINST THE PEOPLE

(1) *Target Figures for the Development of the National Economy of the U.S.S.R. from 1959 to 1965: Theses of N. S. Khrushchev's Report to the 21st Congress of the Communist Party of the Soviet Union, on the Targets of the Seven-Year Plan;* Soviet Booklet No. 43, p. 79. Soviet Booklets, 3 Rosary Gardens, London S.W. 7. December 1958.

(2) Irving R. Levine, *Main Street, U.S.S.R.*, pp. 31–32. New York, Signet Books (New American Library), 1960. A reprint of selections from the original edition published by Doubleday.

(3) Joseph Novak, *The Future Is Ours, Comrade*, pp. 34–35. Garden City, New York, Doubleday, 1960.

(4) V. I. Lenin, *Selected Works*, Vol. IX, p. 137. New York: International Publishers, 1943.

(5) Ibid., Vol. IX, p. 137.

(6) Ibid., Vol. VI, p. 475.

(7) Levine, p. 32.

(8) Lenin, Vol. VI, p. 477.

(9) Hadley Cantril, *Soviet Leaders and Mastery over Men*, p. 23. New Brunswick, Rutgers University Press, 1960.

(10) Cantril, p. 8.

(11) Ibid.

Chapter Fourteen—THE MAKING OF COMMUNIST MAN

(1) Elliot R. Goodman, *The Soviet Design for a World State*, p. 431. New York, Columbia University Press, 1960.

(2) V. I. Lenin, *Works*, Vol. XXI, p. 399. Moscow, 1922.

(3) Ibid., Vol. XXI, p. 260.

(4) Ibid., Vol. XXV, p. 194.

(5) Goodman, pp. 431–432.

(6) *7-Year Plan Target Figures*, Report to the Special 21st Congress of the Communist Party of the Soviet Union and reply to discussion by N. S. Khrushchev, *Soviet Booklet* No. 47, p. 72. Soviet Booklets, 3 Rosary Gardens, London S.W. 7, February 1959.

(7) *7-Year Plan*, p. 73.

(8) *7-Year Plan*, p. 67.

(9) Anastas Mikoyan, Speech at the 21st Congress of the CPSU; *Soviet News*, February 2, 1959. Published by the Soviet Embassy, London.

(10) *7-Year Plan*, p. 91.

(11) Lenin, *Works*, Vol. XXV, p. 441.

(12) *7-Year Plan*, p. 39.

(13) "Resolution of the CPSU Central Committee on the tasks of propaganda in contemporary conditions," USSR *National Affairs*, January 11, 1960, p. 20. Also, *Pravda* and *Red Star*, Moscow, January 10, 1960.

(14) Ralph Waldo Emerson, "Circles," *Essays*, First Series.

(15) J. V. Stalin, *Foundations of Leninism*, 10th Edition, p. 445. Moscow, 1934.

(16) Resolution on Propaganda, p. 11.

(17) Fannie Stearns Davis Gifford, "The Ancient Beautiful Things," *The Ancient Beautiful Things*, New York, Macmillan.

(18) *7-Year Plan*, p. 36.

(19) Ibid., p. 40.

(20) Ibid., p. 35.

(21) Resolution on Propaganda, p. 8.

(22) Evgeni Evtushenko, "Poem," *Back to Life*, Edited by Robert Conquest, pp. 28–29. New York, St. Martin's Press, 1960.

Chapter Fifteen—METHODS OF MIND-MAKING

(1) Hadley Cantril, *Soviet Leaders and Mastery over Man*, pp. 9–10. New Brunswick, New Jersey, Rutgers University Press, 1960.

(2) Ibid., p. 24.

(3) V. I. Lenin, *Selected Works*, Vol. II, p. 105. New York, International Publishers, 1943.

(4) "Resolution of the 21st Congress of the Communist Party of the Soviet Union," *Soviet News*, February 10, 1959, p. 145. Published by the Press Department of the Soviet Embassy, London.

(5) Lenin, *Selected Works*, Vol. VI, p. 71.

(6) *Target Figures for the Development of the National Economy of the U.S.S.R. from 1959 to 1965: Theses of N. S. Khrushchev's Report to the 21st Congress of the Communist Party of the Soviet Union on the Targets of the Seven-Year Plan*, Soviet Booklet No. 43, pp. 81–82. Soviet Booklets, 3 Rosary Gardens, London S.W. 7. December 1958.

(7) *Soviet News*, February 12, 1959, p. 153. Published by the Press Department of the Soviet Embassy, London.

(8) *7-Year Plan Target Figures*, Report to the Special 21st Congress of the Communist Party of the Soviet Union and reply to discussion by N. S. Khrushchev; Soviet Booklet No. 47, p. 91. Soviet Booklets, 3 Rosary Gardens, London S.W. 7. February 1959.

(9) *Theses*, p. 77. Also V. I. Lenin, *Works*, Vol. 19, p. 368. Moscow, 1922.

(10) *Edward P. Morgan and the News*, American Broadcasting Company, July 1, 1960. Mimeographed.

(11) "Resolution of the CPSU Central Committee on the tasks of propaganda in contemporary conditions," USSR National Affairs, January 11, 1960, p. 2. Also, *Pravda* and *Red Star*, Moscow, January 10, 1960.

(12) Resolution on Propaganda, p. 6.

(13) Ibid., p. 7.

(14) Ibid., pp. 8–9.

(15) *7-Year Plan,* p. 43.

(16) *Soviet News,* February 12, 1959, pp. 155–156. Published by the Press Department of the Soviet Embassy, London.

(17) For a more detailed survey of the Soviet attitude toward private saving, see Irving R. Levine, *Main Street, U.S.S.R.,* Chapter 14, pp. ff. New York, Signet Books (New American Library), 1960. A reprint of selections from the original edition published by Doubleday.

(18) Robert Frost, "The Code," *Collected Poems,* p. 91. New York, Holt, 1930.

(19) Wiktor Woroszylski, "Questions of a Party Man," *Pro Prostu,* May 3, 1956. Also, in *Back to Life,* Edited by Robert Conquest, pp. 98–99. New York, St. Martin's Press, 1960.

(20) *7-Year Plan,* p. 29.

(21) Resolution on Propaganda, p. 17.

(22) Lenin, *Selected Works,* Vol. II, p. 139.

(23) Resolution on Propaganda, p. 12.

(24) Lenin, *Selected Works,* Vol. II, p. 89.

(25) Joseph Novak, *The Future Is Ours, Comrade,* p. 12. New York, Doubleday, 1960.

Chapter Sixteen—THE UNITED NATIONS AS TARGET

(1) Theodore Draper, *Ordeal of the UN: Khrushchev, Hammarskjold and the Congo.* In The *New Leader,* November 7, 1960, Section Two. Price 25¢. The New Leader, 7 East 15th Street, New York 3.

(2) Draper, p. 27.

(3) Ibid.

(4) Ibid.

(5) *United Nations Review,* Vol. 7, No. 4, October 1960, pp. 21–28. Published by United Nations Office of Public Information. Price 50¢ per copy.

(6) *United Nations Review,* p. 21.

(7) Ibid., pp. 23–24.

Chapter Seventeen: TOO LATE FOR CREDULITY

(1) G. F. Hudson, "Russia and China: the Dilemmas of Power," *Foreign Affairs,* Vol. 39, No. 1, October 1960, p. 5.

(2) Hudson, p. 5.

(3) Ibid.

(4) Ibid.

(5) E. B. White, "Letter from the West," *The New Yorker*, June 18, 1960, p. 33.

(6) White, p. 35.

(7) Ibid.

(8) Frederick C. Barghoorn, *The Soviet Cultural Offensive*, p. 53. Princeton University Press, 1960.

(9) Barghoorn, p. 53.

(10) Dennis Healey, "Yugoslavia, 1960," *The New Leader*, October 31, 1960, p. 3.

(11) "Developments in the Captive Countries, Highlights and Trends," *ACEN News*, No. 67, October 1960, p. 16. Published by Press Bureau of ACEN (Assembly of the Captive European Nations), 29 West 57th Street, New York.

(12) Tamas Aczel and Tibor Meray, *The Revolt of the Mind*, p. 439. New York, Praeger, 1959.

BIBLIOGRAPHY

BOOKS FROM COMMUNIST SOURCES

Adoratsky, V. *Dialectical Materialism.* International Publishers, New York, 1934.

Guest, David A. *A Textbook of Dialectical Materialism.* International Publishers, New York, 1939.

Lenin, V. I. *Selected Works.* International Publishers, New York, 1943.

Mao Tse-tung. *Selected Works* (Four volumes, Based on Chinese Edition, Peking, 1951). International Publishers, New York, 1954.

Marx, Karl. *Selected Works in Two Volumes.* Prepared by the Marx-Lenin Institute, Moscow. Ed. Adoratsky. International Publishers, New York, 1942.

Mikhailov, N. *The Sixteen Republics of the Soviet Union.* U.S.S.R. Information Bulletin, 1951, Washington, D.C.

Stalin, J. V. *Works.* Foreign Languages Publishing House, Moscow, 1949, 1952, 1953, 1954.

————— *Foundations of Leninism.* International Publishers, New York, 1932.

————— *Problems of Leninism.* International Publishers, New York, 1934.

J. V. Stalin. (A Commemoration volume by the Central Committee, Communist Party of the Soviet Union.) Workers Library Publishers, New York, 1940.

PAMPHLETS FROM COMMUNIST SOURCES

7-Year Plan Target Figures. Soviet Booklet #47, Soviet Booklets, 3 Rosary Gardens, London S.W. 7, 1959.

Target Figures for the Development of the National Economy of the USSR from 1959 to 1965, Theses of N. S. Khrushchev's Report to the 21st Congress of the Communist Party of the Soviet Union. Soviet Booklet #43, Soviet Booklets, 3 Rosary Gardens, London S.W. 7, 1958.

BOOKS FROM NON-COMMUNIST SOURCES

Aczel, Tamas, and Meray, Tibor. The Revolt of the Mind. Praeger, New York, 1959.

A Decade Under Mao Tse-tung. Green Pagoda Press, Hong Kong, 1959.

Alexander, Robert J. Communism in Latin America. Rutgers University Press, 1958.

Almond, Gabriel. Politics of the Developing Areas. Princeton University Press, 1960.

Aron, Raymond. The Century of Total War. Beacon, Boston, 1955.

Barghoorn, Frederick C. The Soviet Cultural Offensive. Princeton University Press, 1960.

Bass, Robert, and Elizabeth Marbury. The Soviet-Yugoslav Controversy, 1948–1958: A Documentary Record. Prospect Books, New York, 1959.

Berlin. Prepared by the United States Mission, Berlin, 1959.

Berliner, Joseph S. Soviet Economic Aid. Praeger, New York, 1958.

Brzezinski, Z. The Soviet Bloc: Unity and Conflict. Harvard University Press, 1960.

Cantril, Hadley. Soviet Leaders and Mastery Over Men. Rutgers University Press, 1960.

Colegrove, Kenneth. *Democracy versus Communism.* Van Nostrand, New York, 1957.

Communism in China. Union Research Institute, Hong Kong, 1959.

Counts, George. *The Challenge of Soviet Education.* McGraw-Hill, New York, 1957.

Crankshaw, Edward. *Russia Without Stalin.* Viking, New York, 1956.

Dallin, David J. *The Changing World of Soviet Russia.* Yale University Press, 1956.

Daniel, Hawthorne. *The Ordeal of the Captive Nations.* Doubleday, New York, 1958.

De Custine, Marquis. *Journey for Our Time.* Regnery, Chicago, 1951.

De Jaegher, R. J., and Irene Corbally Kuhn. *The Enemy Within.* St. Paul Publications, Bombay, Allahabad, 1952.

Delaney, Robert Finley. *This is Communist Hungary.* Regnery, Chicago, 1958.

Dinerstein, H. S. *War and the Soviet Union.* Praeger, New York, 1959.

Djilas, Milovan. *The New Class.* Praeger, New York, 1957.

Draper, Theodore. *American Communism and Soviet Russia.* Macmillan, New York, 1960.

Drummond, Roscoe, and Gaston Coblentz. *Duel at the Brink: John Foster Dulles' Command of American Power.* Doubleday, New York, 1960.

Erfurt, Werner. *Moscow's Policy in Germany.* Bechtle Verlag, Esslingen, Germany.

Fainsod, Merle. *Smolensk under Soviet Rule.* Harvard University Press, 1958.

Garthoff, Raymond L. *Soviet Strategy in the Nuclear Age.* Praeger. New York, 1958.

Goldwin, Robert A. (ed.). *Readings in Russian Foreign Policy.* Oxford, New York, 1959.

Goodman, Elliot R. *The Soviet Design for a World State.* Columbia University Press, 1960.

Hahn, Walter F. and John C. Neff (eds.). *American Strategy for the Nuclear Age.* Doubleday, New York, 1960.

Hechinger, Fred M. *The Big Red Schoolhouse.* Doubleday, New York, 1959.

Hoover, J. Edgar. *Masters of Deceit.* Holt, New York, 1958.

Hostler, Charles W. *Turkism and the Soviets.* Praeger, New York, 1957.

Hunt, R. N. Carew. *The Theory and Practice of Communism.* Macmillan, New York, 1958.

Hunter, Edward. *The Black Book on Red China.* Bookmailer, New York, 1958.

Joy, Admiral Charles Turner. *How Communists Negotiate.* Macmillan, New York, 1955.

Kelsen, Hans. *The Communist Theory of Law.* Praeger, New York, 1955.

Kennedy, John C. *The Strategy of Peace.* Harper, New York, 1960.

Kertesz, Stephen D. *The Fate of East Central Europe.* University of Notre Dame Press, 1956.

Kinkead, Eugene. *In Every War But One.* Norton, New York, 1959.

Kintner, W. R. *The Front is Everywhere.* University of Oklahoma Press, 1950.

Kirkpatrick, E. M. *Target the World.* Macmillan, New York, 1956.

Kong, Alfred. *The Making of a Vagabond.* Hong Kong Viewpoints, Hong Kong, 1958.

Korol, Alexander G. *Soviet Education for Science and Technology.* Wiley, New York, 1957.

Kracauer, Siegfried, and Paul L. Berkman. *Satellite Mentality.* Praeger, New York, 1956.

Laquer, Walter Z. *The Soviet Union in the Middle East.* Praeger, New York, 1959.

Lasky, Melvin J. (ed.). *The Hungarian Revolution.* Martin, Secker and Warburg, London, 1957.

Leites, Nathan. *A Study of Bolshevism.* Free Press, Glencoe, Illinois, 1953.

Lin Yutang. *The Secret Name.* Farrar, Straus and Cudahy, New York, 1958.

Meerloo, Joost A. M. *The Rape of the Mind.* World Publishing Company, New York, 1956.

Nagy, Imre. *On Communism: The Defense of the New Course.* Praeger, New York, 1957.

Novak, Joseph. *The Future is Ours, Comrade.* Doubleday, New York, 1960.

Overstreet, Harry and Bonaro. *What We Must Know About Communism.* Norton, New York, 1958.

Philbrick, Herbert. *I Led Three Lives.* Grosset and Dunlap, New York, 1952.

Possony, Stefan T. *A Century of Conflict.* Regnery, New York, 1953.

Record, Wilson, *The Negro and the Communist Party.* University of North Carolina Press, 1951.

Roberts, Henry L. *Russia and America: Dangers and Prospects.* Council on Foreign Relations, New York, 1956.

Rostow, W. W. *The Dynamics of Soviet Society.* Norton, New York, 1952.

——— *The Stages of Economic Growth, a Non-Communist Manifesto.* Cambridge University Press, New York, 1960.

Schapiro, J. Salwyn. *The World in Crisis.* McGraw-Hill, New York, 1950.

Schapiro, Leonard. *The Communist Party of the Soviet Union.* Random House, New York, 1959.

Seton-Watson, Hugh. *From Lenin to Khrushchev: The History of World Communism.* Praeger, New York, 1960.

———— *Neither War Nor Peace: The Struggle for Power in the Post-War World.* Praeger, New York, 1960.

Soloviev, Mikhail. *My Nine Lives in the Red Army.* Pocket Books, New York, 1957.

Soviet Society Today: A Symposium of the Institute for the Study of the USSR. Munich, 1958.

Spaak, Paul-Henri. *Why NATO?: 1949–1959.* A Penguin Special, S 180. Baltimore, 1959.

Strausz-Hupe, Robert, William R. Kintner, James E. Daugherty, and Alvin J. Cottrell. *Protracted Conflict.* University of Pennsylvania Press, 1959.

Syrup, Konrad. *Springtime in October: The Story of the Polish Revolution of 1956.* Praeger, New York, 1957.

The New India. Planning Commission of the Government of India, Macmillan, New York, 1958.

The Soviet Economic Challenge. Institute for American Strategy, Chicago, 1959.

Trân Tâm. *The Storm Within Communism.* Distributed by The Asian Peoples' Anti-Communist League, Saigon, South Vietnam, 1960.

DOCUMENTS FROM PUBLIC SOURCES

Beware! Tourists Reporting on Russia: An Analysis of Tourist Testimony on Soviet Russia. Prepared by Eugene Lyons for the Senate Internal Security Committee, U. S. Government Printing Office, Washington, D.C., 1960.

Communist Anti-American Riots: Mob Violence as an Instrument of Red Diplomacy: Bogotá—Caracas—La Paz—Tokyo. Staff

Study of the Senate Internal Security Committee. U. S. Government Printing Office, Washington, D.C., 1960.

Communist Party of the United States of America: What It Is, How It Works: A Handbook for Americans. Senate Internal Security Committee, U. S. Government Printing Office, Washington, D.C., 1956.

Concerning the 17th National Convention, Communist Party, U.S.A., December 10–13, 1959. Statement by J. Edgar Hoover, to the Senate Internal Security Committee, U. S. Government Printing Office, 1960.

Confuse and Control: Soviet Techniques in Germany. Department of State Publication 4107, European and British Commonwealth Series 17. Released April 1951. U. S. Government Printing Office, Washington, D.C.

Contradictions of Communism. Report by the Senate Internal Security Committee, Washington, D.C., 1959.

Cultural, Technical, and Educational Exchanges: Agreement, With Exchange of Letters, Between the United States of America and the Union of Soviet Republics, Signed at Washington January 27, 1958. Department of State. U. S. Government Printing Office, Washington, D.C., 1958.

Economic Aspects of Soviet Agriculture: Report of a Technical Study Group: Agricultural Research Service, United States Department of Agriculture. U. S. Government Printing Office, Washington, D.C., 1959.

Exposé of Soviet Espionage, May 1960. Prepared by the Federal Bureau of Investigation, U. S. Department of Justice, J. Edgar Hoover, Director. Transmitted by Direction of the Attorney General for use of the Senate Internal Security Committee. U. S. Government Printing Office, Washington, D.C., 1960.

Facts on Communism: Vol. I, The Communist Ideology. Committee on Un-American Activities, House of Representatives. U. S. Government Printing Office, Washington, D.C., 1959.

Forced Labor in the Soviet Union. United States Information Service, Washington, D.C. (Undated).

From the Work of the Federal Ministry for All-German Affairs: An Excerpt from the Progress Report of the Federal Government of Germany, Bonn, Germany, 1958.

Germany in a Nutshell. Written by Helmut Arntz. Published by the Press and Information Office of the Federal German Government. Bonn, Germany, 1958.

The Great Pretense: A Symposium on Anti-Stalinism and the 20th Congress of the Soviet Communist Party. Prepared and Released by the Committee on Un-American Activities, House of Representatives, U. S. Government Printing Office, Washington, D.C., 1956.

Humanitarian Imperative: Interpellation, Governmental Declaration and Resolution by the Bundestag, Concerning the Situation of the People in the Soviet-Occupied Zone of Germany. Rendered by the Federal Ministry of All-German Affairs, Bonn/Berlin, 1958.

India's New Horizons. Published and distributed by the United States Information Service, India. Albion Press, Kashmere Gate, Delhi.

India's Second Five Year Plan. Government of India Planning Commission. New Delhi, 1956.

India's Third Five Year Plan: A Draft Outline. Government of India Planning Commission. New Delhi, 1960.

Information and Guidance: Military Assistance Program. Department of the Army, Department of the Navy, Department of the Air Force.

Khrushchev's Strategy and Its Meaning for America. Prepared by the Foreign Policy Research Institute of the University of Pennsylvania. Presented by the Senate Internal Security Committee. U. S. Government Printing Office, Washington, D.C., 1960.

Mitten in Deutschland—Mitten Im 20. Jahrhundert (In the Middle of Germany—in the Middle of the Twentieth Century). Edited by the Federal Ministry of All-German Affairs, Bonn, Germany, 1959.

Mutual Security Program, Fiscal Year 1961: A Summary Presentation, March 1960. Department of State, Department of Defense, International Cooperation Administration, Development Loan Fund.

North Atlantic Treaty Organization: The NATO Handbook. North Atlantic Treaty Organization Information Service, Palais de Chaillot, Paris, 1959.

Organization for European Economic Cooperation: A Report by the Secretary-General, April 1959. O.E.E.C., 2, rue Andre-Pascal, Paris 16, France.

Pakistan's Outline of the Second Five Year Plan (1960–65). Government of Pakistan Planning Commission, January 1960. Karachi.

Report of the Special Committee on the Problem of Hungary, General Assembly, United Nations. Official Records: Eleventh Session. Supplement No. 18 (A/3529). New York, 1957.

Scientific, Technical, Educational and Cultural Exchanges: Agreement Between the United States of America and the Union of Soviet Socialist Republics: Signed at Moscow November 21, 1959; Signed at Washington November 24, 1959. Department of State. U. S. Government Printing Office, Washington, D.C., 1959.

Soviet Economic Penetration in the Middle East: A Special Study Prepared at the Request of Senator Hubert H. Humphrey by the Legislative Reference Service of the Library of Congress. Presented by Mr. Humphrey. U. S. Government Printing Office, Washington, 1959.

Soviet Empire: Prison House of Nations and Races. A Study in Genocide, Discrimination, and Abuse of Power. Prepared by the Legislative Reference Service of the Library of Congress at the request of the Senate Internal Security Committee. U. S. Government Printing Office, Washington, D.C., 1958.

The Soviet Note on Berlin: An Analysis. Department of State Publication 6757. European and British Commonwealth Series 52. Released January 1959. U. S. Government Printing Office.

Soviet Political Agreements and Results. Staff Study for the Senate Internal Security Committee. U. S. Government Printing Office, Washington, D.C., 1959.

Soviet World Outlook: A Handbook of Communist Statements. Department of State Publication 6836. European and British Commonwealth Series 56. U. S. Government Printing Office, Washington, D.C., 1959.

Speech of Nikita Khrushchev Before A Closed Session of the XXth Congress of the Communist Party of the Soviet Union on February 25, 1956. Senate Internal Security Committee, U. S. Government Printing Office, Washington, D.C., 1957.

Status of the Hungarian Refugee Program. Senate Internal Security Committee. U. S. Government Printing Office, Washington, D.C., 1958.

The Technique of Soviet Propaganda, by Suzanne Labin. A Study Presented by the Senate Internal Security Committee. U. S. Government Printing Office, Washington, D.C., 1960.

United States and Germany, 1945–1955. Department of State. U. S. Government Printing Office, Washington, D.C., 1955.

The United States Through the Eyes of Soviet Tourists: An Analysis of their Published Reports. Prepared by the Staff of the Senate Internal Security Committee. U. S. Government Printing Office, Washington, D.C., 1960.

PAMPHLETS

Berlin: A Compilation of Analytical Materials. Institute for the Study of the USSR. Mannhardtstrasse 6, Munich, Germany.

Brief on Communism: Marxism-Leninism. American Bar Association. 1155 East 60th Street, Chicago 37, Illinois.

Crimes of the Stalin Era: Special Report to the 20th Congress of the Communist Party of the Soviet Union, by Nikita S. Khrushchev. Annotated by Boris I. Nicolaevsky. The New Leader, 7 East 15th Street, New York.

Germany: Behind the Iron Curtain: The Soviet Occupation Zone. The Countries of the Earth, Edited by Karl Hermann Böhmer. Special Issue. Tellus-Verlag, Essen, Germany.

Hungary Under Soviet Rule III: A Survey of Developments from the Revolution to August 1959. American Friends of the Captive Nations, 510 Madison Avenue, New York 22, New York.

Hungary Under Soviet Rule IV: A Survey of Developments from August 1959 to August 1960. American Friends of the Captive Nations, 510 Madison Avenue, New York 22.

Injustice the Regime: Documentary Evidence of the Systematic Violation of Legal Rights in the Soviet Zone of Germany, 1954–1958. Verlag für Internationalen Kulturaustausch, Berlin-Zehlendorf-West.

Let a Hundred Flowers Bloom, Mao Tse-tung, with Notes and Introduction by G. F. Hudson. *The New Leader,* Section 2, September 9, 1957. 7 East 15th Street, New York City.

Letters from the Communes I, Introduction and Notes by Richard L. Walker. *The New Leader,* Section Two, June 15, 1959. 7 East 15th Street, New York.

Letters from the Communes II: Hunger in China. Introduction and Notes by Richard L. Walker. *The New Leader,* Section Two, May 20, 1960. 7 East 15th Street, New York.

Meaning of Hungary, by Raymond Aron. *The New Leader,* Section Two, March 24, 1958. 7 East 15th Street, New York.

Ordeal of the UN: Khrushchev, Hammarskjold and the Congo, by Theodore Draper. *The New Leader,* Section Two, November 7, 1960. 7 East 15th Street, New York City.

Revolt in Hungary: A Documentary Chronology of Events. Based Exclusively on Internal Broadcasts by Central and Provincial Radios, October 23, 1956–November 4, 1956. Free Europe Committee, 2 Park Avenue, New York 17.

Soviet Society Today: A Symposium of the Institute for the Study of the USSR. Mannhardtstrasse 6, Munich, Germany, 1958.

Studies on the Soviet Union. Institute for the Study of the USSR. Mannhardtstrasse 6, Munich, Germany, 1960.

The Greater Danger: The Post-Stalin Pattern for Communist World Conquest. American Federation of Labor and Congress of Industrial Organizations, Publication No. 37, November 1956.

The New Class in North Vietnam, Edited by Hoang Van Chi. Cong Dan Publishing Company, Saigon, 1958.

The Seventeenth Parallel, By Duong Chau. Cong Dan Publishing Company, Saigon, 1958.

The U. S. versus The U. S. S. R.: Ideologies in Conflict. By Robert A. Fearey, Public Affairs Press, Washington, D.C., 1959.

Tibet: A Few Facts. Committee for Solidarity with Tibet, Kermani Building, P. Mehta Road, Bombay 1, India.

Under Soviet Heel: Destruction of Jewish Life in Eastern Europe, By Peter Meyer. Reprinted from *The Jews in the Soviet Satellites,* By Peter Meyer, Bernard D. Weinryb, Eugene Duschinsky, Nicolas Sylvain. Published by Syracuse University Press. Copyright 1953, American Jewish Congress.

Youth in the Soviet Union: A Collection of Articles. Special Issue of Soviet Affairs Analysis Service, Institute for the Study of the USSR, Mannhardtstrasse 6, Munich, Germany.

PERIODICALS—COMMUNIST

China Reconstructs. Monthly. Imported Publications and Products, 4 West 16th Street, New York 11, New York.

International Affairs: A Monthly Journal of Political Analysis, Moscow. American distributors: Imported Publications and Products, 4 West 16th Street, New York 11, New York.

Mainstream. Monthly. 832 Broadway, New York 3, New York.

Political Affairs. Monthly. New Century Publishers, 832 Broadway, New York 3, New York.

Soviet News. Published by the Press Department of the Soviet Embassy, London.

USSR: Illustrated Monthly, 1706 Eighteenth Street, N.W., Washington 9, D.C.

The Worker. Weekly. 35 East 12th Street, New York 3, New York.

World Marxist Review. Monthly. English Edition of *Problems of Peace and Socialism,* published in Prague. Central Books, Ltd., 37 Gray's Inn Road, London W.C. 1.

PERIODICALS—NON-COMMUNIST

ACEN *News.* A Monthly Review of the Activities of the Assembly of Captive European Nations. Published by the Press Bureau of ACEN, 29 West 57th Street, New York 19, New York.

Asian Culture, Vietnamese Association for Asian Cultural Relations, 201 Le Van Duyet, Saigon, Vietnam.

Bulletin. Institute for the Study of the USSR. Monthly. Mannhardtstrasse 6, Munich, Germany.

Department of State Bulletin: The Official Weekly Record of the United States Foreign Policy. U. S. Government Printing Office, Washington, D.C.,

East Europe: A Monthly Review of East European Affairs. Free Europe Committee, 2 Park Avenue, New York 16, New York.

Foreign Affairs: An American Quarterly Review, 10 McGovern Avenue, Lancaster, Pennsylvania.

NATO Letter. Monthly Publication of NATO. NATO Information Service, Paris. U. S. Department of State, Washington, D.C.

New Leader. Published Weekly by the American Labor Conference on International Affairs, 7 East 15th Street, New York 3, New York.

Problems of Communism. Bimonthly. U. S. Information Service, Washington, D.C.

Quest, 148 Mahatma Gandhi Road, Bombay 1, India.

Russian Review: An American Quarterly Devoted to Russia Past and Present. Hanover, New Hampshire.

Soviet Survey: A Quarterly Review of Cultural Trends. Published by the Congress for Cultural Freedom, 104 Boulevard Haussman, Paris 8e, France.

United Nations Review, Published Monthly by United Nations Office of Public Information, New York City.

RESEARCH CENTERS

GENERAL

International Committee for Information and Social Activity (CIAS); 8 Avenue de l'Arsenal, Luxembourg.

Mid-European Studies, 4 West 57th Street, New York 19.

Rand Corporation, 1625 I Street, N.W., Washington, D.C.

The Institute for the Study of the USSR, Mannhardtstrasse 6, Munich, Germany.

Union Research Institute, 110 Waterloo Road, Kowloon, Hong Kong.

CENTERS ATTACHED TO UNIVERSITIES

Center of International Studies, Princeton University, Princeton, N.J.

Center for International Studies, Massachusetts Institute of Technology, Cambridge, Mass.

Center of Slavonic Studies, University of Montreal, Montreal, Quebec, Canada.

Department of Slavic Studies, Indiana University, Bloomington, Indiana.

East Asian Institute, Columbia University, New York 27.

Hoover Institute and Library, Stanford University, Palo Alto, California.

Russian Institute, Columbia University, New York 27.

Russian Research Center, Harvard University, Cambridge, Massachusetts.

School of Advanced International Studies, Johns Hopkins University, Baltimore, Maryland.

Slavic Institute, University of California, Berkeley, California.

INDEX

Abnormal, Communist usage of, 191–192
Africa, Soviet policy, 50, 53, 56, 58
Agreements, Soviet, 54–56, 160, 175–176, 185, 192, 326
Agriculture, Soviet, 114–115, 117
Albania, 16, 187, 226, 230, 233
Apro, Antal, 330–331
Artists, Soviet, 129
Asia, Soviet policy, 50, 53, 56, 58
Associations, voluntary, 116, 287–289
Atheism, 276–278
Austria, 45, 60, 330
"Authority vacuum," attempts to fill, 308–309, 327
Automation, Soviet stress on, 114

Balance of power, 30–31, 51–54, 57, 97
Baltic states, 16
Barter deals, 53–54
Beria, L. P., 126–127, 129
Berlin, 17, 35, 174–196
  airlift, 185–186
  Allied Command, 179, 181, 185
  blockade, 185–186
  crises created by Soviet, 174–176
  elections, 178–189, 248, 250
  four-power agreements, 175–176, 185–186, 193, 196
  importance to the Soviets, 192–193
  Khrushchev's policies, 48–49, 174–178, 187–196
  occupation zones, 177–178, 179, 185
  relevant dates and events, 177–179
  Western policies, 175–176, 194–195
  Yalta and Potsdam agreements, 177–181, 185, 186
Bolshevik *coup d'état* of 1917, 131–133, 137, 161, 184, 222
Bolshevik Party, 82, 88, 89
"Bourgeois capitalism," 173
Brain-washing, 280–283
Bulgaria, 16, 187, 226, 230, 233
Bureaucracy in the Soviet Union, 89–93
Burma, 322

Cadres, Party, 38, 284–285, 292–293
Cantril, Hadley, 255, 283
Capitalism, 163, 259–260
  Lenin on, 113
  struggle between communism and, 14–15
"Capitalist imperialist nations," 31, 37, 46
Cells, Communist, 134
Censorship, propaganda and, 146, 206–208
Central Committee, 127–129
Chemical industry, 105
Chinese Communists, 33, 35, 56, 79, 97–98, 262–263
  ideological differences with Soviet, 42, 57–58, 97–98
  Tibet, 169
  underdeveloped countries aided by, 58
Chinese People's Republic, 35, 57–58
"Class enemy," 79, 91
"Class morality," 62–63, 71
"Class struggle," 13, 27, 69, 165
Clay, General Lucius, 185–186
Coexistence; *see* Peaceful coexistence
Cold war, 33, 148
  campaign for fostering, 40
Collectivization, 114–116, 128
Collective leadership, 30, 122

Colonialism, 220–240
  colonial territories, 230
  COMECON, 236–238
  difference between Soviet and Western, 221, 239, 307
  economic and political domination, 180, 225–234
  pre-Communist Russia, 220–222
  "rim" countries, 230–233
  satellite countries, 233
  Soviet policy, 84, 172–173
  speech by Khrushchev, 238–239
  subjugation of people, 180, 225–226
COMECON, 236–238
Cominform, 16, 187
Comintern, 15–16, 147, 169–170
Common Market, 237
Communism; *see also* Marxism-Leninism
  competition with other systems, 86
  future of, 76–77
  ideology, 61–77
  ideological geography of, 11–29
  reactionary and dated, 75–77
  two-camp concept, 13–20, 31
  ways of denying victory to, 82–86
  weaknesses, 82–86
Communist International, 15–16, 147–148
Communist man, 196, 255–279
  ability to manipulate, 114
  exchange programs and, 217
  Khrushchev's concept, 262–265
  lacks individuality, 267–268
  Lenin's concept, 258–261
  mass production of, 266–267
  provincialism of, 275
  taught atheism, 276–278
  thinking done for him, 368–369
  traits of, 258–279, 289
Communist movement
  peaceful coexistence stage, 98
  Soviet-Sino differences, 58, 97–98
  world, 17–18, 33, 38
Communist Party, 120–135, 251–252
  cadres, 103–104, 284–285
  citizen participation, 285–286
  conspiratorial purposes, 223
  East zone of Germany, 181
  directives, 40, 134–135
  history of, 120–135
  Khrushchev ideologist of, 61–77
  legal standing, 80
  membership, 286
  never won a free election, 80–81
  problem of bureaucratic dry rot, 89–93
  Soviet policy made by, 15, 110–111, 127
  structure of, 68
  war against the people, 241–257
Communist Youth Festival, Vienna, 24–25
Conformity, 83, 93
Congo, 169
  Soviet penetration, 44, 95–97, 305, 309–311
Conspiracy, 86, 134–135
Constitution, Soviet, 223–224
Consumer goods, 86–87, 95, 105
Counts, George S., 146
Cousins, Norman, 207
Cuba, Soviet penetration, 44, 49–50, 95–97, 193, 305–306
Czechoslovakia, 226, 230, 233, 335
  Communist Party, 81, 211–212
  Soviet occupation, 187

Dallin, David J., 166–167
Democracy, 46–47
  Communist definition, 69, 166–167, 285–286
  Jeffersonian, 333–335
"Democratic centralism," 62–63, 68–69, 71, 89, 111
"Dictatorship of the proletariat," 62, 68–69, 146
Diplomacy, Communist, 13, 17, 54–56, 323–325
Directives, Communist, 40, 134–135
Disarmament negotiations, 42–43, 45, 52, 55, 83–85, 325–328
Draper, Theodore, 59–60, 302–306
Drummond, Roscoe, 303
Dulles, John Foster, 164

East Berlin, 48–49, 174–196; see also Berlin
East Europe, 32, 33
  Soviet occupation, 52–53, 97, 133, 187
East zone of Germany, 18–183
  German Democratic Republic, 186, 189–191
  lacks diplomatic recognition, 195–196
  puppet regime, 174, 230
  sovietization of, 133, 180–183, 330
Economic development, Soviet, 86–89, 328–329
  comparison of U.S. and, 329
Economic warfare, 17, 35, 53–54
  blueprint for, 106, 108–109
Education, 106, 118, 283–284, 293–295
  literacy problem, 146–147
Ehrenburg, Ilya, 204
Eisenhower, Dwight D., 28, 46
Elections, Soviet, 80–81, 162, 166, 242–253
  in Berlin, 178, 183–184, 186–187, 189, 192
Engels, Friedrich, 171, 259
Espionage, Soviet, 23–24, 45, 213
Evtushenko, Evgeni, 275–276
Exchange programs, 197–219
  basic provisions, 202
  advantages for the West, 216–219
  agreements, 201–202
  historical background, 197–202
  indoctrination to counteract effect of, 199, 203–204
  negotiations, 205–209, 212–213
Expansion drive, Soviet, 17–18, 37, 84, 98, 99, 192–193

Family, Communist attacks on, 293–294
Food production, 105
Foreign policy, Soviet, 23, 50, 95–97, 131
Foster, William Z., 139
Free world, 331–332
  meaning of, 320–322
Freedom, Soviet definition of, 66, 257, 320–322
"Friendship," Communist, 134, 204–205, 209, 314
Fronts, Communist, 37, 40, 135, 140, 287, 300

Geneva Conference, 199
German Democratic Republic, 48, 186, 189–191, 195–196
Germany
  Berlin crises, 174–196; see also Berlin
  East zone of Germany; see East zone of Germany
  peace treaty for, 182
  reparations, 182

reunification of, 178, 190, 195
  West Germany; see West Germany
Gigantism, centralized, 112–116
"Good will" tours, 173
Goodman, Elliot R., 260–261

Hammarskjold, Dag, 28, 55, 305–318, 325
Hearst, William Randolph, Jr., 326
"Historic mission" of Communism, 32, 41, 62, 181, 232
History, Communist, 120–135
  disregard of facts, 122–126, 131
  of Soviet Communist Party, 120–135
  workbook for the Party, 130–135
Housing, 105, 274, 294
Hungary, 14, 16, 226, 230, 233, 236, 327, 330
  Soviet occupation, 94, 165–169, 200, 330–331

Ideas, as weapons, 271–272
Ideology, Communist, 11–29, 61–77
  appeal to underdeveloped countries, 75–77
  imposition upon language, 171–172
"Imperialism," Western, 31, 141
Imperialism, Soviet, 54, 63, 141
"Imperialist," 19–20
Incentives, economic, 115, 118
Independent countries; see also Underdeveloped countries
  Soviet attempts to influence, 36–37, 134
India, 17, 233, 322–323, 305
  Communist Party, 96–98
  economic development, 106–113
  U.S. aid to, 277–278
Individual development, 114–116
Indoctrination, 63, 120–121, 146, 292–293
Indonesia, 151, 267
Industrialization, Soviet, 83–84, 114–115, 118
Intellectuals, Soviet, 63, 129
Interference, Communist usage of, 23–24, 167
International Affairs (periodical), 142, 149, 154–155
"Internationalism," proletarian, 98–99, 232
Iron and steel output, 105
Iron Curtain, 20–26, 197
Italian Communist Party, 72–74

Kadar, Hungarian Communist leader, 165–166, 168, 331
Kerensky, Aleksandr, 137, 222
Khrushchev, Nikita, 59, 225, 331–332
  as an agitator, 91–92
  attack on the United Nations, 302–318
  attitude towards Stalin, 17, 31, 71–72, 121, 124–126, 330
  on colonialism, 220
  controls Party, 61–77, 89–93
  diplomacy, 13, 17, 54–56
  intends to be misunderstood, 156
  killer many times, 94
  1959 Party Congress, 16–17
  Paris press conference, 47–48, 303–304
  problems standing in way of, 59, 79, 319–335
  role of, 16–17, 41, 54
  Seven Year Plan; see Seven Year Plan
  success needed by, 78–99
  Summit Conference, 44–45
  threats and professions of "friendship," 49, 190
  two-world social system, 14

at United Nations, 11, 12, 86, 99, 157–158, 161, 229, 239, 302–318
use of Party cadres, 284–290
visit to the United States, 59, 153–155, 157–158, 191
Khrushchevism, 51, 59–60
Kommunist, 58, 64
Komsomol, 245, 286

Labor, Soviet, 38–39, 97, 118
Lacy, Admiral William, 201–202, 212–213, 215
Land program, 114–115
Language, Communist exploitation of, 141, 156–173
Latin America, 39, 50, 53, 56, 58, 151
Lenin, V. I., 122, 131–132, 299
Bolshevik *coup d'état*, 131–132, 184
on Bolshevik Party, 22–23, 89
on capitalism, 113
founded *Comintern*, 15–16
on role of man, 258–261
strategist of the revolution, 13, 133–134
What Is to Be Done? 39, 145
Levine, Irving R., 241–243, 252
Litvinoff, 137
Lvov, Prince, 131

Macmillan, Harold, 46, 252
Malenkov, 17, 129, 188
Man; *see* Communist man
Manchester Guardian, 195–196, 332
Marchand, René, 136–137
Marquand, David, 332–333
Marshall Plan, 19, 52, 236
Marx, Karl, 12–13, 76, 212, 258–259
Marxism-Leninism, 33, 61–77, 79, 134
obstacle to progress, 87–88
Seven Year Plan and, 111
"world view," 13–29
Mass production, stress on, 266–267
Materialism, 76, 83
Mazurov, K., 203
Menzies, Robert G., 220, 239
Middle class, 116
Mikoyan, trip to U.S., 39–40, 215
Mind-making, methods of, 280–301
attitude of Communist Party, 270–271
psychological study of, 283–284
standardizing the citizen, 296–298
Minorities, Communist, 97, 251
Molotov, 17, 200, 252
Mongolia, 230, 233–234
"Monolithic unity," 116

National-revolutionary movements, 306, 309
Nationalism, Soviet, 132–133
NATO, 16, 17, 44, 170, 190, 193
Negotiation, Communist usage of word, 159–160, 322–323
Nehru, Jawaharlal, 233, 305
Neutralism and neutrality, 152, 307–308
Newspapers, Soviet, 58, 143–146, 148, 181
Non-Communist orbit, 27, 149
Novak, Joseph, 244, 300
Nuclear weapons, control of, 32, 326–327

Pakistan, 106–110, 322, 323
Parinaud, André, 203, 210
Paris, Summit conference, 44–49
Party; *see* Communist Party
Party and class, definition, 250–251
Patience, Khrushchev's idea of, 51, 256
Peace, Communist usage of word, 24, 30, 56, 170–171

"Peace offensive," of Stalin, 148, 187
Peaceful coexistence, 13–14, 27–28, 30–60
Communist meaning of, 30–43, 170–171, 203, 208
directives to Party members, 34–35, 37–38, 40
second era of, 45, 60
stalemate coexistence replaces, 50–53
in underdeveloped countries, 36–37
veiled warfare, 299
"Penetrating without being penetrated," 22–24, 167, 200
People, Communist usage of word, 170–171
daily life watched, 244–246
in Soviet Union, 241–257
Philippines, 152
Pieck, Wilhelm, 141
Poland, 222, 226, 230, 233
Soviet occupation, 16, 187
uprisings, 17
Police, secret, 249
Polish-Soviet Friendship Meeting, 190
Politburo, 122, 127
Ponomarev, B., 38–39
Pravda, 20, 104–105, 121, 188, 204
Press, Communist, 91, 136–155, 198
censorship and propaganda, 146
conspiratorial, 146, 152
in the U.S., 137–142, 149–150
Press, free-world, 47–49
Production, Soviet, 112–113
"Progressive elements," 68, 95, 104–135
Propaganda, Communist, 27, 30, 56–60, 81, 136–155
censorship and, 146
"escape clause," 210
on the home front, 91, 298–301
major shift in, 50, 56–60
in underdeveloped countries, 49–50
Property
private, 272–274
state ownership, 116
Psychology, Soviet, 266, 283–284
Public opinion, 322
Public organizations, 287
Purges, Communist, 73–74, 124–126, 128–129, 229

RB-47 case, 45
Radio, jamming of Western broadcasts, 21, 22, 26, 81, 198, 218
Red Army, 225–227, 327
Religion in U.S.S.R., 218, 276–278
Reparations, German, 182, 186
Reuter, Ernst, 183–184
Reuther, Walter, 210
"Revisionism," 35–36, 58, 67–71, 106
"Revolutionary vanguard," 162
Robert, Chalmers, 303
Robinson, Edwin Arlington, 64, 130
Roosevelt, Franklin D., 140
Roschin, Alexei, 318
Rumania, 16, 44, 226, 230, 233
Soviet occupation, 186–187
Russell, Bertrand, 164
Russification program, 180, 226

Sanakoyev, Shalva, 154–155
Satellite countries, 16, 79, 82–83, 327
economic and political domination by Moscow, 54, 233–236
Stalin takes over, 186–187
Schapiro, Leonard, 62, 224
Schlegel, Frederick von, 138
Scientists, Soviet, 129

"Sectarianism," Communist, 36
Self-determination, Communist usage of word, 161–163
Self-indulgence, Western ways of, 82–86
Semenov, Soviet High Commissioner, 189
Seton-Watson, Hugh, 85, 87
Seven Year Plan, 17, 70, 103–119
  blueprint for economic warfare, 106, 108–109, 119
  chances for success, 117–118
  compared to plans in other countries, 106–116
  meaning to West, 108, 118–119
  "selfless dedication" by people to, 104, 117
  target figures, 33, 105–106, 117
  Theses, Khrushchev's, 103–104
Silone, Ignazio, 200
Slave labor camps, 247, 328
Slogans, 60, 146
Sobolev, Arkady, 317
Socialism, 14, 262
"Socialist internationalism," 275
"Socialist realism," 62
"Socialist solidarity," 35–36, 71, 98, 321, 322
Sokolovsky, Marshal, 185
South Vietnam, 84
Soviet citizens, 241–257
  contact with the West, 129
"Spirit of Camp David," 56, 58–59, 191
Sputniks, 17
Stalin, Joseph, 16, 199, 271
  on aid given by U.S., 328–329
  consolidation of power, 52, 96
  "cult of personality," 124
  death of, 120–121
  de-Stalinization by Khrushchev, 17, 31, 71–72, 121, 124–126, 330
  tyranny of, 125, 129
Stalin-Hitler non-aggression pact, 13–14, 141
Standard of living, 42, 83, 94, 108–109, 272–273
Standardization, idolatry of, 265–266
State, modern, 66
Steel output, 105
Strikes, 94, 235
Subversion, 27, 86
Summit conferences, 42–47, 174–175, 191, 324
Suslov, Mikhail, 214, 288

Tensions, created by Communists, 28, 56–57
Terrorism, 93–95, 244–247, 330–331
Textbooks, as weapons, 147, 153
Tibet, 169
Tito, Marshal, 14
Togliatti, Italian Communist, 72–74
Tourists to Soviet Union, 25
Treaties, U.S.S.R., not respected, 84, 327
Trials and purges, 124–128
Turkestan, 228
Twentieth Congress of the CPSU, 30, 124, 127
Twenty-First Congress of CPSU, 14, 32–35, 61, 103–104, 130
"Two-camp theory" of Communism, 13–20, 31

U-2 affair, 23–24, 45, 55, 58–59, 191
Underdeveloped countries
  Communist activity, 33, 36–37, 53, 75–77, 88–89, 95–97, 305–318
  labor movement, 39
  Soviet appeal to, 132–134
  Soviet economic offensive, 53–54, 88–89, 305–318

"United front" movements, 37, 40, 135, 140
United Nations, 45, 54, 169
  General Assembly, 11–12, 308
  Khrushchev's attack on, 27, 55, 160, 302–318
  Khrushchev's temper tantrum, 86, 99, 158, 229, 239
  RB-47 case, 45
  Soviet attempt to wreck, 97–98, 302–318
  vetoes by Soviet, 185, 311, 315
United States
  aid to U.S.S.R., 19–20, 328–329
  Communist plan to overthrow, 139
  Communist Party, 40, 207
  Communist press, 137–142
  culture, 322–333
  exchange programs, 197–219
  Mikoyan's trip to, 39–40
  policy towards Red China, 35

Vanguard Party, 23, 68
Vietnam, 84
Virgin-land program, 17, 114, 117–118
Voting in U.S.S.R.; see Elections

"Warmongering," 19–20, 31, 172, 312
West, Soviet citizens exposed to, 129
West Berlin, 174–196; see also Berlin
  Soviet blockade of, 185–186
West Germany
  Berlin crises, 174–196
  included in NATO, 190
  Soviet plans for, 192–193
West Side Story, 209
Western nations, 53, 321–322
  "rigidity" of, 99
  Soviet policy, 46, 85
  ways of preventing Communist victories, 82–86
White, E.B., 325, 327–328, 331
Wolfe, Bertram D., 122–123
Words, 156–173
  corruption of language, 171–173
  decoding, 157, 159
    abnormal, 191–192
    agreement, 160
    democracy, 166–167
    interference, 167
    international, 169–170
    negotiation, 159–160
    peace, 170–171
    people, 163–166
    self-determination, 161–163
  double-talk, 156–159
Workers' societies, 134, 138, 141, 150
Working-classes, 35, 38
World, Communist view of, 11–29
World War I, 131–132
World War II, Soviet plundered East Europe, 133
Woroszylski, Wiktor, 297
Writers, Soviet, 129

Yalta Agreement, 161, 162, 177–181, 185, 186, 196
Young Communist League, 286–288
Youth groups, Soviet, 180
Yugoslavia, 14, 106
  economic growth, 329–330
  revisionists, 35–36

Zaharov, Soviet Commandant, 194
Zaroubin, G. N., 201
Zhdanov, 16, 19, 199
Zhukov, Georgi, 26, 203–204, 207–210